Hans-Christian Petersen (ed.)
Spaces of the Poor

Mainz Historical Cultural Sciences | Volume 17

Editorial

The **Mainzer Historische Kulturwissenschaften** [Mainz Historical Cultural Sciences] series publishes the results of research that develops methods and theories of cultural sciences in connection with empirical research. The central approach is a historical perspective for cultural sciences, whereby both epochs and regions can differ widely and be treated in an all-embracing manner from time to time. The series brings together, among other things, research approaches in archaeology, art history and visualistic, philosophy, literary studies and history, and is open for contributions on the history of knowledge, political culture, the history of perceptions, experiences and life-worlds, as well as other fields of research with a historical cultural scientific orientation.
The objective of the **Mainzer Historische Kulturwissenschaften** series is to become a platform for pioneering works and current discussions in the field of historical cultural sciences.

The series is edited by the Co-ordinating Committee of the Special Research Group Historical Cultural Sciences (HKW) at the Johannes Gutenberg University Mainz.

Hans-Christian Petersen (ed.)
Spaces of the Poor
**Perspectives of Cultural Sciences
on Urban Slum Areas and Their Inhabitants**

[transcript]

The Print was sponsored by the Research Focus Historical Cultural Sciences.

Bibliographic information published by the Deutsche Nationalbibliothek
The Deutsche Nationalbibliothek lists this publication in the Deutsche Nationalbibliografie; detailed bibliographic data are available in the Internet at http://dnb.d-nb.de

© 2013 transcript Verlag, Bielefeld

All rights reserved. No part of this book may be reprinted or reproduced or utilized in any form or by any electronic, mechanical, or other means, now known or hereafter invented, including photocopying and recording, or in any information storage or retrieval system, without permission in writing from the publisher.

Cover layout: Kordula Röckenhaus, Bielefeld
Layout: Mark-Sebastian Schneider, Bielefeld
Printed by Majuskel Medienproduktion GmbH, Wetzlar
ISBN 978-3-8376-2473-1

Contents

Introduction
HANS-CHRISTIAN PETERSEN | 7

A Janus-Faced Institution of Ethnoracial Closure
A Sociological Specification of the Ghetto
LOÏC WACQUANT | 15

The Subalterns Speak Out
Urban Plebeian Society in Late Imperial Russia
ILYA V. GERASIMOV | 47

"... not intended for the Rich"
Public Places as Points of Identification for the Urban Poor –
St. Petersburg (1850-1914)
HANS-CHRISTIAN PETERSEN | 71

Blood in the Air
Everyday Violence in the Experience of the Petersburg Poor,
1905-1917
MARK D. STEINBERG | 97

Outcast Vienna 1900
The Politics of Transgression
WOLFGANG MADERTHANER | 121

Revisiting Campbell Bunk
JERRY WHITE | 135

Creating the City of Delhi
Stories of Strong Women and Weak Walls
SONJA WENGOBORSKI/JASPAL NAVEEL SINGH | 147

Urban Meeting Locations of Nicaraguan Migrants in Costa Rica's Metropolitan Area and the Spatial Effects on their Social Support Networks
HAUKE JAN ROLF | 169

Urban Poverty and Gentrification
A Comparative View on Different Areas in Hamburg
INGRID BRECKNER | 193

Europe's only Megacity
Urban Growth, Migration and Gentrification in 21st Century Moscow
JULIA RÖTTJER/JAN KUSBER | 209

Contributors | 237

Introduction

HANS-CHRISTIAN PETERSEN

What do we know about the urban impoverished areas of the world and the people living in them? When looking at research reports available so far, the answer to this question is relatively sobering. Still, one narration is dominating according to which the habitats of the urban poor were solely places of dull backwardness, characterised by spatial and mental narrowness. The world of the people at the bottom rung of society appears to be widely homogeneous and is drawn in grey and black colours. Queries beyond this are rarely found so that Markus Schroer correctly speaks of "a reproduction of always the same images"[1] in respect of ghettos, favelas and banlieues.

When applying this perspective, the question of what these 'narrow habitats' meant for their inhabitants, is ignored. The view from the outside is blind to the perspective from the inside. This starts already with the language and the terms in which we describe the world surrounding us. The word *slum*, mentioned in the subtitle of this volume, has never been an absolute and neutral term since its emergence in the first half of the 19th century, but conveyed stigmatising associations from the very beginning. *Slums* were not only places of urban blight and utmost poverty, but at the same time 'conglomerations' of the 'outcasts' of society, of the 'undeserving poor' who stood outside of society and who could not expect any help from it.[2] This is why Alan Gilbert has pointed out that language matters,[3] especially when we are talking about poverty and the people struck by it. Terms such as *slum* are predestined for political instrumentalisation – to mention only the so called 'slum clearances' as a wrongly perceived 'solution' to the

---

1 SCHROER, 2006, p. 250.
2 Cf. amongst others: DYOS, 1967; JONES, 1971; GASKELL, 1990; GREEN, 1995; LINDNER, 2004; KOVEN, 2006.
3 Cf. GILBERT, 2007.

problem, be it in Victorian London of the 19th century[4] or in current-day Rio de Janeiro, where the favelas are 'cleaned' by the forces of police and military for the FIFA World Cup 2014 as well as the Olympic Games 2016.

If the term gets used in this volume despite its problematic etymology, it is due to the circumstance that it is de facto the common description for an urban spatial concentration of poverty. This is true historically as well as today and is not limited to the English-speaking world, as is demonstrated by the contributions to this volume. This is not designed to advocate a perpetuation of the associations inherent to the term, but quite the contrary, these are taken by the authors as the starting point for critical reflections and looks behind the allegedly unambiguous facade of the slums.

The volume at hand is the outcome of a conference which was organised by the Research Unit *Historical Cultural Sciences* (Historische Kulturwissenschaften, HKW) of the Johannes Gutenberg University Mainz from March 30th until April 1st 2012.[5] Almost all of the speakers have prepared their papers for publication. Additionally, there are three articles by authors who were contacted for the conference, but were unable to attend due to scheduled obligations and by those who decided to write a contribution after having taken part in the conference (Loïc Wacquant, Sonja Wengoborski and Jaspal Naveel Singh, Julia Röttjer and Jan Kusber). The main concern of the conference was an interdisciplinary dialogue on the topic as to how far approaches of cultural sciences can contribute to overcome the "exotification"[6] of the urban poor and to look at heterogeneities and individuality instead of alleged unambiguousness. The concept follows pioneering studies by Pierre Bourdieu[7], Loïc Wacquant[8] and others, who perceived the inhabitants of slum districts as individuals, as actively engaged people who shape the precarious social conditions around them themselves in a process of purposeful adoption.

The contributions to the volume at hand do not apply a uniform approach, but represent just that multiperspectivity which was intended. This is not synonymous with arbitrariness, but results from the consideration that a broad discussion of different theories and methods is the best way to achieve a picture of the urban poor as multifaceted as possible. However, all texts have in common a

---

4   Cf. YELLING, 1986; ALLEN, 2008.
5   Cf. the conference report by PAUL FRIEDL, in: H-Soz-u-Kult, 27.06.2012: http://hsozkult.geschichte.hu-berlin.de/tagungsberichte/id=4281, 07.05.2013.
6   WACQUANT, 1998, p. 203.
7   BOURDIEU et al., 1993.
8   WACQUANT, 2004.

concurrent examination of structures and individual agency. Processes of social polarisation and displacement are linked with the question of what we can say about those who are struck by this development. With this in mind, the volume is also an appeal for a return of the social question as it has been discussed in the English-speaking debate since the middle of the 1990s – for a "New Social History", which preserves the critical impetus of social history without abandoning the cultural-historical progresses of knowledge gained in the last decades.[9]

The chronological frame of the contributions ranges from the 19th to the 21st century. As well as a number of historical analyses, there are also articles focusing on present-day developments. Geographically, case studies of North and Latin American, European as well as Indian cities are included, which naturally covers only a part of a global theme. Hopefully, the publication of the volume may be an incitement for further research in the future.

At the beginning of the volume stands a text of LOÏC WACQUANT, in which the already mentioned question of terminology is examined in detail. Wacquant develops an analytical concept of the ghetto as a spatially based implement of ethno-racial closure. At the same time, he strongly argues against an intermixture of the terms *ghetto* und *slum* by emphasising "that not all ghettos are poor and not all poor areas are (inside) ghettos". In this context he advises against an indiscriminate transfer of concepts and terms, originating from the US American debate on other - for instance European - societies in order not to dilute the analytical categories. Looking at the *ghetto*, Wacquant makes an argument for a perspective which sees the ghetto simultaneously as a sword (in the sense of an instrument of isolating certain groups of the population) as well as a shield (in the sense of a potential place of mutual support for its inhabitants).

The following texts are investigating further the possibilities and limits of writing about the urban poor. On the basis of examples from early 20th century Russian cities Nizhny Novgorod, Kazan, Vilnius and Odessa, ILYA V. GERASIMOV opposes applying discourse-analytical methods on the main sources (i.e. newspaper reports, police and court documents) for the social history of the urban poor. Referring to the concept of *subalternity*, he argues that since lower strata did not use discourse, the method of discourse analysis would produce misinterpretations. Instead, one would have to go beyond the texts to see actual (non-discursive or non-verbal) social practices and their users in a wider con-

---

9   Cf. amongst others: ELEY, 2005, as well as the correspondent discussion of his theses in the forum of the AMERICAN HISTORICAL REVIEW, 2008. As a brilliant German-speaking, combative representative is to be named: MADERTHANER/ MUSNER, 2007.

text. Since these practices, the "body talk" of the subalterns as he calls it, also carry meanings, and since the historian can learn to understand them, they too are open to interpretation.

My contribution is shedding light on another Russian example: St. Petersburg, the capital of late imperial Russia. Looking at two types of sources that are quite different at first sight (on one hand a series of articles from a Petersburg newspaper and on the other several petitions submitted by 'itinerant peddlers' from Petersburg's Haymarket), the epistemic possibilities and limitations are discussed to discover the urban poor of former times by documents we find in the archives today. The method suggested in the article is a spatial approach, by looking at concrete places. Beyond stylistic devices, both types of sources provide us with information about places which were important to their inhabitants and which they regarded as 'their own'.

MARK D. STEINBERG is also dealing with St. Petersburg, namely with a phenomenon which was characterised by Petersburg's newspapers at the beginning of the 20th century as a "traumatic epidemic of blood and violence". On the basis of a rich collection of contemporary articles, he demonstrates to which extend everyday violence shaped the life of the inhabitants, particularly in the poor districts of the city, how this development was perceived at that time and which explanations can be found from today's point of view. According to Steinberg, the violence can be understood best as a blocked agency, resulting from the extensive exclusion of the poor from the urban discourse. At the same time he is rather sceptical in reading too much into the violence from a retrospective viewpoint, concerning, for example, the political dimension of such an agency.

WOLFGANG MADERTHANER takes the well-known picture of *Fin de Siècle Vienna* as a place gathering central cultural innovations of modernity as a starting point for shedding light on the 'other', the poor Vienna. He makes an argument for reading the metropolis as a social text in order to develop an understanding of the mass culture of the city. According to Maderthaner, descriptions of Vienna can be found especially in the new genre of urban reportage, developed by figures such as Emil Kläger or Max Winter, which draw another picture of the city than the myth produced by elitist discourses and the tourism industry. At the same time, reports about these phenomena reflect changes in political culture, e.g. when the poor masses, which first showed up only as chaotic hordes in hunger revolts, became the grass roots of figures such as Franz Schuhmeier and Karl Lueger, who, although with quite diverging purposes, now made politics with the support of the masses.

JERRY WHITE presents Campbell Bunk, a street in the North London district Islington, which became one of the poorest slums of 19th century London.

White, having worked himself as a public health inspector in Islington in the 1970s, some 15 years after Campbell Bunk had been demolished, brings in a special perspective. Starting his job, he soon realised that the reputation of the former slum was hardly less vivid than it had been. He kept on hearing stories about it, and in 1986 he published a fascinating study on Campbell Bunk between the wars based on interviews he conducted with the local inhabitants. His contribution to the volume at hand can be characterised as a reappraisal after 25 years – from the viewpoint of the 'practitioner', the historian as well as the people living in Campbell Road today.

The article by SONJA WENGOBORSKI and JASPAL NAVEEL SINGH also covers the gamut up to the present. They examine the development of the Indian metropolis Delhi from two different perspectives: In the first part of the article, Wengoborski and Singh are drawing on official documents of city planning and academic or journalistic writings to characterise the city's management of urban poverty. In the second part, this viewpoint is contrasted with insights of modern Hindi literature, which emphasise the lived experiences of the individual social actors in the poor milieus of Delhi. In this way, the important role women play in keeping families and communities functioning becomes clear – an important corrective as against the dominating narrative of official city planners, politicians and other 'strong men.'

HAUKE JAN ROLF addresses the issue of the spatial organisation of Nicaraguan immigrants in Costa Rica's metropolitan area. Based on interviews he conducted with the local inhabitants during his many years of research, he offers an intriguing insider perspective on the social networks of the immigrants and the importance of certain places for their solidarity. Using the examples of a suburban squat, a baseball stadium in San José as well as an inner-city park, Rolf is able to demonstrate how Nicaraguan immigrants shape the respective quarters and the different functions these places hold. Among others, he identifies *transnationalised places* – evidence that opens new perspectives for future research.

The two concluding articles are focusing on urban socio-spatial developments at the beginning of the 21st century and particularly on gentrification processes. INGRID BRECKNER presents three Hamburg city districts as examples of a polarised urban development that is in different stages of gentrification. Ottensen experienced urban renewal since the 1970s and gentrification from inside as well as from outside. The same process is much younger in St. Pauli, where gentrification started after the closing of a huge brewery, which created space for new construction process. Something similar is expected or feared to happen in Wilhelmsburg – up to now the 'district of outcasts' – where two big international exhibitions have opened this year. At the same time the examples of Ottensen and St. Pauli make it clear that resolute and enduring protest is not without influence and that it can at least partially change the direction of the development of city districts.

JULIA RÖTTJER and JAN KUSBER are dealing with similar developments in 21st Century Moscow, the only Megacity in the European context. Looking at urban growth, migration and gentrification, they manage to successfully combine historical perspectives with those of the social sciences and to shed light on processes that make a currently lacking comparison with Western Europe on these topics look promising. The final assessment of Röttjer and Kusber, namely that the development of today's Moscow can serve as "an example of neoliberal growth and the absence of comprehensive urban planning", is appropriate for other cities as well. The same can be said for their appraisal that the article is at the same time an appeal for a closer collaboration of historical and social sciences mainly dealing with the phenomena in question.

Three further contributions, by Johannes Niedbalski (Berlin) on "Funfairs and Amusement Parks. A Social Topography of Pleasure in Early 20th Century Berlin", by Monika Murzyn-Kupisz (Cracow) on urban development and gentrification processes in today's Poland and by Yury Basilov (St. Petersburg) on 21st century St. Petersburg could not be realized for personal reasons, respectively just due to lack of time. As regrettable as this may be for the volume at hand, it is at the same time absolutely understandable. Maybe these yet unwritten texts can serve as stimulation for further research and collaboration.

Concluding, I would like to express my gratitude to the Research Unit *Historical Cultural Sciences* (HKW) of the Johannes Gutenberg University Mainz. The financing of the conference as well as the admission of this volume in the series "Mainz Historical Cultural Sciences" (Mainzer Historische Kulturwissenschaften) were the indispensable basis for the publication at hand. The two colleagues working in the Research Unit's Office, Kristina Müller-Bongard and Cathleen Sarti, were at all times very kind and competent advisors – thanks a lot to both of you for the wonderful collaboration! Furthermore I would like to thank the head of the Department for East European History at the Historical Institute of the Johannes Gutenberg University Mainz, Jan Kusber, for his valuable support in developing and realising the project. I am grateful to my colleague Christof Schimsheimer for the assistance during the conference and to Diana and Helga Weilepp for their patient and very competent replies to quite a few questions from my side during the translation of my text. The Department for Research and Technology Transfer of the Johannes Gutenberg University Mainz offered the opportunity to proof read the contributions to this volume – a process highly appreciated by all authors. And last but not least I am grateful to all authors who – despite so many other obligations – found the time and the energy to revise their presentations for publication. It would be great if this would prove to be a beginning for future collaboration.

Literature

AMERICAN HISTORICAL REVIEW FORUM, Geoff Eleys' *A Crooked Line*, in: American Historical Review 113, 2 (2008), p. 391-437.

ALLEN, MICHEL, Cleansing the City: Sanitary Geographies in Victorian London, Ohio 2008.

BOURDIEU, PIERRE et al., La misère du monde, Paris 1993.

DYOS, HAROLD J., The Slums of Victorian London, in: Victorian Studies 11, 1 (1967), p. 5-40.

ELEY, GEOFF, A Crooked Line: From Cultural History to the History of Society, University of Michigan, Ann Arbor 2005.

GASKELL, MARTIN (ed.), Slums, Leicester et al. 1990.

GILBERT, ALAN, The Return of the Slum: Does Language Matter?, in: International Journal of Urban and Regional Research 31, 4 (2997), p. 697-713,

GREEN, DAVID R., From Artisans to Paupers: Economic Change and Poverty in London, 1790-1870, Aldershot, Brookfield 1995.

JONES, GARETH STEDMAN, Outcast London: A Study in the Relationship between Classes in Victorian Society, Oxford 1971.

KOVEN, SETH, Slumming: Sexual and Social Politics in Victorian London, Princeton 2006.

LINDNER, ROLF, Walks on the Wild Side. Eine Geschichte der Stadtforschung, Frankfurt/Main, New York 2004.

MADERTHANER, WOLFGANG/MUSNER, LUTZ, Die Selbstabschaffung der Vernunft. Die Kulturwissenschaften und die Krise des Sozialen, Wien 2007.

SCHROER, MARKUS, Räume, Orte, Grenzen. Auf dem Weg zu einer Soziologie des Raums, Frankfurt/Main 2006.

YELLING, JAMES ALFRED, Slums and Slum Clearance in Victorian London, London et al. 1986.

WACQUANT, LOÏC, Drei irreführende Prämissen bei der Untersuchung der amerikanischen Ghettos, in: Die Krise der Städte. Analysen zu den Folgen desintegrativer Stadtentwicklung für das ethnisch-kulturelle Zusammenleben, ed. by WILHELM HEITMEYER et al., Frankfurt/Main 1998, p. 194-211.

ID., Body & Soul: Notebooks of an Apprentice Boxer, Oxford 2004.

FRIEDL, PAUL, Conference Report: Looking Behind the Facade of the Ghetto: Perspectives of Cultural Sciences on Urban Slum Areas and Their Inhabitants. 30.03.2012-01.04.2012, Mainz, in: H-Soz-u-Kult, 27.06.2012: http://hsozkult.geschichte.hu-berlin.de/tagungsberichte/id=4281, 07.05.2013.

A Janus-Faced Institution of Ethnoracial Closure
A Sociological Specification of the Ghetto[1]

LOÏC WACQUANT

> The scientific mind must form itself by continually reforming itself.
> (Gaston Bachelard, Psychoanalyse de l'esprit scientifique, 1938)

It is a paradox that, while the social sciences have made extensive use of the "ghetto" as a *descriptive term*, they have failed to forge a robust *analytical concept* of the same. In the historiography of the Jewish diaspora in early modern Europe and under Nazism, the sociology of the black American experience in the twentieth-century metropolis, and the anthropology of ethnic outcasts in East Asia and Africa, its three traditional domains of application, the term "ghetto" variously denotes a bounded urban ward, a web of group-specific institutions, and a cultural and cognitive constellation (values, mind-set, or mentality) entailing the sociomoral isolation of a stigmatized category as well as the systematic truncation of the life space and life chances of its members. But none of these strands of research has taken the trouble to specify what makes a ghetto *qua* social form, which of its features are constitutive and which are derivative, as they have, at each epoch, taken for granted and adopted the *folk concept* extant in the society under examination.

---

1   First published in HAYNES/HUTCHISON, 2012, p. 1-33.

This explains that the notion, appearing self-evident, does not figure in most dictionaries of social science.[2] It is also why, after decades employing the word, sociologists remain vague, inconsistent, and conflicted about its core meaning, perimeter of empirical pertinence, and theoretical import. The recent "Symposium on the Ghetto" organized by *City & Community* in the wake of Mario Small's critique of the central theses of my book *Urban Outcasts* richly documents the myriad observational anomalies and analytic troubles spawned by the unreflective derivation of social-scientific from ordinary constructs.[3] These troubles are not resolved but redoubled when the *composite US imagery* of the (black) ghetto (after its collapse) gets transported to Western Europe and Latin America, and they are trebled when scholars attempt cross-national comparisons of patterns of urban marginality and/or ethnoracial inequality based on the national common sense of their home societies as to the meaning of "the ghetto".[4] This debate vividly demonstrates that the ghetto is not a *contested concept* à la Gallie[5] so much as a *confused conception* that comes short of the level of analytic specificity, coherence, and parsimony minimally required of a scientific notion.

This chapter clears up this confusion by constructing a rigorous sociological concept of the ghetto as a spatially based implement of ethnoracial closure. After spotlighting the semantic instability and slippage of the notion in American culture and scholarship, I extract the structural and functional similarities presented by three canonical instances of the phenomenon: the Jewish ghetto of Renaissance Europe, the black American ghetto of the Fordist United States, and the reserved districts of the Burakumin in post-Tokugawa Japan. Against thin *gradational* conceptions based on rates (of ethnic dissimilarity, spatial concentration, poverty, etc.), which prove promiscuous and prone to metaphorical bleeding as well as inchoate, I elaborate a thick *relational* conception of the ghetto as a

---

2   Remarkably, "ghetto" receives no entry in the nineteen-volume International Encyclopedia of the Social and Behavioral Sciences published in the United States just as the country was being shaken to its core by a wave of ghetto riots, cf. SILLS/ MERTON 1968. Even specialized dictionaries of racial and ethnic studies give the notion short shrift: definitions in them are typically terse, limited to the mention of ethnic segregation in space and to a descriptive denotation of particular ghettos (those of the Jewish and black diasporas).

3   Cf. HAYNES/HUTCHISON, 2008.

4   An extended argument in favor of epistemological rupture as the only viable solution to the 'demarcation problem' in the comparative sociology of urban marginality is WACQUANT, 2008(1), p. 7-12, 135-162, 233-235, 272-276.

5   Cf. GALLIE, 1956.

sociospatial institution geared to the twin mission of isolating and exploiting a dishonored category. So much to say that the ghetto results not from ecological dynamics but from the inscription in space of a material and symbolic *power asymmetry*, as revealed by the recurrent role of collective violence in establishing as well as challenging ethnoracial confinement. Next, I unscramble the connections between ghettoization, segregation, and poverty, and I articulate an ideal-typical opposition between ghetto and ethnic cluster with which to carry out measured comparisons of the fates of various stigmatized populations and places in different cities, societies, and epochs. This points to the role of the ghetto as organizational shield and cultural crucible for the production of a unified but tainted identity that furthers resistance and eventually revolt against seclusion. I conclude by proposing that the ghetto is best analogized not with districts of dereliction (which confuses ethnoracial seclusion with extraneous issues of class, deprivation, and deviance) but with other devices for the forcible containment of tainted categories such as the prison, the reservation, and the camp.

A fuzzy and evolving notion

A brief recapitulation of the strange career of "the ghetto" in American society and social science, which has dominated inquiry into the topic both quantitatively and thematically, suffices to illustrate its semantic instability and dependency on the whims and worries of urban rulers. For the past century, the range and contents of the term have successively expanded and contracted in keeping with how political and intellectual elites have viewed the vexed nexus of ethnicity and poverty in the city.[6]

At first, in the closing decades of the nineteenth century, the ghetto designated residential concentrations of European Jews in the Atlantic seaports and was clearly distinguished from the "slum" as an area of housing blight and social pathology.[7] The notion dilated during the Progressive era to encompass all inner-city districts wherein exotic newcomers gathered, namely, lower-class immigrants from the southeastern regions of Europe and African Americans fleeing the Jim Crow regime of racial terrorism in the US South. Expressing upper-class worries over whether these groups could or should assimilate into the predominant Anglo-Saxon pattern of the country, the notion referred then to the intersection between the ethnic neighborhood and the slum, where segregation was

---

6   Cf. WARD, 1989.
7   Cf. LUBOVE, 1963

believed to combine with physical disrepair and overcrowding to exacerbate urban ills such as criminality, family breakdown, and pauperism, and thwart participation in national life. This conception was given scientific authority by the ecological paradigm of the emerging Chicago school of sociology. In his classic book *The Ghetto*, Louis Wirth assimilates to the Jewish ghetto of medieval Europe the "Little Sicilies, Little Polands, Chinatowns, and Black Belts in our large cities"[8], along with the "vice areas" hosting deviant types such as hobos, bohemians, and prostitutes. All of them are said to be "natural areas" born of the universal desire of different groups to "preserve their peculiar cultural forms" and each fulfills a specialized "function" in the broader urban organism.[9] This is what one may call *Wirth's error*: confounding the mechanisms of sociospatial seclusion visited upon African Americans and upon European immigrants by conflating two urban forms with antinomic architectures and effects, the ghetto and the ethnic cluster. This initial error enabled the ecological paradigm to thrive even as the urbanization of African Americans blatantly contradicted its core propositions.[10] It would be repeated cyclically for decades and persistently obfuscate the specificity of ghettoization as an exclusive type of enclosure.

The notion contracted rapidly after World War II under the press of the Civil Rights movement to signify mainly the compact and congested enclaves to which African Americans were forcibly relegated as they migrated into the industrial centers of the North. The growth of a "Black Metropolis in the womb of the white" wherein Negroes evolved distinct and parallel institutions to compensate for and shield themselves from unflinching exclusion by whites[11] contrasted sharply with the smooth residential dispersal of European Americans of foreign stock. And the mounting political mobilization of blacks against continued caste subordination made their reserved territory a central site and stake of sociopolitical struggles in the city as well as a springboard for collective action against white rule. Writing at the acme of the black uprisings of the 1960s, Kenneth Clark made this relationship of ethnoracial subordination epicentral to his dissection of the *Dark Ghetto* and its woes: "America has contributed to the concept of the ghetto the restriction of persons to a special area and the limiting of their freedom of choice on the basis of skin color. The dark ghetto's invisible walls have been erected by the white

---

8   WIRTH, 1928, p. 6.
9   A useful analytic survey of the works of the Chicago school on this front is HANNERZ, 1980; a cutting critique of the biotic naturalism of Park, Burgess and Wirth is in LOGAN/MOLOTCH, 1987, chap. 1.
10 Cf. WACQUANT, 1998.
11 Cf. DRAKE/CAYTON, (1945) 1993.

society, by those who have power."¹² This diagnosis was confirmed by the Kerner Commission, a bipartisan task force appointed by President Johnson whose official report on the "civil disorders" that rocked the American metropolis famously warned that, because of white racial intransigence, America was "moving toward two societies, one black, one white – separate and unequal."¹³

But over the ensuing two decades the dark ghetto collapsed and devolved into a barren territory of dread and dissolution due to deindustrialization and state policies of welfare reduction and urban retrenchment. As racial domination grew more diffuse and diffracted through a class prism, the category was displaced by the duet formed by the geographic euphemism of "inner city" and the neologism of "underclass," defined as the substratum of ghetto residents plagued by acute joblessness, social isolation, and antisocial behaviors.¹⁴ By the 1990s, the neutralization of the "ghetto" in policy-oriented research culminated in the outright expurgation of any mention of race and power to redefine it as any tract of extreme poverty ("containing over 40 % of residents living under the federal poverty line"), irrespective of population and institutional makeup, in effect dissolving the ghetto back into the slum and rehabilitating the folk conception of the early twentieth century.¹⁵ This paradoxical "deracialization"

---

12 CLARK, 1956, p. 11.
13 KERNER COMMISSION, 1968, p. 2. This formula was intended as an inverted echo of the Supreme Court decision Plessy v. Ferguson (1896) which proclaimed racial segregation congruent with the country's Constitution, provided that the dual institutional tracks thus spawned be "separate but equal" (which they never were, not surprisingly since the same court studiously omitted to specify any criteria of equality or the means to bring it about). This ruling provided the juridical basis for the establishment of six decades of legal segregation in the United States, until the 1954 decision Brown v. Board of Education found that racial separation by itself implies an inegality that violates constitutional principles. It points to the pivotal role of the state in the (un)making of the black ghetto and of ethnoracial domination more generally.
14 Cf. WILSON, 1987.
15 Cf. JARGOVSKY, 1997. At the same time, the ostensibly deracialized conception of 'the ghetto' as a district of widespread destitution kept the focus squarely on the African-American (sub)proletariat by adopting as its operational cut-off point the bureaucratic category of a census tract with a 40-percent poverty rate, which coincidentally ensured its empirical overlap with the remnants of the historic Black Belt. Like the discovery of the 'underclass' a decade earlier, this conceptual move validated the special worries of state elites about the management of

of a notion initially fashioned, and until then deployed, to capture ethnoracial partition in the city resulted from the combination of the crumbling of the historic dark ghetto of the industrial era and the correlative political censorship of race in policy-oriented research after the ebbing of the Civil Rights movement. This "gutting of the ghetto"[16] was then taken one step further by the rash proposal to abandon the notion altogether, instead of clarifying it, on grounds that it cannot capture the complexity, heterogeneity, and fluidity of "poor black neighborhoods" in the United States[17] – as if ghettoization were a flat and static synonym for impoverishment, occurred only in the United States, and could not encompass, or partake of, a fluid and differentiated urban formation.

Meanwhile the term was extended to the study of the distinctive sociocultural patterns elaborated by homosexuals in the cities of advanced societies "in response to both stigma and gay liberation"[18] after the Stonewall riots. It has also made a spectacular return across western Europe in heated scholarly and policy debates over the links between postcolonial immigration, postindustrial economic restructuring, and spatial dualization as the fear of the "Americanization" of the metropolis swept the continent.[19] That European social scientists took to invoking "the ghetto" to stress the growing potency and specificity of ethnoracial division in their countries just when their American colleagues were busy extirpating race from the same notion is an irony that seems only to further muddle its meaning. Yet one can extract out of these varied literatures common threads and recurrent properties to *construct a relational concept* of the ghetto as an *instrument of closure and control* that clears up most of the confusion surrounding it and turns it into a powerful tool for the social analysis of ethnoracial domination and urban inequality. For this it suffices to return to the historical inception of the word and of the phenomenon it depicted in Renaissance Venice.

A janus-faced institution of ethnic closure and control

Coined by derivation from the Italian *giudecca*, *borghetto* or *gietto* (or from the German *gitter* or the Talmudic Hebrew *get*: the etymology is disputed), the

---

   black marginality in the inner city while eliding the latter's roots in ethnoracial domination and regressive state policies.
16 WACQUANT, 2002.
17 Cf. SMALL, 2009.
18 LEVINE, 1979, p. 31.
19 Cf. MUSTERD et al., 2006; SCHIERUP et al., 2006.

word "ghetto" initially referred to the forced consignment of Jews to special districts by the city's political and religious authorities. In medieval Europe, Jews were commonly allotted quarters wherein they resided, administered their own affairs, and followed their customs. Such quarters were granted or sold as a privilege to attract them into the towns and principalities for which they fulfilled key roles as money-lenders, tax collectors, and long-distance tradesmen. But, between the 13th and the 16th century, in the wake of the upheavals caused by the Crusades, favor gradually turned into compulsion.[20] In 1516 the Senate of Venice ordered all Jews rounded up into the *ghetto nuovo*, an abandoned foundry on an isolated island enclosed by two high walls whose outer windows and doors were sealed while watchmen stood guard on its two bridges and patrolled the adjacent canals by boat.[21] Jews were henceforth allowed to come out to pursue their occupations by day, but they had to wear a distinctive garb that made them readily recognizable and return inside the gates before sunset on pain of severe punishment. These measures were designed as an alternative to expulsion to enable the city-state to reap the economic benefits brought by the presence of Jews (including rents, special taxes, and forced levies) while protecting its Christian residents from contaminating contact with bodies perceived as unclean and dangerously sensual, carriers of syphilis and vectors of heresy, in addition to bearing the taint of money-making through usury, which the Catholic Church equated with prostitution.[22]

As this Venetian model spread in cities throughout Europe and around the Mediterranean rim,[23] territorial fixation and seclusion led, on the one hand, to overcrowding, housing deterioration, and impoverishment as well as excess morbidity and mortality, and, on the other, to institutional flowering and cultural consolidation as urban Jews responded to multiplying civic and occupational restrictions by knitting a dense web of group-specific organizations that served as so many instruments of collective succor and solidarity, from markets and business associations, to charity and mutual aid societies, to places of religious worship and scholarship. The *Judenstadt* of Prague, Europe's largest ghetto in

---

20   Cf. STOW, 1992.
21   Cf. CURIEL/COOPERMAN, 1990.
22   Cf. SENNET, 1994, p. 224.
23   Cf. JOHNSON, 1987, p. 235-245. A functional variant arose with the ghetto of Rome, which was founded in 1555 on the banks of the Tiber and abolished in 1870. It purported to foster the religious conversion and cultural dissolution of Jews, but it ended up having the opposite effects and it did not diffuse geographically. Cf. STOW, 2001.

the eighteenth century, even had its own city hall, the *Rathaus*, emblem of the relative autonomy and communal strength of its residents, and its synagogues were entrusted not only with the spiritual stewardship but also with the administrative and judicial oversight of its population. Social life in the Jewish ghetto was turned inward and verged "on overorganization"[24], so that it reinforced both integration within and isolation from without.

One can detect in this inaugural moment the four constituent elements of the ghetto, viz., (i) *stigma*, (ii) *constraint*, (iii) *spatial confinement*, and (iv) *institutional parallelism*. The ghetto is a social-organizational device that employs space to reconcile two antinomic functions: (1) to maximize the material profits extracted out of a category deemed defiled and defiling; and to (2) minimize intimate contact with its members so as to avert the threat of symbolic corrosion and contagion they are believed to carry. If the target population did not serve an essential economic function, it could be kept out of the city or expelled from it – as Jews had been periodically in medieval history. If that same group was not irremediably tainted, it would simply be exploited and allowed to mingle in the city in accordance with its position in the division of labor. It is the conflictive combination of economic value and symbolic danger that made handling Jews problematic and spurred the invention of the ghetto.

These same four building blocks and the same dual rationale of *economic extraction cum social ostracization* governed the genesis, structure, and functioning of the African-American ghetto in the Fordist metropolis during the half-century after World War I. Blacks were actively recruited into northern cities of the United States cities at the outbreak of World War I because their unskilled labor was indispensable to the industries that formed the backbone of a factory economy fed by booming military production but starved of hands by the interruption of European migration.[25] Yet there was no question of them mixing and consorting with whites, who regarded them as inherently vile, congenitally inferior, and shorn of ethnic honor owing to the stain of slavery.[26] As blacks moved in from the South in the millions, white hostility increased and

---

24 WIRTH, 1928.
25 Cf. MARKS, 1989.
26 The following disquisition on the 'Negro character' published in the journal of the Hyde Park Property Owners' Association (cited in SPEA, 1968, p. 220) captures the tenor of the view of African Americans held by white Chicagoans at the close of the Great War: "There is nothing in the make-up of a Negro, physically or mentally, which should induce anyone to welcome him as a neighbor. The best of them are insanitary. [...] Ruin alone follows their path. They are proud as peacocks, but

patterns of discrimination and segregation that had hitherto been informal and inconsistent hardened in housing, schooling, and public accommodations and were extended to the economy and polity.[27] African Americans were forcibly funneled into reserved districts that quickly turned homogeneously black as they expanded and consolidated. They had no choice but to seek refuge inside the bounded perimeter of the Black Belt and to endeavor to develop in it a network of separate institutions to procure the basic needs of the castaway community. Thus arose a duplicate city anchored by black churches and newspapers, black block clubs and lodges, black schools and businesses, and black political and civic associations, nested at the core of the white metropolis yet sealed from it by an impassable fence built of custom, legal suasion, economic discrimination (by realtors, banks, and the state), and violence, as manifested in the beatings, fire-bombings, and riots that checked those who dared to stray across the color line.

This forced institutional parallelism predicated on enveloping and inflexible spatial seclusion – not extreme poverty, housing blight, cultural difference, or mere residential separation – is what has distinguished African Americans from every other group in US history, as noted by leading students of the black urban experience from W.E.B. Du Bois and E. Franklin Frazier to Drake and Cayton to Kenneth Clark and Oliver Cox.[28] It also characterizes the trajectory of the Burakumin in the Japanese city after the close of the Tokugawa era.[29] As the lineal descendants of the *eta* and *hinin*, two categories locked out of the fourfold estate order of feudal Japan (composed of warriors, peasants, artisans, and merchants), the Burakumin were untouchables in the eyes of the Buddhist and Shinto religions.[30] As a result, they suffered centuries of virulent prejudice, discrimination,

---

      have nothing of the peacock's beauty. [...] Niggers are undesirable neighbors and entirely irresponsible and vicious."

27   Cf. SPEAR, 1968; OSOFSKY, 1971.
28   Cf. WACQUANT, 1998.
29   Cf. HANE, 1982.
30   The eta ("filth eternal") were permanent and hereditary pariahs descended from the occupational guilds tainted by the handling of death, blood, leather, and armor. The hinin ("nonhuman") were temporary and nonhereditary pariahs tainted by criminal punishment (typically banishment for ten to twenty years). The exact origins, composition, and evolving status of the Burakumin are the objects of fierce debates in Japanese historiography in relation with contemporary political battles and policy alternatives (cf. NEARY, 2003), and the topic continues to be as sulfurous as the category.

segregation, and violence that kept them cloistered in social and physical space. By the nineteenth century, they were legally confined from sundown to sunup in out-of-the-way hamlets (*buraku*) that were omitted from official maps; they were obliged to wear a yellow collar and to walk barefoot; they were expected to drop on their hands and knees when addressing commoners; and they could be killed virtually without sanction. Crucially, the Burakumin were barred from entering shrines and temples and they were restricted to wedding solely among themselves, based on the belief that the filth of their ancestors was indelible and communicated by blood. Although they are phenotypically indistinguishable from other Japanese, they can be identified through the marriage registries established and diffused during the Meiji era (1868-1912), as well as by their patronym and place of provenance or residence.

The Burakumin were officially emancipated in 1871, but as they moved into cities they were funneled against their will into notorious neighborhoods near garbage dumps, crematoria, jails, and slaughterhouses, that were widely viewed as nests of criminality and immorality. There, they were barred from industrial employment and locked in low-paying and dirty jobs, sent to separate schools, and compelled to remain largely endogamous,[31] effectively leading constricted lives encased by a network of parallel and inferior institutions. By the late 1970s, according to the Burakumin Defense League, they were estimated to number 3 million, trapped in 6000 *buraku* districts in some thousand cities across the main island, with strong concentrations in the Kyoto region. After a full decade of vigorous programs of affirmative action launched in 1969, one-fifth of the Burakumin were still employed as butchers, shoemakers and in the leather trades, and over one-half worked as street sweepers, trash collectors, and public works employees. As a result, their rates of poverty, welfare receipt, and mortality stood far above the national average.[32]

Spread over three continents and five centuries, the Jewish, African-American, and Burakumin cases demonstrate that the ghetto is not, *pace* Wirth, a "natural area" arising via environmental adaptation governed by a biotic logic "akin to the competitive cooperation that underlies the plant community"[33] The mistake of the early Chicago school here consisted in falsely "converting history into natural history" and passing ghettoization off as "a manifestation of human nature" virtually coterminous with "the history of migration"[34], when it is a

---

31   Cf. DeVos/Wagatsuma, 1966.
32   Cf. Sabouret, 1983.
33   Wirth, 1928, p. 284f.
34   Ibid., p. 285.

highly peculiar form of urbanization warped by asymmetric relations of power between ethnoracial groupings: a special form of *collective violence concretized in urban space*. That ghettoization is *not* an "uncontrolled and undesigned"[35] process, as Robert E. Park asserted in his preface to *The Ghetto*, became especially visible after World War II in the United States when the black American ghetto was reconstructed from the top down, and its shelf-life extended by another quarter-century, through state policies of public housing, urban renewal, and suburban economic development intended to bolster the rigid rigid spatial and social separation of blacks from whites.[36] It is even more glaring in the instance of the "caste cities" built by colonial powers to inscribe in space the hierarchical ethnic organization of their overseas possessions, such as Rabat under French rule over Morocco and Cape Town after the passage of the Group Areas Acts under the apartheid regime of South Africa.[37]

Recognizing that it is a product and instrument of group power makes it possible to appreciate that, in its full-fledged form, the ghetto is a *Janus-faced institution* as it plays opposite roles for the two collectives it binds in a relation of asymmetric dependency. For the dominant category, its rationale is to *confine and control*, which translates into what Max Weber calls the "exclusionary closure" of the subordinate category.[38] For the latter, however, it is a *protective and integrative device* insofar as it relieves its members from constant contact with the dominant and fosters consociation and community-building within the constricted sphere of intercourse it creates. Enforced isolation from the outside leads to the intensification of social exchange and cultural sharing inside. Ghettos are the product of a mobile and tensionful dialectic of external hostility and internal affinity that expresses itself as ambivalence at the level of collective consciousness. Thus, although European Jews consistently protested relegation

---

35 IBID., p. viii.
36 Cf. HIRSCH, 1983.
37 Cf. ABU-LUGHOD, 1980; WESTERN, 1981. Colonial societies form a vast yet largely uncharted domain for the comparative study of the dynamics and forms of ghettoization for three reasons. First, in their settler variant, they were 'geographic' social formations, predicated on land spoliation, close control of the circulation of goods and people, and the rigid regimentation of space. Second, they were founded on sharp, stiff, and salient ethnoracial divisions that were projected onto the spatial organization of the city. Lastly, urban forms were major vehicles for social engineering and identity crafting in the colony. Cf. for illustrations the complementary studies of French dominions by WRIGHT, 1991, and ÇELIK, 1997.
38 Cf. WEBER, 1922/1978.

within their outcast districts, they were nonetheless deeply attached to them and appreciative of the relative security they afforded and the special forms of collective life they supported: Francfort's ghetto in the eighteenth century was "not just the scene of confinement and persecution but a place where Jews were entirely, supremely, at home"[39] Similarly black Americans took pride in having "erected a community in their own image," even as they resented the fact that they had done so under duress, as a result of unyielding white exclusion aimed at warding off the specter of "social equality," that is, sexual mixing.[40]

"I love Harlem because it belongs to me"

The sentiment of being "home" inside the ghetto, in a protected and protecting space, is expressed with verve in the narrative of the daily foibles of Jesse B. Semple or Simple, the character created by the poet Langston Hughes to give voice to the aspirations of urban black Americans at the mid-century point. Thus when he exclaims about Harlem :

> "'It's so full of Negroes, I feel like I got protection.' – 'From what?' – 'From white folks', said Simple. I like Harlem because it belongs to me. [...] You say the houses ain't mine. Well, the sidewalk is – and don't you push me off. The cops don't even say, 'Move on,' hardly no more. They learned something from them Harlem riots[41]. [...] Here I ain't scared to vote – that's another thing I like about Harlem. [...] Folks is friendly in Harlem. I feel like I got the world in a jug and the stopper in my hand! So drink a toast to Harlem!"[42]

Acknowledging the double-sidedness of the ghetto spotlights its role as organizational matrix and symbolic incubator for the production of a "spoiled identity" in Erving Goffman's sense of the term.[43] For the ghetto is not only the concrete means and materialization of ethnoracial domination through the spatial segmentation of the city; it is also a site of intense cultural production and a potent *collective identity machine* in its own right. It helps to incrustate and

---

39 GAY, 1992, p. 67.
40 Cf. DRAKE/CAYTON, (1945) 1993, p. 115
41 In 1935 and 1943, the residents of Harlem rose up against racial exclusion made unbearable by the economic collapse of the Great Crisis, cf. GREENBERT, 1991.
42 HUGHES, 1957, p. 20f.
43 Cf. GOFFMANN, 1963.

elaborate the very division of which it is the expression in two complementary and mutually reinforcing ways. First, the ghetto sharpens the boundary between the outcast category and the surrounding population by deepening the sociocultural chasm between them: it renders its residents objectively and subjectively more dissimilar from other urban dwellers by submitting them to unique conditionings, so that the patterns of cognition and conduct they fashion have every chance of being perceived by outsiders as singular, exotic, even "aberrant",[44] which feeds prejudicial beliefs about them.

Next, the ghetto is a cultural combustion engine that melts divisions amongst the confined population and fuels its collective pride even as it entrenches the stigma that hovers over it. Spatial and institutional entrapment deflects class differences and corrodes cultural distinctions within the relegated ethnoracial category. Thus Christian ostracism welded Ashkenazic and Sephardic Jews under an overarching Jewish identity such that they evolved a common "social type" and "state of mind" across the ghettos of Europe.[45] Similarly, America's dark ghetto accelerated the sociosymbolic amalgamation of mulattos and Negroes into a single unified "race" and turned racial consciousness into a mass phenomenon fueling community mobilization against continued caste exclusion.[46]

Yet this unified identity cannot but be stamped with ambivalence as it remains tainted by the very fact that ghettoization proclaims what Weber calls the "negative evaluation of honor"[47] assigned to the group confined. It is therefore wont to foster among its members sentiments of self-doubt and self-hatred, dissimulation of one's origin through "passing," the pernicious derogation of one's kind, and even fantastical identification with the dominant.[48] The ghetto is home, but it remains an inferior home, built under duress, that exists at the order and sufferance of the dominant. Its residents know that, as it were, in their bones.

---

44 Cf. SENNETT, 1994, p. 244; WILSON, 1987, p. 7f.
45 Cf. WIRTH, 1928, p. 71-88; IBID., 1956/1964
46 Cf. DRAKE/CAYTON, (1945) 1993, p. 390.
47 WEBER, 1922/1978.
48 Cf. CLARK, 1965, p. 63-67. The phenomenon of "passing" among the Burakumin is an explosive question in the historical sociology and politics of Japan's "invisible race", cf. NEARY, 2003. An abiding sense of disgrace born of the internalization of stigma is a prevalent theme in the autobiographies of Burakumin activists (e.g., HANE, 1982, p- 163-171).

Disentangling poverty, segregation, and ethnic clustering

Articulating the concept of ghetto as sociospatial mechanism of ethnoracial closure makes it possible to disentangle the relationship between ghettoization, urban poverty, and segregation, and thence to clarify the structural and functional differences between ghettos and ethnic neighborhoods. I tackle each of these questions in turn.

1. *Poverty is a derivative and variable characteristic of ghettos*: The fact that many ghettos have historically been places of endemic and often acute misery owing to the paucity of space, the density of settlement, and the economic restrictions and statutory maltreatment of their residents does not imply that a ghetto is necessarily a place of destitution, nor that it is uniformly deprived. Indeed the very opposite is true: ghettos have more often than not been vectors of economic amelioration, even as they imposed multifarious restrictions on their residents. The *Judengasse* of Frankfurt, instituted in 1490 and abolished in 1811, went through periods of prosperity no less than penury, and it contained sectors of extraordinary opulence as court Jews helped the city become a vibrant center of trade and finance – part of its glamour to this day comes from it being the ancestral home of the Rothschild dynasty.[49] Being forced to dwell within the walled compound of the *mellah* did not prevent the Jews of Marrakech from thriving economically: many of its business leaders were renowned throughout Morocco for their wealth.[50] Turning to the United States, James Weldon Johnson insisted that the Harlem of the 1930s was "not a slum or a fringe" but the "cultural capital"[51] of black America, a place where "the Negro's advantages and opportunities are greater than in any other place in the country." Similarly, Chicago's "Bronzeville" at the mid-twentieth-century point was not only far more prosperous than the Southern black communities from which its residents had migrated; it harbored the largest and most affluent African-American bourgeoisie of its era.[52]

The ghetto arises through the *double assignation of category to territory and territory to category*, and therefore purports to contain the gamut of classes evolved by the confined group. It follows that, to the degree that this group

---

49 Cf. WIRTH, 1928, chapter 4.
50 Cf. GOTTREICH, 2006, p. 102-105.
51 JOHNSON, 1930, p. 4.
52 Cf. DRAKE/CLAYTON, (1945) 1993.

experiences socioeconomic dispersion, its reserved district offers extensive avenues for economic betterment and upward mobility in its internal social order. Indeed, in the case of African Americans, ghettoization, class differentiation, and collective enrichment proceeded apace: in addition to allowing the conversion of peasants into industrial workers, the rise and consolidation of the ghetto fostered the growth of a black middle class of business owners, professionals, politicians, teachers, and preachers servicing a captive clientele of lower-class coethnics that the dispersed rural communities of the South could have never sustained.[53] Whether a ghetto is poor or not, and to what degree, depends on the overall economic standing of the category it cloisters, its distribution in the division of labor, and on extraneous factors such as demography, ecology, state policies, and the shape of the surrounding economy.

Conversely, not all dispossessed and dilapidated urban districts are ghettos – and if they are such, it is not by dint of their level of deprivation. Declining white neighborhoods in the deindustrializing cities of the US Midwest and the British Midlands, depressed rural towns of the former East Germany and southern Italy, and the disreputable *villas miserias* of greater Buenos Aires at the close of the twentieth century are territories of working-class demotion and decomposition, not ethnic containers dedicated to maintaining an outcast group in a relationship of seclusive subordination.[54] They are not ghettos other than in a purely metaphorical sense, no matter how impoverished and how isolated their residents may be. If extreme rates of concentrated poverty breeding social isolation sufficed to make a ghetto, as argued by William Wilson,[55] then the backcountry of Alabama, Native American reservations, large chunks of the former Soviet Union and most Third-World cities would be gargantuan ghettos. More curiously still, by that definition neither Venice's *ghetto nuovo* nor Chicago's Bronzeville at the peak of their historical development would be ghettos![56]

---

53   The ghetto of Chicago thus produced the country's first black national newspaper, "The Chicago Defender", whose owner, Robert S. Abbott, was also the city's first black millionaire, cf. SPEAR, 1968, p. 165-167.

54   Cf. the case of Buenos Aires dissected by AUYERO, 2000.

55   Cf. WILSON, 1996.

56   Another anomaly generated by the income-based (re)definition of the ghetto is the following: the same neighborhood, harboring the same population and institutions, and fulfilling the same functions in the metropolitan system, would alternately become a ghetto and cease being one with wide variations of its poverty rate caused by cyclical fluctuations of the economy. This conception not only leaves out the canonical cases of the ghetto: by making ghettoization a derivative property of

The *favelas* of the Brazilian metropolis are often portrayed as segregated dens of dereliction and disorganization, overrun by drugs and violence, but upon close observation they turn out to be variegated working-class wards with finely stratified webs of ties to industry and to the wealthy districts for which they supply household service labor. They display considerable variety in levels of segregation and situations of collective "socioeconomic vulnerability".[57] As in the *ranchos* of Venezuela and the *poblaciones* of Chile, families that dwell in these squatter settlements span the color continuum and have extensive genealogical bonds to higher-income households; they are "not socially and culturally marginal, but stigmatized and excluded from a closed class system"[58]. In any case, neither their poverty rate nor the mix of functions they fulfill in the metropolis, from viable reservoir of labor power to warehouse for the rejects of "regressive deindustrialization," qualifies them as ghettos. The same demonstration applies to the *ciudad perdida* in Mexico, the *cantagril* in Uruguay, and the *pueblo jóven* in Peru.[59]

Given that not all ghettos are poor and not all poor areas are (inside) ghettos, one cannot collapse the analysis of ghettoization into the study of slums, impoverished estates, and assorted districts of dispossession in the city. This conflation is precisely the mistake committed by those European observers who, smitten with a vague and emotive vision of the black American ghetto as a territory of urban dissolution and social dread – that is, with the barren *vestiges* of the dark ghetto *after its implosion* at the close of the 1960s – conclude that "ghettoiza-

---

economic inequality and income distribution, it fails utterly to identify a distinctive sociospatial form.

57 Cf. MARQUES/TORRES, 2005; KOWARICK, 2009.
58 PERLMA, 1976, p. 195. Cf. also ZALUAR/ALVITO, 1998.
59 Cf. WACQUANT, 2008(1), p. 7-12. There are at least three major interlinked reasons why ghettos did not emerge in Latin American cities – a fact attested by Gilbert, cf. GILBERT, 1998; IBID., 2011. First, the countries with significant dishonored populations (descendants of African slaves and native peasants) have evolved gradational systems of ethnoracial classification based on phenotype and a host of sociocultural variables, as opposed to categorical systems based on descent (as define Jews in Europe and blacks in the United States), resulting in fuzzy and porous ethnic boundaries. Second, and correlatively, they sport low and inconsistent patterns of residential segregation, and solid segregation is a necessary stepping stone to ghettoization. Third, Latin American states have spawned sharply asymmetric conceptions of citizenship, but they have typically not given legal imprimatur to ethnoracial classification and discrimination.

tion" has struck the lower-class zones of the urban periphery of Europe due to rising unemployment, immigrant segregation, and festering delinquency, or, worse, because they adopt the fleeting impressions of their residents who think of themselves as "ghetto" since this is how depressed and defamed neighborhoods are now publicly labelled in public debate.

"The ghetto" comes to France: How "everyday usage" drowns out sociology

Didier Lapeyronnie's thick book on the alleged coalescence of the "urban ghetto" in France announces a study of "segregation, violence and poverty" in that country but contains not a shred of data and no analysis on these trends and their overlap.[60] Instead, it uses the word ghetto as a loose synonym for declining lower-class estates branded as such by journalists and by some of their residents (who themselves have learned the label from the media). The notion then inexplicably devolves into a subjective concept pertaining to lifestyle, self-conception, and "the shared feeling of having been betrayed" by dominant institutions:

> "The term ghetto belongs to the everyday vocabulary of the *banlieue* [lower-class periphery]. It is used to designate a difficult social or personal situation, even a psychological situation stamped by disorder, poverty, and sometimes violence. It is not necessarily associated with urban segregation and confinement in a territorial sense [...]. Many residents can be of the ghetto without living in the ghetto. They can live it partially, as a function of moments and interactions.... By following this everyday usage, we understand the ghetto to be a dimension of individual and collective behaviors [...]. The ghetto is not a situation, it is a category of action in an array of social relations [...]. We shall seek to evaluate and to define the ghetto as a function of its effects on the self-construction effected by its residents, as a function of the capacity of individuals to name themselves and to assert an 'I', to establish or not a positive relationship to self [...]. We shall seek the truth, or rather the truths, of the ghetto, in the words and in the reflections of its residents"[61]

Characterizing the ghetto as a matter of subjective orientation, "a psychological situation stamped by disorder, poverty, and sometimes violence," is both

---

60   Cf. LAPEYRONNIE, 2007.
61   IBID., 2010, p. 22-24, 26.

incoherent and inconsistent with the established conceptual usage of the term. By that definition, neither the Jewish ghetto of Venice nor the black ghetto of Chicago in their full bloom would be ghettos; any population invoking the idiom of the ghetto is *eo ipso* ghettoized; and consequently the simple remedy to ghettoization is for the residents of lower-class districts to change their representations of themselves. Not to mention that French citizens residing outside the country's "sensitive neighborhoods" who feel "betrayed" by leading institutions would be surprised to discover that, unbeknownst to them, they "live the ghetto."

Echoing Lapeyronnie (on whose views he relies), the sensationalist book by *Le Monde* journalist Luc Bronner entitled *The Law of the Ghetto* provides a selective account of street delinquency and a long litany of clashes between unemployed youths and the police in a few *banlieues* brashly labelled "ghettos" because of the shock value of the term to describe territories of "social, political, and economic violence": "We must dare this term which so frightens the Republic" to describe "our Gomorra."[62] When the so-called law of the ghetto denotes the imprint of low-grade criminality, the flourishing of an informal economy, and assorted urban disorders, we know we have reached the point where the word has been emptied of any sociological meaning to serve as an ordinary *categoreme*, a term of accusation and alarm, pertaining not to social science but public polemic, that serves only to sell books and to fuel the spiral of stigmatization enmeshing the unpoverished districts of the urban periphery.

2. All ghettos are segregated but not all segregated areas are ghettos: The select boroughs of the West of Paris, the exclusive upper-class suburbs of Boston, Berne or Berlin, and the "gated communities" that have mushroomed in global cities such as Milan, Miami, São Paulo, and Cape Town are monotonous in terms of wealth, income, occupation, and very often ethnicity, but they are not for all that ghettos. Segregation in them is entirely voluntary and elective, and for that very reason it is neither all-inclusive nor perpetual. Fortified enclaves of luxury package "security, seclusion, social homogeneity, amenities, and services" to enable bourgeois families to escape what they perceive as "the chaos, dirt, and danger of the city"[63]. These islands of privilege serve to enhance, not curtail, the life chances and protect the lifestyles of their residents, and they radiate a positive aura of distinction,[64] not a sense of infamy and dread. In terms

---

62   BRONNER, 2010, p. 249, 23.
63   CALDEIRA, 2000, p. 264f.
64   Cf. LOW, 2004.

of their causal dynamics, structure and function, they are the very antithesis of the ghetto. To call them such, as with variations on the expression "gilded ghetto," invites confusion and stretches the semantics of the term to the point of meaninglessness.[65]

This indicates that residential segregation is a necessary but not a sufficient condition for ghettoization. For a ghetto to emerge spatial confinement must first be *imposed and all-encompassing*; then it must be overlayed with a distinct and *duplicative set of institutions* enabling the population thus cloistered to reproduce itself within its assigned perimeter. If blacks are the only ethnic category to be "hypersegregated" in American society,[66] it is because they are the only community in that country for which involuntary segregation, assignment to a reserved territory, and organizational parallelism have combined to entrap them in a separate and inferior social cosmos of their own, which in turn bolstered their residential isolation, as well as enforced their extreme marital isolation, virtually unique in the world among major ethnic groups.[67]

That even forcible segregation at the bottom of the urban order does not mechanically produce ghettos is demonstrated by the fate of the declining lower-class *banlieues* of France after the mid-1970s. Although they have been widely described and disparaged as "ghettos" in public discourse and their inhabitants share a vivid feeling of being cast out in a "penalized space" suffused with boredom, anguish, and despair,[68] relegation in these depressed concentrations of public housing laid fallow at the urban periphery is based first on class, and only secondarily on ethnicity, and it is remarkably impermanent. Proof is that the residents who move up the class structure typically move out of the neighborhood – so much so the rate of geographic mobility among the households of "sensitive neighborhoods" surpasses the national average.[69] As a result these degraded districts are culturally heterogeneous, typically harboring a mix of native French families with immigrants from three to six dozen nationalities. And their inhabitants suffer not from institutional duplication and enclosure but, on

---

65   PINÇON-CHARLOT/PINÇON's, 2007, dissection of the dense web of associations, clubs, and councils through which the upper crust of the French bourgeoisie bulwarks its secluded spaces (exclusive urban enclaves, parks and castles, beaches and gardens) shows that the "ghettos of the gotha" are no ghettos. This catchy coinage makes for good marketing copy but muddies the sociological waters.
66   Cf. MASSEY/DENTON, 1993
67   Cf. PATTERSON, 1998.
68   Cf. PÉTONNET, 1982.
69   Cf. OBSERVATOIRE DES ZONES URBAINES SENSIBLES, 2005.

the contrary, from the lack of an ingrown organizational structure capable of sustaining them in the absence of gainful employment and adequate public services. Like the German *Problemquartier*, the Dutch "*krottenwijk*", and the British "sink estates," France's deteriorating *banlieues* are, sociologically speaking, *anti-ghettos*.[70]

The anti-ghettos of Western Europe and the Roma exception

If and when an urban district turns into a ghetto, it should display five mutually reinforcing properties resulting from the reciprocal asssignation of category and territory: (1) growing ethnic homogeneity; (2) increased encompassment of the target population; (3) rising organizational density; (4) the production and adoption of a collective identity; (5) and impermeable boundaries. On all five dimensions, the formerly industrial *banlieues* of France harboring rising shares of immigrants have been *moving steadily away from the pattern of the ghetto*.[71]

Over the past 30 years, these defamed districts have become more diverse in their ethnic composition; the proportion of all foreigners living in them has stagnated or decreased (depending on geographic location and national provenance); and they have lost most of the dense web of organizations that they harbored at the bloom of the age of the industrial "Red Belt." Most strikingly, notwithstanding political campaigns periodically denouncing "multiculturalism" and the media obsession with "Islamicization," these districts have failed to spawn a collective idiom and vision that would unify their residents on grounds of ethnicity, nationality, religion or postcolonial status.[72] Lastly, families experiencing upward mobility, whether through education, employment, or entrepreneurship, have crossed the boundaries of these districts in droves to move up the ladder of neighborhoods and diffuse in metropolitan space. With national variations and regional twists, this French pattern of a multilevel drift

---

70 Cf. WACQUANT, 2008(1).
71 Cf. IBID., 2008(2).
72 Identification based on territory, often cited as a ground for ethnogenesis among lower-class immigrant youths, turns out to be weak: it is defensive, situational and labile; it is closely linked to lifecycle and evaporates upon entry into the labor market or migration out of the neighborhood, cf. LEPOUTRE, 1997.

antithetical to ghettoization fits the trajectories of most immigrant "minorities" throughout Western Europe.[73]

The French analysts who, caught in the political mood and fed by swirling media rumor, bemoan the morphing of the declining working-class districts of the urban periphery into fearsome "immigrant ghettos" wed conceptual confusion and historical amnesia.[74] First, they conflate territories of dereliction (marked by increased unemployment, the deterioration of the housing stock, and the devalorization of their public image) with ethnic segmentation, and they mistake mere segregation, produced by the conjoint press of class and ethnonational origin, for territorial assignation and institutional parallelism – whose absence is then obfuscated by the hazy and sulfurous category of "communautarianism," or by the invocation of the loose journalistic category of "Muslim communities" that exists only in the worried minds of outsiders. Next, they conveniently forget that ethnically marked populations issued from the former colonies were notably *more* segregated spatially and *more* isolated socially (in terms of social ties, marital unions, and institutional participation) in the 1960s and 1970s than they are today. A half-century ago, these immigrants lived separated lives tightly encased in the peripheral sectors of the secondary labor market and in the parallel institutions of the shanty-towns (*bidonvilles*) and reserved housing compounds of the SONACOTRA, the state agency entrusted with housing workers migrating from the Maghrib.[75] Indeed, in sharp contraposition to the black American hyperghetto, it is the growing mixing of native and immigrant populations at the bottom of the structure of classes and places, and the correlative *closing* of social distance and disparities between them in the context of the decomposition of traditional "working-class territories" that are the source of the xenophobic tensions and conflicts that stamp these urban zones.[76]

If there is one category whose experience deviates sharply from this pattern to veer toward ghettoization, it is the Roma of Eastern Europe. This population of 3 to 5 million, dispersed mostly across Romania, Bulgaria, Hungary, Czekoslovakia, and the Balkans has long been marginalized in both monoethnic rural villages and urban districts combining the four structural components of stigma, constraint, spatial enclosure and institutional parallelism. After the collapse of the Soviet empire, the destruction of the safety net and the abrupt social polarization wrought by the market economy have reactivated anti-Roma prej-

---

73 Cf. MUSTERD/KEMPEN, 2009; PEACH, 2009; HARTOG/ZORLU, 2009
74 E.g. MUCCHIELLI/LE GOAZIOU, 2007; LAPEYRONNIE, 2007.
75 Cf. SAYAD/DUPUY, 1995; BERNADOT, 1999
76 Cf. WACQUANT, 2008(1).

udice (as a "criminal race"), animosity, and discrimination and territorial fixation has flared anew as Gypsies sank into unemployment and destitution.[77] But there are also counter-tendencies: many Romas have passed undetected among the non-Gypsy population while others have experienced upward class mobility against the backdrop of a fuzzy ethnic hierarchy enforced with variable stringency in the different nations. Overall, class and country prove to be stronger determinants of the trajectory of Gypsies than race and space.[78] Nonetheless, the controversial policy of the Berlusconi government to reinstitute state-run camps to corral Gypsies on the outskirts of Italian cities and the heinous campaign of destruction of "illegal Rom encampments" launched by President Nicolas Sarkozy in France in the summer of 2010 to curry favor with electors of the far right are there to remind us that the Roma remain prime candidates for the (re) activation of sociospatial enclosure even in western Europe.[79]

3. Ghettos and ethnic neighborhoods sport divergent structures and serve opposite functions: Moving beyond a gradational perspective to scrutinize the peculiar patterning of social relations within the ghetto as well as between it and the surrounding city throws into sharp relief the differences between the ghetto and the ethnic clusters or immigrant neighborhoods such as newcomers to the metropolis have formed in countless countries. The foreign "colonies" of interwar Chicago that Robert Park, Ernest Burgess, and Louis Wirth – and after them the liberal tradition of assimilationist sociology and historiography[80] – mistook for so many white "ghettos" were scattered and mobile constellations born of cultural affinity and occupational concentration, more so than prejudice and discrimination. Segregation in them was partial and porous, a product of immigrant solidarity and ethnic attraction instead of being rigidly imposed by sustained outgroup hostility. Consequently residential separation was neither uniformly nor rigidly visited upon these groups: in 1930, when the all-black Bronzeville harbored 92 % of the city's African-American population, Chicago's Little Ire-

---

77 Cf. GHEORGE, 1991.
78 Cf. LADÁNYI/SZELÉNYI, 2006.
79 The prototype Rom "village" of Castel Romano outside of Rome, home to some 800 Gypsies, with its prefabricated huts laid out in a grid and surrounded by a high metal fence patrolled round the clock by a special police force, and the subjection of its residents to a special census and fingerprinting are strongly redolent of the early modern Italian ghetto. Cf. CLOUGH MARINARO, 2009; CALAME, 2010: http://places.designobserver.com, 07.05.2013.
80 Cf. MILLER, 1992.

land was "an ethnic hodge-podge" of 25 nationalities composed of only one-third Irish persons and containing a paltry 3 % of the city's denizens of Irish ancestry. The eleven dispersed districts making up Little Italy were 46 % Italian and contained just under one-half of Chicagoans of Italian origin. Thus both of these clusters were ethnically plural and monolithically white, and both contained a minority of the population supposedly ghettoized in them.[81]

This pattern was not unique to Chicago but repeated itself in every major industrial center of the Midwest and Northeast of the United States. For instance, the typical Italian immigrant to Philadelphia in 1930 resided amongst "14 percent other Italian immigrants, 38 percent Italian stock, 23 percent all foreign born persons and 57 percent all foreign stock"[82]. Except for marginal and local peculiarities, there were no white "ethnic" neighborhoods in the American metropolis wherein members of one European community were thoroughly isolated from native whites and monopolized space and local institutions to the exclusion of urbanites of other national origins.[83] What is more, the distinctive institutions of European immigrant enclaves were turned outward: they operated to facilitate adjustment to the novel environment of the US metropolis. They neither replicated the organizations of the country of origin nor perpetuated social isolation and cultural distinctiveness. And so they typically waned within two generations as their users gained access to their American counterparts and climbed up the class order and the corresponding ladder of places.[84] All of which is in sharp contrast with the immutable racial exclusivity and enduring institutional alterity of the Black Belt. This Chicago illustration dramatizes the fact that the immigrant neighborhood and the ghetto serve diametrically opposed functions: the one is a springboard for *assimilation* via cultural learning and social-cum-spatial mobility, the other a material and symbolic isolation ward geared toward *dissimilation*. The former is best figured by a bridge, the latter by a wall.[85]

---

81 Cf. PHILPOT, 1978, p. 141-145.
82 HERSCHBERG et al., 1981, p. 200.
83 Cf. WARNER/BURKE, 1969.
84 Cf. NELLI, 1970.
85 Cf. for full documentation of the sharp divergence between the black ghetto and the 'colonies' formed by European immigrant (Jews from Eastern countries, Poles, Italians, and the Irish) in the first half of the twentieth century in the United States LIEBERSON, 1980; BODNAR et al., 1982; ZUNZ, 1986, and GERSTLE, 2001, esp. chap. 5. Workers of Belgian, Italian, Polish, and Iberian provenance underwent a very similar process of spatial diffusion via class incorporation in the French industrial

From shield to sword

It is fruitful, then, to think of *ghetto and ethnic cluster as two ideal-typical configurations situated at opposite ends* of the homological continua of constraint and choice, entrapment and self-protection, exclusivity and heterogeneity, encompassment and dispersal, inward and outward orientations, rigidity and fluidity, along which various populations (themselves differently marked) can be pegged or travel over time depending on the intensity with which the forces of stigma, constraint, spatial confinement, and institutional parallelism impinge upon them and coalesce with one another. We can then shift the analysis from the ghetto as a topographic object, a static state, to *ghettoization* as a sociospatial dynamic, a *multilevel process* liable to empirical specification and measurement. A population that formed mobile clusters out of cultural affinity and inconsistent hostility can find itself subjected to stringent ostracization and territorial fixation such that it evolves permanent sites for comprehensive seclusion: such was the experience of Jews in early modern Europe and of African Americans in the northern metropolis of the United States at the dawn of the Fordist era as they shifted from segregation to ghettoization.

Conversely, ghettoization can be attenuated to the point where, through gradual erosion of, and disjunction between, its spatial, social, and mental boundaries, the ghetto devolves into an elective ethnic concentration operating as a springboard for structural integration and/or cultural assimilation into the broader social formation. This describes well the trajectory of the Chinatowns of the United States from the early to the late twentieth century[86] and the status of the Cuban immigrant enclave of Miami which fostered integration through biculturalism after the Mariel exodus of 1980.[87] It also characterizes the "Kimchee Towns" in which Koreans converged in the metropolitan areas of Japan, which sport a blend of features making them a hybrid of ghetto and ethnic cluster:[88] they are places of infamy that first arose through enmity and constraint, but over

---

city of the first half of the twentieth century in spite of being subjected to virulent xenophobia and widespread collective violence during phases of economic turmoil, cf. NOIRIEL, 1988. Over the past quarter-century, postcolonial migrants have been following a germane trajectory in cities throughout Europe, characterized by low to moderate segregation from nationals and stagnant to decreasing spatial concentration, cf. MUSTERD, 2005.

86 Cf. ZHOU, 1994.
87 Cf. PORTES/STEPICK, 1993.
88 Cf. DEVOS/CHUNG, 1981.

the years their population has become ethnically mixed; residential mingling has in turn enabled Koreans to socialize and intermarry with Japanese neighbors as well as obtain Japanese citizenship through naturalization.

This analytic schema allows one to assess the degree to which a given urban configuration approximates one or the other pure type and on what dimension(s). Thus the so-called gay ghetto is more aptly characterized as a "quasi-ethnic community," since "most gay persons can 'pass' and need not be confined to interacting with their 'own kind'"[89] and none are forced to reside in the areas of visible concentration of gay institutions based on their sexual orientation. Indeed, the vast majority of gays do not live in, or even patronize, these districts, which are local clusters of commercial establishments and public spaces catering to the preferences of gays in matters of consumption and sociability. Their degree of closure, mutual orientation, and collective organization are highly variable and often contested, both without and within the gay district, as illustrated by the case of Le Marais in Paris.[90]

The double-sidedness of the ghetto as *sword* (for the dominant) and *shield* (for the subordinate) implies that, to the degree that its institutional completeness and autonomy are abridged, its protective role is diminished and risks being swamped by its exclusionary modality. In situations where its residents cease to be of economic value to the controlling group, extraction evaporates and no longer balances out ostracization. Ethnoracial encapsulation can then escalate to the point where the ghetto morphs into an apparatus merely to warehouse the spoiled and supernumerary population, as a staging ground for its expulsion, or as a springboard for the ultimate form of ostracization, namely, physical annihilation.

The first scenario fits the evolution of America's "Black Metropolis" after the peaking of the Civil Rights movement in the mid-1960s. Having lost its role as a reservoir of unskilled labor power, the dark ghetto crashed and broke down into a dual sociospatial structure composed of (i) the *hyperghetto*, entrapping the marginal fractions of the black working class in the barren perimeter of the historic ghetto; (ii) and the *black middle-class satellites* that burgeoned at the latter's periphery, in the areas left vacant by white outmigration, where the growing African-American bourgeoisie achieved spatial and social distance from its lower-class brethren.[91] The hyperghetto is a novel sociospatial configuration, doubly segregated by race and class, devoid of economic function, and

---

89 MURRAY, 1979, p. 169.
90 Cf. SIBALIS, 2004.
91 Cf. WACQUANT, 2008(1), p. 11, 51f., 117f.

thus stripped of the communal institutions that used to provide succor to its inhabitants. These institutions have been replaced by the social control institutions of the state (increasingly staffed by the black middle class), and in particular by the booming prison and its disciplinary tentacles. As the authorities turned from the social welfare to the penal regulation of racialized marginality in the city, the hyperghetto became deeply penetrated by and symbiotically linked to the hypertrophied carceral system of the United States by a triple relationship of structural homology, functional surrogacy, and cultural fusion.[92] The second and third scenarios, wherein the ghetto devolves into a means of radical ostracization, were those implemented by Nazi Germany when it revived the *Judenghetto* between 1939 and 1944, first, to impoverish and concentrate Jews with a view toward relocation and later, after mass deportation turned out to be impractical, to funnel them toward extermination camps as part of the "final solution".[93]

The unchecked intensification of its exclusionary thrust attendant upon the loss of its shielding capacity suggests that the ghetto might be most profitably studied not by analogy with urban slums, lower-class districts, and immigrant enclaves but alongside the reservation, the camp, and the prison, as belonging to a broader genus of institutions for the *forced confinement of dispossessed and dishonored groups*.[94] It is not by happenstance that the Bridewell of London (1555), the Zuchthaus of Amsterdam (1654), and the Hospital général of Paris (1656), designed to instill the discipline of wage work in vagrants, beggars, and criminals via incarceration, were invented around the same time as the Jewish ghetto. It is not by coincidence that today's sprawling refugee camps in Sierra Leone, Sri Lanka, and the occupied territories of Palestine and the Gaza Strip look ever more like a cross between the ghettos of early modern Europe and gigantic gulags.[95] And that retention camps for unlawful immigrants have mushroomed throughout Europe as the European Union moved to treating transnational peregrination from the global South as a matter of material security and ethnonational status.[96]

---

92   Cf. WACQUANT, 2001.
93   Cf. FRIEDMAN, 1980; BROWNING, 1986.
94   WACQUANT, 2010, sketches an analytic framework that brings together into a single model forms of sociospatial seclusion at the top (gated communities, upper-class districts) and at the bottom (slum, ethnic cluster, ghetto, prison), as well as urban and rural forms (among which figure preserves, reservations, and camps).
95   Cf. AGIER, 2008; ROZELIER, 2007.
96   Cf. LE COUR GRANDMAISON et al., 2007.

A robust analytic concept of the ghetto as an organizational device for the spatial enclosure and control of a stigmatized group offers a way out of the semantic morass and empirical confusion created by the unreflective adoption of the shifting folk notions of the same among political and intellectual elites. It allows us, not only to describe, differentiate, and explain the diverse urban forms developed by tainted populations as they come into the city without falling into the many traps set by the metaphorical and rhetorical usages of "the ghetto." By spotlighting the tangled nexus of space, power and dishonor, it also gives us the means to grasp the structural and functional kinship between the ghetto, the prison, and the camp just as the state managers of the advanced societies are increasingly resorting to borders, walls, and bounded districts as the means to define, confine, and control problem categories.

Literature

ABU-LUGHOD, JANET L., Rabat, Urban Apartheid in Morocco, Princeton, NJ 1980.
AGIER, MICHEL, Gérer les indésirables. Des camps de réfugiés au gouvernement humanitaire, Paris 2008 (Engl. transl.: Managing the Undesirables: Refugee Camps and Humanitarian Government, Polity, 2011).
AUYERO, JAVIER, Poor People's Politics: Peronist Survival Networks and the Legacy of Evita, Durham, NC 2000.
BERNARDOT, MARC, Chronique d'une institution: la 'Sonacotra' (1956-1976), in: Sociétés contemporaines 33-34 (1999), p. 39-58.
BODNAR, JOHN et al., Lives of Their Own: Blacks, Italians, and Poles in Pittsburgh, Urbana, IL 1986.
BRONNER, LUC, La Loi du ghetto. Enquête dans les banlieues françaises, Paris 2010.
BROWNING, CHRISTOPHER R., Nazi Ghettoization Policy in Poland, 1939-1941., in: Central European History 19, 4 (1986), p. 343-368.
CALAME, JON, The Roma of Rome: Heirs to the Ghetto System, in: The Design Observer, December 2010: http://places.designobserver.com, 07.05.2013.
CALDEIRA, TERESA, City of Walls: Crime, Segregation and Citizenship in São Paulo, Berkeley 2000.
ÇELIK, ZEYNEP, Urban Forms and Colonial Confrontations: Algiers Under French Rule, Berkeley 1997.
CLARK, KENNETH B., Dark Ghetto: Dilemmas of Social Power, New York 1956.

CLOUGH MARINARO, ISABELLA, Between Surveillance and Exile: Biopolitics and the Roma in Italy, in: Bulletin of Italian Politics 1, 2 (2009), p. 265-87.

CURIEL, ROBERTA/COOPERMAN, BERNARD DOV, The Ghetto of Venice, New York 1990.

DEVOS, GEORGE/CHUNG, DEAKYUN, Community Life in a Korean Ghetto, in: Koreans in Japan: Ethnic Conflict and Accomodation, ed. by CHANGSOO LEE and GEORGE DEVOS, Berkeley, CA 1981, p. 225-251.

DEVOS, GEORGE/WAGATSUMA, HIROSHI (eds.), Japan's Invisible Race: Caste in Culture and Personality, Berkeley, CA 1966.

DRAKE, ST. CLAIR/CAYTON, HORACE R., Black Metropolis: A Study of Negro Life in a Northern City (1945), Chicago, IL 1993.

FRIEDMAN, PHILIP, The Jewish Ghettos of the Nazi Era., in: Id./Fridman, Ada June (eds.), Roads to Extinction: Essays on the Holocaust, New York 1980, p. 59-87.

GALLIE, W.B., Essentially Contested Concepts, in: Proceedings of the Aristotelian Society 56 (1956), p. 167-198.

GAY, RUTH, The Jews of Germany: A Historical Portrait, New Haven, CT 1992.

GERSTLE, GARY, American Crucible: Race and Nation in the Twentieth Century, Princeton, NJ 2001.

GILBERT, ALAN, The Latin American City, New York 1998.

ID., On the Absence of Ghettos in Latin America, in: HAYNES, BRUCE D./HUTCHISON RAY (eds.), The Ghetto: Contemporary Global Issues and Controversies, Boulder, Colorado 2012, p. 191-225.

GHEORGHE, NICOLAE, Roma-Gypsy Ethnicity in Eastern Europe, in: Social Research 58, 4 (1991), p. 829-844.

GOFFMAN, ERVING, Stigma: Notes on the Management of Spoiled Identity, New York 1963.

GOTTREICH, EMILY, The Mellah of Marrakesh: Jewish and Muslim Space in Morocco's Red City, Bloomington 2006.

GREENBERT, CHERYL LYNN, Or Does it Explode? Black Harlem in the Great Depression, New York, Oxford 1991.

HANE, MIKISO, Peasants, Rebels, and Outcastes: The Underside of Modern Japan, New York 1982.

HANNERZ, ULF, Soulside: Inquiries into Ghetto Culture and Community. New York 1969.

HARTOG, JOOP/ZORLU ASLAN, Ethnic Segregation in the Netherlands: An Analysis at Neighbourhood Level, in: International Journal of Manpower 30,1/2(2009), p. 15-25.

HAYNES, BRUCE D./HUTCHISON RAY (eds.), The Ghetto: Origins, History, Discourse, in: City & Community 7, 4 (2008), p. 347-398.
ID. (eds.), The Ghetto: Contemporary Global Issues and Controversies, Boulder, Colorado 2012.
HERSCHBERG, THEODORE et al., Philadelphia: Work, Space, Family, and Group Experience in the 19th Century, Oxford, New York 1981.
HIRSCH, ARNOLD, Making the Second Ghetto: Race and Housing in Chicago 1940-1970. Cambridge 1983.
HUGHES, LANGSTON, Simple Stakes a Claim, New York et al. 1957.
JARGOWSKY, PAUL A., Poverty and Place: Ghettos, Barrios, and the American City, New York 1997.
JOHNSON, JAMES WELDON, Black Manhattan (1930), New York 1981.
JOHNSON, PAUL, A History of the Jews, New York 1987.
KERNER COMMISSION, The Kerner Report. The 1968 Report of the National Advisory Commission on Civil Disorders (1968), New York 1989.
KOWARICK, LÚCIO, Viver em risco. Sobre a vulnerabilidade socioeconômica e civil, Sâo Paulo 2009.
LADÁNYI, JANOS/ SZELÉNYI, IVAN, Patterns of Exclusion: Constructing Gypsy Ethnicity and the Making of an Underclass in Transitional Societies of Europe, New York 2006.
LAPEYRONNIE, DIDIER, Ghetto urbain. Ségrégation, violence, pauvreté en France aujourd'hui. Paris 2007.
LE COUR GRANDMAISON et al. (eds.), Le Retour des camps. Sangatte, Lampedusa, Gantánamo, Paris 2007.
LEPOUTRE, DAVID, Cœur de banlieue. Codes, rites et langages, Paris, 1997.
LEVINE, MARTIN P., Gay Ghetto, in: Journal of Homosexuality 4, 4 (1979). Reprinted in expanded form as: 'YMCA': The Social Organization of Gay Male Life, in: Gay Macho: The Life and Death of the Homosexual Clone, New York 1998, p. 30-54.
LOGAN, JOHN R./MOLOTCH, HARVEY L., Urban Fortunes: The Political Economy of Place, Berkeley, CA 1987.
LOW, SETHA M., Behind the Gates: Life, Security and the Pursuit of Happiness in Fortress America, New York 2004.
LIEBERSON, STANLEY, A Piece of the Pie : Blacks and White Immigrants since 1880, Berkeley 1980.
LUBOVE, ROY, The Progressives and the Slums: Tenement House Reform in New York City, 1890-1917, Pittsburgh, PA 1963.
MARKS, CAROL, Farewell – We're Good and Gone: The Great Black Migration. Bloomington, IN 1989.

MARQUES, EDUARDO AND HAROLDO TORRES, São Paulo: segregação, pobreza e desigualdades sociais, São Paulo 2005.
MASSEY, DOUGLAS/DENTON, NANCY, American Apartheid: Segregation and the Making of the Underclass, Cambridge, MA 1993.
MILLER, Z. L., Pluralism, Chicago School Style: Louis Wirth, the Ghetto, the City, and Integration., in: Journal of Urban History 18, 3 (1992), p. 251-279.
MUCCHIELLI, LAURENT/LE GOAZIOU, VÉRONIQUE, Quand les banlieues brûlent. Retour sur les émeutes de novembre 2005, Paris 2007.
MURRAY, STEPHEN O., The Institutional Elaboration of a Quasi-Ethnic Community, in: International Review of Modern Sociology 9 (1979), p. 165-177.
MUSTERD, SAKO, Social and Ethnic Segregation in Europe: Levels, Causes, and Effects, in: Journal of Urban Affairs 27, 3 (2005), p. 331-348.
ID./VAN KEMPEN, RONALD, Segregation and Housing of Minority Ethnic Groups in Western European Cities, in: Tijdschrift voor Economische en Sociale Geografie 100, 4 (2009), p. 559-566.
ID. et al. (eds.), Neighbourhoods of Poverty: Urban Social Exclusion and Integration in Europe, London 2006.
NEARY, IAN, Burakumin at the End of History, in: Social Research 70, 1 (2003), p. 269-294.
NELLI, HUMBERT S., Italians in Chicago: A Study in Ethnic Mobility, New York, Oxford 1970.
NOIRIEL, GÉRARD, Le Creuset français, Paris 1998 (English tr. The French Melting Pot, Ithaca 1996).
OBSERVATOIRE DES ZONES URBAINES SENSIBLES, Rapport 2005, Paris 2005.
OSOFSKY, GILBERT, Harlem: The Making of a Ghetto – Negro New York, 1890-1930, 2nd ed., New York 1971.
PATTERSON, ORLANDO, Broken Bloodlines, in: ID., Rituals of Blood: Consequences of Slavery in Two American Centuries, New York 1998, p. 1-167.
PEACH, CERI, Slippery Segregation: Discovering or Manufacturing Ghettos?, in: Journal of Ethnic and Migration Studies 35 (2009), p. 1381-1395.
PERLMAN, JANICE, The Myth of Marginality: Urban Poverty and Politics in Rio de Janeiro, Berkeley, CA 1976.
PÉTONNET, COLETTE, Espaces habités. Ethnologie des banlieues, Paris 1982.
PHILPOTT, THOMAS LEE, The Slum and the Ghetto: Neighborhood Deterioration and Middle-Class Reform, Chicago 1880-1930, New York, Oxford 1978.
PINÇON-CHARLOT, MONIQUE/PINÇON, MICHEL, Les Ghettos du gotha. Comment la bourgeoisie défend ses espaces, Paris 2007.
PORTES, ALEJANDRO/STEPICK, ALEX, City on the Edge: The Transformation of Miami, Berkeley, CA 1993.

Rozelier, Muriel, Naplouse Palestine. Chroniques du ghetto, Paris 2007.

Sabouret, Jean-François, L'autre Japon: les Burakumin, Paris 1983.

Sayad, Abdelmalek/Dupuy, Éliane, Un Nanterre algérien, terre de bidonvilles, Paris 1995.

Schierup, Carl-Ulrik et al., Migration, Citizenship and the European Welfare State: A European Dilemma, Oxford 2006.

Sennett, Richard, Fear of Touching, in: Id., Flesh and Stone: The Body and the City in Western Civilization, New York 1994, p. 212-251.

Sibalis, Michael, Urban Space and Homosexuality: The Example of the Marais, Paris' 'Gay Ghetto', in: Urban Studies 41, 9 (2004), p. 1739-1758.

Sills, David/Merton, Robert (eds.), International Encyclopedia of the Social Sciences, New York 1986.

Small, Mario, Four Reasons to Abandon the Idea of 'the Ghetto', in: City & Community 7, 4 (2009), p. 389-398.

Spear, Allan H., Black Chicago: The Making of a Negro Ghetto, 1890-1920, Chicago, IL 1968.

Stow, Kenneth R., Alienated Minority: The Jews of Medieval Latin Europe, Cambridge, MA 1992.

Stow, Kenneth, Theater of Acculturation: The Roman Ghetto in the Sixteenth Century, Seattle 2001.

Wacquant, Loïc, A Black City Within the White': Revisiting America's Dark Ghetto, in: Black Renaissance 2, 1 (1998), p. 141-151.

Id., Gutting the Ghetto: Political Censorship and Conceptual Retrenchment in the American Debate on Urban Destitution, in : Globalisation and the New City: Migrants, Minorities and Urban Transformations in Comparative Perspective, ed. by Malcolm Cross and Robert Moore, Basingstoke 2002, p. 32-49.

Id., Urban Outcasts: A Comparative Sociology of Advanced Marginality. Cambridge 2008(1).

Id., Ghettos and Anti-Ghettos: An Anatomy of the New Urban Poverty, in: Thesis Eleven 94 (2008)(2), p. 113-118.

Id., Designing Urban Seclusion in the 21st Century, in: Perspecta: The Yale Architectural Journal 43 (2010), p. 165-178.

Id., Deadly Symbiosis: Race and the Rise of the Penal State, Cambridge 2011.

Warner, Sam Bass, Jr./Burke, Colin B., Cultural Change and the Ghetto, in: Journal of Contemporary History 4 (1969), p. 173-187.

Ward, David, Poverty, Ethnicity, and the American City, 1840-1925, Cambridge 1989.

WEBER, MAX, Economy and Society (1922), 2 vols., ed. by GUENTER ROTH and CLAUS WITTICH, Berkeley, CA 1978.
WESTERN, JOHN, Outcast Cape Town, Minneapolis, MN 1981.
WILSON, WILLIAM JULIUS, The Truly Disadvantaged: The Inner City, the Underclass and Public Policy, Chicago, IL 1987.
ID., When Work Disappears: The World of the New Urban Poor. New York 1996.
WIRTH, LOUIS, The Ghetto, Chicago, IL 1928.
ID., The Ghetto (1956), in: On Cities and Social Life, ed. by ALBERT J. REISS, JR., Chicago, IL 1964, p. 84-98.
WRIGHT, GWENDOLYN, The Politics of Design in French Urban Colonialism. Chicago 1991.
ZALUAR, ALBA/ALVITO, MARCOS (eds.), Um século de favela, Rio de Janeiro 1998.
ZHOU, MIN, Chinatown: The Socioeonomic Potential of an Urban Enclave, Philadelphia, PA 1992.
ZUNZ, OLIVIER, The Changing Face of Inequality: Urbanization, Urban Development, and Immigrants in Detroit, 1880-1920, Chicago 1986.

The Subalterns Speak Out
Urban Plebeian Society in
Late Imperial Russia

ILYA V. GERASIMOV

Urban slum areas of today, just as a hundred years ago, house the kind of people who largely evade regular documentation of their lives, and very rarely produce written accounts of their feelings, desires, and concerns. This should present a major difficulty for historians who write about the slum inhabitants of the past, and who, unlike contemporary sociologists or anthropologists, cannot produce their own data by conducting surveys and interviews. Historians have to rely on existing sources, which are authored mostly by the educated middle classes whose values and rationality these sources reflected (as well as biases and misconceptions). This fundamental deficiency of 'authentic' or at least first-hand evidence should pose a major problem for attempts to write histories of the lower classes, which makes it all the more surprising that such histories are not only numerous but also often written without any concern for the epistemological and methodological impasse presented by the task.

This unshattered optimism can be explained by the origins of social history in the research of premodern epochs. Historians have long been accustomed to studying social groups and entire societies who were illiterate or had an insignificant number of literate members. The revolutionizing effect produced by Medieval Studies in the mid-twentieth century (associated mostly with the Annales School), which laid the ground for new social history and the anthropological turn in history writing, was based in good part on new approaches to the study of the popular masses that had left only scarce written evidence of their lives. 'The silent majority' and 'the people without history' have become legitimate topics of study, no less respectable than traditionally celebrated kings, aristocrats, and literati.[1] The study of muted groups within the medieval communal-based society was continued by historians of the lower (and equally 'speechless') classes during the industrial age.[2] Today, it has become standard to write about all kinds of disenfranchised social groups that left no elaborated self-descriptive narratives that reconstruct their distinctive cultures and even their subjectivity.

Russian history is particularly prominent for this type of scholarship – both because of the heavy impact left on the field by Marxism (with its fixation on the lower classes), and because of the low literacy rates of the pre-1917 population. Many of the generalizations about prerevolutionary workers' culture and subjectivity have been made on the basis of a single document, which is quite outstanding in all senses – the autobiography of one Semen Kanatchikov.[3] Those historians who, in their studies, have analyzed a broader number of written sources produced by workers still dealt with the 'conscious workers' or even 'plebeian intelligentsia', rather than with the entire social group.[4] Peasant studies do not have such an authoritative and self-conscious text, which does not preclude scholars from making generalizations about the peasants' inner self and collective identity on a grand scale.[5] The underworld or just the 'gray zone' social sphere of a late imperial city can be studied on the basis of several dozen newspaper feuilletons written by lower-middle-class journalists.[6] Criticism of these approaches from within the historical profession usually questions the sufficiency of the analyzed evidence for reaching such broad conclusions. The discussion is framed in terms of the 'representativeness of sources', which cannot be definitively resolved in most cases: how many examples (case studies, written testimonies) are 'enough' to substantiate a historian's claim?[7]

The very question of whether those written accounts of mores and deeds of the commoners, produced by educated and usually upper-class observers,

---

1   Cf. WHITE, 1967; WOLF, 1982.
2   Cf. for classic studies of the proletariat and the peasantry THOMPSON, 1968; SHANIN, 1972.
3   A RADICAL WORKER IN TSARIST RUSSIA, 1986.
4   Cf. STEINBERG, 1992; ID., 2002, Chapter I.
5   Cf. for one of the most recent examples RETISH, 2008. Cf. for criticism of bold discursive generalizations and projections in peasant studies GERASIMOV, 2004.
6   For example, in Odessa: SYLVESTER, 2005.
7   This problem has been particularly acute in Microhistory, which substantiates broad generalizations by the meticulous analysis of just one or several cases. Cf. on the problem of relations between a unique case and the general social norm in microhistorical studies EGMOND/MASON, 1997, p. 2f. et al; GINZBURG, 1993.

are meaningful at all as a 'source' is not recognized, and perhaps will not be even understood by many historians. The basic 'credibility check' of a primary source implies examining whether the author was an eyewitness or had firsthand access to reliable information, or personal reasons to distort the picture, and also determining the author's purpose and circumstances of writing down the document. The idea that those different groups of the lower social orders might be completely misrepresented and misinterpreted even by the most sympathetic and scrupulous observers from the ranks of the educated upper classes would strike a historian – and particularly a historian of Russia – as groundless. Why should testimony by an aristocrat or a cleric of the early Middle Ages be seen as a more adequate source on the history of peasants of that epoch than an early twentieth-century newspaper feuilleton by a university graduate on the history of urban slums of the same period? After all, aristocrats lived in castles separated by spatial and cultural distance from the village, while newspaper journalists could dwell just around the corner from a flophouse.

The difference between the two examples is the nature of the social organization and the character of the production of knowledge in the Middle Ages and at the turn of the twentieth century. In the former case, both the 'silent majority' and their educated overlords shared a vision of the society as composed of half-isolated communes characterized by a universally recognized set of rights, obligations, cultural norms, and distinctive economic functions. By contrast, Russian society during the late imperial period (as other European societies of the time) was characterized by economic dislocations, intensive social mobility, and a multiplicity of "cultures in flux."[8] Social identities in this society are multifaceted and transitional, greatly differing in the ways they are viewed 'from the outside' (by the legislator or the police) and are experienced 'from within'. At the same time, unlike the medieval literati, the educated elite of the turn of the twentieth century belonged to the common public sphere sustained by the circulation of public discourses and engaged in the production of discourses. This is a radically new situation in comparison with the premodern world, where the closest analogue to a modern public hegemonic discourse was theology, equally alienated from the serf and the lord as its subjects, and almost equally embracing both of them as its objects. The modern hegemonic discourses of nation and culture, class and politics structure the ways in which educated members of the public sphere perceive the social reality and navigate through it, but they are alien and all but irrelevant for those outside the public sphere – which means for the absolute majority of the population.

---

8   Cf. FRANK/STEINBERG, 1994.

According to the rigid criteria upheld by social historians–purists of the Habermas model, only 2 or 3 percent of the inhabitants of Russian provincial cities (such as Kazan in the Middle Volga region) belonged to the public sphere at the beginning of the twentieth century.[9] This figure may be viewed as too low, and there can be alternative methods for assessing the size of the public sphere. It is clear, however, that the majority of the urban inhabitants could not belong to any public sphere in principle, for basic technical reasons. To begin with, only 51 percent of the population of Kazan was literate in 1897, and the rate of literacy was not much higher even ten years later, given the influx of mostly illiterate migrants from the countryside.[10] Furthermore, the cumulative print run of major newspapers in Kazan reached its peak in 1913, with about 25,000 copies at a time of about ten titles being published – for a city that had about 158,000 inhabitants over the age of ten, or 120,000 older than age twenty.[11] This means that only 16 to 20 percent of adult Kazanians would have had access to newspapers in principle, which by itself did not make them active participants in the public sphere, but was a sine qua non for those who wished to participate in it. It can be added that in terms of formal social status, only 10 percent of the urban population in Russia did not belong to nonprivileged social groups: peasants or petty commoners (*meshchane*).

Thus, 2 to 20 percent of the urban population participated or could participate in the public sphere, having access to public discourses on a regular basis and perceiving reality in discursive categories. For them, "textuality has become a metaphor for reality in general"[12]. The rest could be exposed to discourses and the world of ideologies and bureaucratic document-based procedures, but they were not properly socialized into this world, and did not fully interiorize its "geography" and "physics." At least they did not rely on discourses and textuality in their everyday lives. This majority cannot be identified with a particular class, legal estate, occupation, or confession – or any other categories of modern social discourse. They are most accurately defined in the vaguest terms as the "lower classes" or "plebeian society." This is exactly the structural situation that

---

9   When the public sphere is effectively limited to a tiny layer of urban 'bourgeoisie' participating in town council elections and formally registered associations of bicycle riders or lawn tennis clubs. Cf. HAUSMANN, 2002; HÄFNER, 2004.

10 Cf. TROINITSKII, 1904, p. x.

11 Cf. AMIRKHANOV, 1999, p. 312-320. I have projected the demographic structure of the city population as revealed by the 1897 census on the population of Kazan in 1913. Cf. TROINITSKII, 1904, p. 10f.

12 Quoted from ELEY, 2005, p. 43.

is central for Subaltern Studies: "The term 'subaltern' [...] is used [...] to refer to subjects, working people, the lower classes: the demographic difference", as Ranajit Guha put it in the first volume of *Subaltern Studies*, "between the total [...] population and all those [...] described as the 'elite'"[13].

The original "subalterns" as conceptualized within the South Asian Subaltern Studies project were subjugated by the alien colonial rule imposed by foreigners, who had imposed their own alien cultural norms, social divisions, and political regime.[14] Today, thirty years later, the condition of subalternity is understood more broadly and at the same time more specifically as a state of alienation from the modern epistemological regime imposed and sustained through hegemonic discourses. Colonial domination has been reconsidered as primarily a discursive hegemony, and as such has lost a formal connection to the actual occupation or colonization of the country by foreigners. The advent of modernity as an elite intellectual and cultural phenomenon could draw a dynamic frontier between the elite of the moderns socialized into the nation of the common public sphere and the subalterns still living in the nondiscursive world of local knowledge, now being conceptualized as "traditions". This collision could take place in any modernizing society. Thus, back in 2008, a prominent Ottomanist, the late Donald Quataert suggested that workers and peasants of the Anatolian "heartland" of the empire could be productively conceptualized as "subalterns" despite "the centrality of the Turkish state in the minds of many scholars"[15]. Recently, Nora Lafi has attempted (if only somewhat cursorily) to reframe the urban history of the late Ottoman period in terms of Subaltern Studies.[16] In the context of Russian studies, Alexander Etkind makes the metaphor of "internal colonization" (based on a somewhat outdated reading of postcolonial theory and subaltern studies) the central theme of the Russian history of the post-Petrine period.[17]

The significance of "subalternity" well exceeds the role of yet another fashionable way of 'repackaging' the same old empirical material. It is not a new name for the urban poor – it is a recognition of the fundamental difficulty in describing a social sphere structured by absolutely different rules and rationality, and yet closely integrated with the discourse-based modernized part of the community. In the words of Princeton historian Gyan Prakash, "we should

---

13 PANDEY, 2005, p. 411.
14 Cf. GUHA, 1982.
15 QUATAERT, 2008, p. 379.
16 Cf. LAFI, 2011.
17 Cf. ETKIND, 2011.

understand subalternity as an abstraction used in order to identify the intractability that surfaces *inside* the dominant system—it signifies that which the dominant discourse cannot appropriate completely, an otherness that resists containment."[18]

Inhabitants of urban slums in imperial Russia were not colonized representatives of a different race from exotic islands: as individuals, they participated in the social interactions and hierarchies sanctioned by imperial officialdom as the regime of modern knowledge. They were licensed as petty craftsmen and peddlers, employed as manual workers or shop assistants, drafted into the military or prosecuted as criminals under the imperial penal code and according to the standard juridical procedure. Yet they did not have a common name as a group, nor did they have a common subjectivity or a sense of universal solidarity. Or at least there was no way to frame and express that commonality discursively, even if called "subaltern": "Subalternity cannot be generalized according to hegemonic logic."[19] Clarifying this thesis, Gayatri Chakravorty Spivak further complicates the seemingly unresolvable conundrum of the subalterns as the "One-That-Must-Not-Be-Named" social stratum, and hence elusive to the point of nonintelligibility: "Subalternity is a position without identity. [...] No one can say 'I am a subaltern' in whatever language. And subaltern studies will not reduce itself to the historical recounting of the details of the practice of disenfranchised groups and remain a study of the subaltern. Subalternity is where social lines of mobility, being elsewhere, do not permit the formation of a recognisable basis of action."[20]

The very aspiration to grasp the nature of subalterns (even if by means of invalid 'discursive' instruments) stems from the broadly shared conviction that such a community is real, at least as a commonality of lived life experiences. We cannot easily grasp this commonality of the 'plebeian society' conceptually, but we do not question its reality, as we observe it personally or get a sense of it in the past from reading between the lines of our primary sources. The most indirect, primarily spatial characteristic of this community – 'slums' – may work as a fairly all-embracing catchword in some instances, particularly today, but the concept would be of little help in the case of Russian imperial society, for example. In every city there were neighborhoods and whole districts of shacks populated by the most marginal social types, but they were not the exclusive ghettos: people of low socioeconomic status resided all over the city, while certain cat-

---

18 PRAKASH, 2000, p. 287.
19 SPIVAK, 2005, p. 475.
20 IBID., p. 476.

egories of the modernized could live in the slums (for example, poor students, teachers, or 'conscious' factory workers). The fundamental conflict between the vitality of the 'unspeakable' collectivity and the impossibility of framing it through generalizations was famously captured by Spivak in her essay "Can the Subaltern Speak?" Commenting on the main idea of this text almost two decades later, Spivak explained: "The focus of subalternity in the essay remained the singular woman who attempted to send the reader a message, as if her body were a 'literary' text."[21]

This phrase revealed the disciplinary limitations of the subaltern studies approach as influenced by methodologies developed primarily within text-centered literary studies (which Spivak herself duly acknowledges), and implicitly suggested a way out of the seemingly unresolvable predicament of subalternity. Indeed, the subaltern seems impenetrable for analysis only from the 'colonial' perspective of an observer who cannot even conceive of any other mode of thinking except those determined by hegemonic discourses, and cannot proceed beyond merely registering the existence of some 'dark matter' within the social universe. (Spivak herself admits the role of her social position and cultural horizon in setting the limits of her analytical perspective.[22]) There is, however, reality beyond the public sphere structured by hegemonic discourses, and there are methods of analysis not constrained by the availability of 'literary texts' as primary sources. Moreover, the construction of one's social persona as a representation of certain fixed collective identities scaled down to the level of the individual (e.g., 'a heterosexual middle-aged sales assistant of Orthodox faith and monarchist political leaning') is only one possible way of presenting the interaction of a person with the society. Why do social historians not finally make a step from the essentialist structuralism of Newton-age physics to at least the state of the mid-twentieth-century mode of scientific thinking that, for example, accepts the idea of an electron performing simultaneously as a particle and a wave, and never having fixed coordinates but only a different 'probability of finding an electron at a given place'?

In other words, studying people who existed in the situation preceding the formation of modern social groups (nations, classes, subcultures) as some sort of 'elementary particles' should be different from studying individuals who have been formed by and within these groups, and therefore perceive themselves as a function of those collectives. Subalterns as members of a seemingly amor-

---

21 IBID., p. 478.
22 "In search of the subaltern I first turned to my own class: the Bengali middle class […]. From French theory that is all I could do." IBID., p. 481.

phous plebeian society cannot be meaningfully categorized in terms of their fixed 'state' (be it ethnicity or occupation), but they can be 'stabilized' as coherent social elements by the study of their life trajectories and the choices they make along the way. Subalterns rarely reveal their 'inner self' in writing, but taking the idea of perceiving one's body as a 'literary text' seriously opens the way to finally hearing the subalterns speaking out. To understand this 'body talk' we need first to decipher a peculiar language of self-description and self-representation composed of individual social gestures as 'words', interconnected sequences of actions as 'sentences', and stable social practices as its grammar.

The necessary prerequisite for this task is a truly massive array of sources documenting the lives of subalterns, even if, as Gyan Prakash warns, "what historical records present us with are palimpsests of the subaltern, impressions of the subversive force exerted by the 'minor,' never the force itself"[23]. This is only natural, as there can be no narrative sources consistently depicting subaltern society as a 'thing', and we are looking into actions that left traces in historical records, not into ready interpretations of intentions, much less the subjectivities of the subalterns. Actions too can be misinterpreted and misrepresented in the sources, but the chances of compensating for these flaws through the simultaneous usage of alternative sources and their analysis in a broader historical context are incomparably higher than in the case of misinterpretations of someone's thoughts and intentions. And what kinds of actions of the slum inhabitants other than vital statistics (of births and deaths) have been best registered? Only one: instances of their breaking the law.

Thus criminality (or what was perceived as 'criminal' by certain social groups, in certain epochs) offers a unique window on social practices as a particular language of self-expression and self-representation unmediated by traditional institutions and not concealed by dominant public discourses, including those supported by present-day historians and custodians of 'national purity'. This approach may raise legitimate objections: criminality, a deviant behavior by definition, seems to be at odds with the very idea of typicality of social practices (unless we assume that the lower social strata are inherently criminal and immoral).

To this, it is necessary to point out that no other types of social actions can be regarded as 'typical' in the usual sense when it comes to subalternity, that is, when a sampling of actors or actions is viewed as representative of the entire

---

23 PRAKASH, 2000, p. 294.

group. As Spivak put it, "The subaltern has no 'examples'. The exemplary subaltern is hegemonised, even if (and not necessarily) in bad faith."[24]

Of no less importance is the focus suggested in this essay on the ways people responded to certain situations, rather than on the situations themselves as communicating a certain preexisting 'meaning'. It can be a fistfight, church attendance, labor culture, or courting rituals – the question is not which of these activities were more 'typical' of the subalterns-members of urban plebeian society, but what choices they made when faced with such an opportunity. Did they reveal any patterns of group solidarity, a coherent moral economy, or rational choice under the circumstances?

Last but not least, the very structure of recordkeeping in the epoch and society we are talking about made criminal behavior grossly overrepresented in documents. The newspapers registered no other episodes of private lives with similar breadth and intensity. The richest archival collections were formed by the police and various courts, and all focused mostly on instances of breaching the law. Nobody cared about documenting the everyday relationships of merchants' employees of different ethnoconfessional background until somebody committed a crime. The ensuing police investigation documented, inter alia, invaluable elements of regular social practices: this makes criminality a good occasion to discuss much broader and more typical aspects of people's lives. It so happened, that both the authorities and the public were attracted mostly by conflicts; we can use this specific interest to our advantage by preserving a broader focus and remembering that conflicts (and criminality) formed only a tip of the iceberg of complex social interactions we are about to explore.

Without succumbing to the relativization of the 'criminal', my research focuses on the responses to a misdemeanor, rather than on its inherent 'intention'. A closer look at social conflicts identified as criminal can shed light on the process of ascribing meaning to personal confrontations and making sense of cultural and social differences. What becomes 'the exemplary' (or 'typical') is not the people and the situations they got into, but the social practices they demonstrated in the process of engaging with each other and different situations. To reveal and review the variety of possible responses to a wide range of situations and encounters, a very substantial survey of registered incidents is required. We are speaking about thousands and thousands of cases reported by the police, by newspapers, or described in the court records, which should be analyzed qualitatively, rather than processed quantitatively as statistical aggregations.

---

24   SPIVAK, 2005, p. 484.

I have pursued exactly this type of research for the past twelve years, which resulted in the book titled *Ethnic Crime, Imperial City: Practices of Self-Organization and Paradoxes of Illegality in Late Imperial Russia, 1905-1917*. Its main protagonist is the elusive and ever-escaping subaltern – urban plebeian society – whose distinctive collective profile is reconstructed indirectly through the multiple imprints it had left interacting with the 'textual' and discourse-based modern segment of society.

Because the Russian empire was vast and extremely heterogeneous, any choice of a locality for a case study raises the question of its typicality: does it reflect the realities of Siberia (western on eastern?), the situation in the Caucasus (Northern Caucasus or Transcaucasia?), or in the Western Borderlands (in Poland or in Belarus?), and so on? The fundamental fragmentedness of the imperial social sphere, unmediated by universal (and hegemonic) public discourses, has made the problem of representativeness of examples selected for analysis particularly acute and unresolvable in principle through accumulating any statistically significant number of examples. It is impossible to meaningfully process data from hundreds of loci from all over the vast Russian empire in qualitative analysis (as quantification already implies a certain politics of grouping and agglomeration of facts and actors). As a practical solution to this conundrum, I explore the situation on the ground in four different locations, two pairs of imperial cities that both resemble each other and highlight mutual differences: Kazan (today the capital of the national Republic of Tatarstan in the Russian Federation), Nizhny Novgorod (the most 'ethnically Russian' city in the Middle Volga region), Odessa (the Black Sea port in Southern Ukraine), and Vilna (today, Vilnius, the capital of Lithuania). This sampling is as random as it is carefully assorted: obviously, representing only a small fraction of all of the empire's urban centers, these cities have much in common but also are very different.

Odessa (in Ukraine) and Vilna (today Vilnius, the capital of Lithuania) were located in the pale of Jewish settlement in the Russian empire, the territory where Jews were allowed to reside without special permission (at least, in urban areas). Jews constituted over 30 percent of their inhabitants. No other ethnic group had a bigger share in Vilna, where Poles and East Slavs (Russians, Belarusians, Ukrainians) had approximately the same share. In Odessa, Jews were the largest ethnic minority, while Russians and Ukrainians (often poorly differentiated statistically) constituted a majority. Both Vilna and Odessa became Russian imperial cities in the late 18th century, as a result of Russia's imperial expansion southward and westward, but Vilna had had a long prehistory as an important political and cultural center of the Polish-Lithuanian Commonwealth, while Odessa was founded virtually from scratch as a colonial outpost. Poles and Jews claimed Vilna as their ancestral town, and the rising Lithuanian nationalist movement challenged them, despite a mere 2 percent of ethnic Lithuanians among the city population. In Odessa, neither 'Great Russians' coming from the empire's internal provinces, nor Ukrainian migrants, nor Jews fleeing from the overpopulated shtetls in the Pale, nor Moldavians coming from neighboring Bessarabia could claim this territory as their 'ancestral' land; all newcomers were compelled to adjust to the new terrain, new climate, and new socioeconomic environment.[25]

Nizhny Novgorod and Kazan were two provincial centers in the Middle Volga region, as much the imperial 'heartland' as could be imagined. Still, the specificity of the Russian imperial situation was characterized by the absence of any ethnic or cultural homogeneous 'center': almost 40 percent of Kazan province's population were Tatars. In Nizhegorod province, about 10 percent were non-Russians, while over 6 percent of ethnic Russians belonged to various sects of Old Believers – a very significant factor of social and cultural differentiation, particularly in pre-1905 imperial Russia. At the beginning of the twentieth century, Nizhny Novgorod and Kazan represented two types of Russianness. The former was as 'ethnically Russian' as was possible in the Russian empire (slightly yielding only to Moscow with its 95 percent of native Russian speakers in 1897). The latter was a key imperial administrative and cultural center, and in this respect was perceived as the backbone of the Russian state and society (despite its 25 percent non-Russian and non-Christian population).[26]

---

25   MINCZELES, 2000; STALIUNAS, 2006; WEEKS, 2006. Cf. for a general survey of Vilnius history (with only cursory treatment of the imperial period) BRIEDIS, 2009. Cf. for Vilnius as a palimpsest-like agglomeration of sites of memory SCHULZE WESSEL et al., 2010. A classic, if somewhat outdated already history of Odessa is HERLIHY, 1986. Cf. for the early twentieth century history of Odessa from the vantage point of radical politics WEINBERG, 1993, and for a history of the "local community" of the educated middle class HAUSMANN, 1998. Since the 1990s, scholars show much more interest not in the history of the city itself but in the 'Odessa myth': SYLVESTER, 2005; TANNY, 2011.

26   Probably because of the restrictions barring foreigners from visiting these cities before 1991, Kazan and Nizhny Novgorod missed the wave of writing histories of Russian imperial urban centers in the mid-1980s and early 1990s. The studies appearing now usually ignore the immediate pre-1917 decade, or focus on specific aspects of urban history (e.g., the history of landscape, of religious groups, etc.). The noticeable exception is presented by the monograph by KÜNTZEL, 2001. Still, even this book is structured as a collection of sketches dedicated to various strata

The similarities and differences between the two pairs of towns, as well as within these pairs, allow us to identify stable elements and important variations within the patterns of ethnically marked conflicts and cooperation in Russian imperial society. The comparative perspective of the study also offers a clue for in-depth interpretations of certain social phenomena, beyond various organicist explanations. For example, the preponderance of Jews in Vilna prostitution, the reputation of Tatars as prone to deadly violence in Kazan, the persistence of Russian ultranationalist ("black hundreds") organizations – are either explained by some 'innate' qualities of those ethnic groups, or most often, are ignored by historians and national activists alike. The comparative perspective on four urban centers relativizes the uniqueness of many ethnically marked practices, and also offers alternative explanations by social context and specific historical circumstances.

The very category of ethnicity, just as all other markers of difference (confession, legal estate, occupation, regional identification, or gender) are used here not as self-referential entities, but as concepts that must be treated differently depending on their usage as categories of practice or categories of analysis. We cannot do without them: just as the educated elite of the modernized society of the past, we rely on analytically produced generalizations to make sense of reality, but this does not imply that we have to perceive our generalizations as normative reconstruction of the past "as it actually happened" (*wie es eigentlich gewesen*). Reconstructing subalterns from the imprints left by their activities, we become engaged in the complex work of translating subalterns' social ac-

---

and loci of the Nizhegorod society and presented in isolation from each other: a chapter on the monasteries, another on the Nizhegorod Fair, the next deals with the Sormovo industries, and so on. To this day, the most comprehensive narrative of the history of Nizhny Novgorod at the turn of the twentieth century, written in Russian, belongs to Dmitrii Smirnov (1891-1990), see SMIRNOV 2007. Cf. for a useful survey in English DEHAAN: http://www.opentextnn.ru/space/nn/?id=542, 07.05.2013. Despite its primary focus on an earlier (pre-1905) period, the comprehensive survey of the "Nizhegorod civilization" by Catherine Evtuhov offers useful background information on the city of Nizhny Novgorod as well. Cf. EVTUHOV, 2011. Kazan was luckier in getting scholars' attention, but comprehensive urban studies of Kazan are also rare. A detailed structuralist social history of Kazan during the late imperial period can be found in HÄFNER, 2004. Cf. for a pioneering attempt at studying the history of everyday life in Kazan in the longue durée VISHLENKOVA et al., 2008. Cf. for a more conventional narrative of urban history VISHLENKOVA et al., 2007.

tions – through the categories used by the records-keepers of the past – into an analytically construed model. This process can be called the "paleontology of knowledge," as we have to reconstruct from scattered evidence a species profoundly alien to our world, forsaken and forgotten, that cannot even be theoretically revived in its original form here (as subalternists energetically insist). Therefore, our reconstruction cannot pretend to be a realistic replica of the original, but rather is an approximated model demonstrating our own understanding of how individual fragments and known parameters of the 'prehistoric' social body could be meaningfully combined together.

In practical terms this metaphor means that primary sources use all kinds of attributes in describing protagonists of various actions: self-descriptive and formally upheld by bureaucratic procedures, scientific categories and literary clichés. In our translation job we treat them all as categories of practice, that is, as markers of difference that made sense only for a particular cultural context and under specific circumstances. 'A Tatar' or 'a Jew' frequent in documents produced in all four locations of my study, but these terms are absolutely meaningless and hollow by themselves, outside the specific pocket of local knowledge and the exact circumstances of every usage of the term – and every incident that provoked its usage. For instance, when in January 1908 the police solved the case of a recent "expropriation" attack by revolutionaries on the office of the Kazan city forester, they prepared to arrest the leader, known by the Russian alias "Aleksey." Aleksey turned out to be the Tatar Aligulla Bililiatdinov, a 26 year old worker wearing "Russian" dress.[27] The local nationalist newspaper expressed less indignation about the actual "revolutionary robbery" than about the "imposter," whom the paper depicted in Orientalist terms as a typical Tatar criminal: tall, dark-skinned, gloomy, Mongoloid-looking, and "of Muhammad's faith"[28]. Curiously, before the arrest, the three attackers had been described by five witnesses (who saw them at close range and talked to them) as "representatives of the [Russian] intelligentsia" "judging by the color of their faces and their speech"[29]. There was no mention of the typical Mongoloid facial characteristics of the leader, or the primitive mores of his two accomplices, who turned out to be twenty-year-old simple Russian workers.[30] This example can tell us much about the limits of applicability of even such 'objective' categories of practice as Russians and Tatars, or *intelligenty* and workers. The question is not whether

---

27   Cf. KAZANSKII TELEGRAF, No. 4452, 01.01.1908, p. 3.
28   IBID., No. 4453, 03.01.1908, p. 3.
29   VOLZHSKII LISTOK, No. 564, 22.12.1907, p. 3.
30   Cf. IBID., No. 653, 17.04.1908, p. 3.

the witnesses or authors of newspaper reports wrongly understood the concept of ethnicity or class, but how they used the available repertoire of categorizing differences to mark out situational and structural divides in a particular case.

From hundreds of similar cases we can compose a more or less detailed map of such divides and group solidarities that may coincide or not coincide with categories of difference employed in the sources. This is a dynamic map, like satellite weather images: group boundaries shift in time, and local knowledge circulates through migrations and partial access of the subalterns to the mass media. How should we perform the next step of our 'paleontological' reconstruction and translate the assembled catalogue of qualities and features into a coherent model of the plebeian society of subalterns living inside and outside urban slums? Unfortunately, we can rely only on the same concepts of ethnicity, confession, occupation, and so on, only this time we should work with them as categories of analysis: analytically elaborated, with explicitly defined connotations and parameters of applicability. The task is to explain, *how* that society worked, not *what* it looked like as a totality. None of the analytical categories we use can cope with the task individually, but there is no need to invent elaborated hybrid mega-models. Instead of "strategic essentialism" of self-fashioning by national and other modernized groups,[31] and the "realism of the group" as practiced by nation-centered social sciences,[32] the new imperial history takes as its departure point the principle of "strategic relativism" of the imperial situation: the impossibility of unquestionable belonging to only one particular social hierarchy or group.[33] Thus, the only accurate way to outline a social persona in this situation of the absence of absolute hegemony of any 'hegemonic discourses' (at least over the plebeian society of subalterns) is to reconstruct it as a composite and multifaceted one.

This is not exactly the hybridity so much celebrated in postcolonial studies, which is envisioned in accordance with what Ernest Gellner called "Modigliani's map," when multicolored blocks of different sizes and shapes (but with clear boundaries and internally homogeneous) form a giant mosaic of cultural (and social) diversity. These blocks are located on the same plane and are grouped according to clear departments.[34] In the department of "peoples," this diversity is represented in the case of the Russian Empire by "Jews," "Ukrainians," "Tatars," and "Russians"; in the department of "social structure," it fea-

---

31   Cf. SPIVAK, 1987, p. 205.
32   Cf. BRUBAKER, 1994, p. 3-14.
33   Cf. GERASIMOV et al., 2009, p. 20.
34   Cf. GELLNER, 1984, p. 139f.

tures "nobles," "peasants," "petty commoners," and so on. As it becomes increasingly clear from modern historical and anthropological studies, "poverty," "Russianness," "slums," and "youth" do not belong to four different and separate 'planes of diversity' (thus forming isolated spaces of social differentiation and hybridization), but combine to produce universal composite social identities. These hybrid identities formed in different times from different components with different characteristics are the main protagonists of new imperial history as pursued in my study.

Looking from this vantage point, the task of reconstructing the composite social sphere of the plebeian society appears to be very different from assembling a priori assigned blocks (class/confession/gender/nationality, etc.) in a certain way. Rather, we have to envision this society as differentiated into groups that are distinguished only when (or every time) certain criteria of otherness become relevant in the context of a specific situation, when these criteria are actually used for marking groupness. In the first case, the matrix of differences is imposed by the researcher, and is more or less sensitive to the nuances of the past, from the outside. In the second case, differences are recognized as such and registered only if they are actually manifested in practice, in a specific situation. Ideally, these differences should be described in the analytical language of contemporary social sciences and interpreted within the framework of a contemporary theoretical model, but it is equally important to avoid anachronistic ascriptions of today's criteria of groupness to motivations of the actions of people in the past.

The best illustration of the dynamic nature of sociocultural hybridity and relativism of criteria of groupness (both as a category of analysis and a category of practice) can be found in the strange case of a fraudulent check cashed by a stranger in August 1906 at the Kazan Merchant Bank. Someone withdrew the handsome sum of 8200 rubles (equivalent to three annual salaries of an upper-middle-class civil servant or professional) from the bank account of the wealthy Tatar merchant Akhmet Khusainov (1835-1906).[35] The police failed to crack this case, which resembles an Agatha Christie mystery: in the seemingly patriarchal firm, every employee close to the head of the business was under suspicion.[36] Ethnicity played a prominent part in the logic of the investigation, but proved futile in the end. The missing sum was discovered by a Jewish law-

---

35 Akhmet was the eldest of the three Khusainov brothers, a successful entrepreneur worth several million rubles by the time of his death. Cf. SHAIDULLINA, 2010.

36 Cf. NATIONAL ARCHIVE OF THE REPUBLIC OF TATARSTAN (NART), f. 79, op. 1, vol. 2, del. 805.

yer, Alexander Bat, who was auditing the firm's finances in March 1907, after the death of its head. Two of the late merchant's Tatar assistants (or rather confidants), who had vague duties, were in charge of keeping the checkbook and the personal seal of Akhmet Khusainov, but these respected gentlemen were beyond the suspicions of Mr. Bat. He suggested that the clerk Mukhamet-Valei Saidashev (also a Tatar) had the opportunity to steal a check when he was summoned to the main office: on his meager salary of 35 rubles a month, in the fall of 1906, Saidashev made a few expensive purchases, and then moved to Semipalatinsk (in present-day Kazakhstan).[37]

The director of the Kazan Merchant Bank, the ethnic Russian Boris Sapozhnikov, defending the bank's reputation, suggested that the check had been accepted because it was authentic: what else could explain how for more than half a year nobody had noticed the misappropriation of such a considerable sum? Sapozhnikov declared that after so long a time neither he nor his employees would recognize the person who had cashed the check but suggested that he was dressed like a Russian, had a "French beard," and did not look "like a Tatar"[38]. The only person fitting this description was Mukhamed Davletshin, one of the confidants of the merchant Khusainov, looking after the checkbook. As it turned out, on his small salary of 50 rubles a month, Davletshin had the means to pay for his wife to live in a spa in Groznyi, and in the fall of 1906 he loaned more than 1000 rubles to another employee. Davletshin spoke Russian without an accent and lived with his Russian lover in Kazan in a predominantly Russian neighborhood.[39] Naturally, Davletshin denied all accusations (he claimed that he had won the money gambling) and pointed out that while the Russian signature on the check in question was quite typical of Khusainov's, the second, Tatar signature was very different and had been done by someone unable to write in Tatar (i.e., in Arabic script). There was a Russian capable of doing the forgery – the accountant Kliucharev, who for some reason did not request statements from the bank for six months, which was a direct violation of his duties and resulted in the overly late discovery of the missing money.[40] The investigation reached a dead end after interrogations of a dozen people had uncovered no decisive evidence to put forward official charges. The very date of the crime received two interpretations: August 11, 1906, was Friday, the Muslim holiday. Some saw this as proof that the perpetrator belonged to the Tatar "circle" around Khusainov,

---

37   IBID., ll. 1-2.
38   IBID., ll. 14-16 ob.
39   IBID., ll. 34-37, 39.
40   IBID., l. 39 ob.

who had cunningly arranged a perfect alibi for himself.[41] Others perceived it as revealing a "Russian trail" of evidence. The real problem was the meaninglessness of ethnic markers as self-explanatory codes of social practice: what kinds of patriarchal relations end up in a fraudulent financial scheme? What does someone's "Tatarness" mean if a person has a Russian lover, gambles, and probably steals from his brethren? How can a Russian steal if the checkbook and the seal are kept by two Tatar confidants of the boss? It is quite possible that the entire affair was a collective enterprise, requiring the cooperation of both Russians and Tatars.

The "Khusainov affair" proves that analytically constructed social identities (and even those consciously interiorized by historical actors) are fairly independent from actions and individual choices. This disconnection between the static social persona and dynamic behavior is characteristic of the "subaltern" and nondiscursive plebeian society.

In the situation of composite and fluid social identities, the only stable element appears to be not any fixed 'proportion of hybridity' but the general trend of actions and life choices. Thus, scholars debate the degree of integration and emancipation of Jews in Odessa at the beginning of the twentieth century, and the exact meaning of Jewishness. Leaving the question of the essence or the correct definition of Jewishness aside, I suggest focusing instead on what possible difference the alleged Jewishness made in the actions of people, and under what circumstances. My study of Odessa revealed the involvement of Jews in criminal violence and murders on a massive scale, contrary to the old and recent myths about Jews being prone to 'peaceful' white-collar crimes. Jewish gangsters murdered scores of people in cold blood, but what is really important is not the brutality of Jewish thugs, but their choice of victims. In over a thousand cases that I have reviewed, not a single Gentile was murdered by Jews in Odessa.[42] In light of the studies on ethnic gangsters in the United States,[43] this fact can be interpreted as an indicator of important mental mapping. Despite the outstanding record of Odessa Jews as pioneers of emancipation and integration into the larger society,[44] it appears that they did not cross one important psychological boundary between 'us' and 'them', as can be seen in the extreme (and thus even more important) case of choosing victims 'of our own kind'. There was one telling exception to this rule, though: Jews who were members

---

41　IBID., l. 2.
42　Cf. GERASIMOV, 2010.
43　Cf. COHEN, 1999; ROCKAWAY, 1993.
44　Cf. ZIPPERSTEIN, 1985.

of revolutionary anarchist gangs killed Gentiles, when attacking under the cover of revolutionary slogans. Quitting the sphere of the subaltern isolation from hegemonic discourses and acting on behalf of the future common revolutionary nation, they overcame the invisible and probably unconscious barrier of their self-alienation. However deviant and violent, these social practices allow us to trace the dynamic intergroup boundaries and see their dependence on mental mapping and ideological contexts.

Social practices *were* the universal language binding the urban plebeian society together, substituting for the virtually unavailable discourses. Nobody briefed a recent migrant about the rules of behavior in town: he or she picked up this nonverbalized wisdom by literally rubbing shoulders with more experienced peers, by getting punched for every mistake, and negotiating a new arrangement through close physical contact, including violence. The nonverbal and very 'bodily' foundation of social practices eventually created a developed metalanguage of self-expression and self-representation of individuals and social groups – we just need to learn how to read this language. On the basis of thousands of documented cases I identify several key strategies, or social practices that helped to communicate meaning within the plebeian society, and structure it, sustaining social order in the unstable and unruly milieu of recent migrants to the city slums.

One practice can be identified as "the middle ground" – to use the concept elaborated by Richard White in his classic study of the intercultural communication and conflict in the North American Great Lakes region.[45] As he put it:

> "The middle ground is the place in between: in between cultures, peoples, and in between empires and the nonstate world of villages. [...] People try to persuade others who are different from themselves by appealing to what they perceive to be the values and the practices of those others. They often misinterpret and distort both the values and the practices of those they deal with, but from these misunderstandings arise new meanings and through them new practices – the shared meanings and practices of the middle ground."[46]

Thus understood, the middle ground is not literally a particular "place" or a "process" (unlike frontier), but rather a state of relationships and dialogue of actors attempting to bridge the deep cultural gap and social divide. We can see this practice at work in all four of the principal locations of my study and particu-

---

45 Cf. WHITE, 1991.
46 IBID., p. x.

larly in Kazan, where neither Russian, Orthodox Christian population, nor Tatar Muslim community had means and guts to impose their own norms and values on the other. Hence they had to negotiate and seek a compromise, creating a new common reality of "creative misunderstanding".

Another practice can be called "patriarchality" (in the sense of both archaism and male domination). The social practice of patriarchality did not imply that social relations and motivations of people employing this practice were actually "patriarchal": naive, archaic, irrational, and completely male-controlled. Rather, it was a sustained attempt to keep the isolation of the subaltern society from penetration of the modern public sphere of public discourses. This was particularly important in Vilna, where this integration implied mobilization into one of the competing powerful nationalist projects (Polish, Jewish, Russian, or Lithuanian), with potentially devastating consequences for the urban community. These consequences were fully realized in the 1930s and 1940s, with the dismantling of pseudo-archaic patriarchality and subalternity.

The social practice of patriarchality employed in Late Imperial Russia sustained parochialism that did not allow for generalizing and institutionalizing the categories of belonging (to a national community) and otherness (of aliens). It also sanctified authority defined in nonnational categories of seniority, male domination, and formal office-holding. Up to a certain point, this practice was capable of accommodating elements of urban modernity that equally downplayed the importance of nationality – be it the union movement or commerce. Balancing between these two often-overlapping cognitive modes in the social practice of patriarchality, Russian late imperial society managed to accommodate the challenges of modernity surprisingly well, at the cost of a relatively low level of mobilization of intergroup confrontation.

The persistence of violence in the urban plebeian society allows us to treat it as the third fundamental, albeit morally and legally intolerable, social practice in its own right. As such, violence is anything but 'senseless', as has been shown by the modern anthropology of violence.[47] Violence served as a marker of belonging to a common social space and, more rarely, as a stigma of otherness. Even in the latter case, this was not about the indication of ultimate alienation, but, so to speak, of 'a second-choice voting'. It may sound paradoxical, but violence can communicate even friendliness, albeit only in a most awkward way, as the following episode shows. In September 1908, in the Bolshoi Fontan seafront neighborhood of Odessa, a Jew, Nutovich, met his Ukrainian neighbor, the shopkeeper Stetsenko, on the street. Because of their prehistory of heated argu-

---

47   Cf. BLOK, 2001.

ments, this time Stetsenko picked up a stone and smashed Nutovich in the face with it. Formally (and actually) this was a hate crime, but it was also something more: a gentile shopkeeper used the last argument to induce his Jewish neighbor to become his customer, not to ban him from his shop, as can be assumed from a general outline of the incident.[48]

In the subaltern plebeian society, violence as a social practice was multifaceted, playing the important common role of a communicative medium. As such, it was excessively "expressive," spoken in the body language of injuries, rape, and mutilations, but it was the only alternative to the verbalized communication based on borrowed discourses with built-in explanatory schemes. It was mostly an extreme way to express one's individual position, and as such is invaluable for a study of social arrangements beyond the normative groupings into ethnicities, confessions, legal estates, or classes. The language of violence tells the story of intensive contacts and spontaneously emerging power fields of social solidarity and confrontation across the conventional map of social composition. The social practice of violence did not have the constructive potential of the middle ground or even of patriarchality, the latter being more about sustaining the status quo and stability of a heterogeneous social milieu. On the other hand, rarely employed in the course of politicization of ethnicity as collective action with a single uniform target and goals, in late imperial plebeian society, violence did not fully unleash its destructive force capable of splitting communities or mobilizing one group against another. This would change once the former subaltern society became integrated into the political nation by imposing a normative discourse, or rather an ideological canon. Then, habitual tolerance to violence and the low threshold for its unleashing brought about truly gruesome consequences.

The subalterns from Russian plebeian society were capable of rationally processing information and making informed decisions, only they did it by using different cognitive mechanisms, and different concepts of rationality. This is an important lesson that the Russian imperial situation can teach scholars thinking about subalternity: whenever a suspicion arises that someone in the society "cannot speak" (in any sense of the word), it is a sure indicator that the observer cannot listen. The vast majority of those, who did not succeed in mastering even the basics of the elite discursive sphere (or perhaps did not want to), could be perceived as 'dumb' – but only by those, who identify themselves with the elite stratum of the educated society. Paradoxically, in the absence of any universal public sphere, the diverse social milieu of the subaltern plebeian society was

---

48   Cf. ZVERSKOE IZBIENIE, 1908, p. 2f.

fairly coherent and predictable to migrants from different localities, representing different ethnoconfessional groups, regions, or subcultures. What they all had in common as the universally recognizable basic element of the 'primary modeling system' was their body (both physical and social) and its functions. As a medium, the emerging 'secondary modeling system' of the plebeian society used not words, but semiotically meaningful social practices.

The Bolshevik revolution removed the entire layer of the elitist (middle-class) 'patrician society' with its hegemonic discourses, just as some activists of subaltern studies would recommend as a solution against isolationism of subalternity. This move, however, did not make the former plebeian society less autistic or more interventionist in its dealing with public discourses (suffice it to reread the prose of Mikhail Zoshchenko or studies of amateur correspondents of Soviet newspapers). Thus, the Russian case defies the rigidly structuralist or post-stucturalist reading of the subaltern: it is not a caste, and not a stigma, and the 'space of difference' that subalterns inhabit cannot be imagined as completely isolated and unreadable to Others. Subalternity is rather a social condition and epistemological stance that can be changed or exchanged for a different one.

Literature

AMIRKHANOV, R. U., Nasledie, dostoinoe izuchenie: Kazanskie dorevoliutsionnye periodicheskie izdaniia na russkom iazyke (1881–1917), in: Ekho vekov 1 (1999), p. 312-320.

BLOK, ANTON, Honor and Violence, Cambridge 2001.

BRIEDIS, LAIMONAS, Vilnius: City of Strangers, Budapest 2009.

BRUBAKER, ROGERS, Rethinking Nationhood: Nation as Institutionalized Form, Practical Category, Contingent Event, in: Contention 4, 1 (1994), p. 3-14.

COHEN, RICH, Tough Jews: Fathers, Sons, and Gangster Dreams, New York 1999.

EGMOND, FLORIKE/MASON, PETER, The Mammoth and the Mouse: Microhistory and Morphology, Baltimore, London 1997.

ELEY, GEOFF, Is All the World a Text? From Social History to the History of Society Two Decades Later, in: Practicing History: New Directions in Historical Writing After the Linguistic Turn, ed. by GABRIELLE M. SPIEGEL, New York, London, p. 35-62.

ETKIND, ALEXANDER, Internal Colonization: Russia's Imperial Experience, Cambridge 2011.

EVTUHOV, CATHERINE, Portrait of a Russian Province: Economy, Society, and Civilization in Nineteenth-Century Nizhnii Novgorod, Pittsburgh 2011.
FRANK, STEPHEN/STEINBERG, MARK D. (eds.), Cultures in Flux: Lower-Class Values, Practices, and Resistance in Late Imperial Russia, Princeton 1994.
GELLNER, ERNEST, Nations and Nationalism, Oxford 1984.
GERASIMOV, ILYA V., On the Limitations of a Discursive Analysis of 'Experts and Peasants' (An Attempt at the Internationalization of One Discussion in Kritika), in: Jahrbücher für Geschichte Osteuropas 52, 2 (2004), p. 261-273.
ID. et al., New Imperial History and the Challenges of Empire, in, Empire Speaks Out: Languages of Rationalization and Self-Description in the Russian Empire, ed. by ILYA V. GERASIMOV et al., Leiden, Boston 2009, p. 3-33.
ID., Ethnic Crime, Imperial City: Practices of Self-Organization and Paradoxes of Illegality in Late Imperial Russia, in: Imperial Victims – Empires as Victims: 44 Views, ed. by ANDRZEJ NOWAK, Krakow 2010, p. 97-129.
GINZBURG, CARLO, Microhistory: Two or Three Things That I Know about It, in: Critical Inquiry 20 (1993), p. 10-34.
GUHA, RANAJIT (ed.), Subaltern Studies. Writings on South Asian Society and History, Volume I, Delhi, Oxford 1982.
HÄFNER, LUTZ, Gesellschaft als lokale Veranstaltung: Die Wolgastädte Kazan' und Saratov, 1870-1914, Köln et al. 2004.
HAUSMAN, GUIDO (Ed.), Universität und städtische Gesellschaft in Odessa, 1865-1917. Soziale und nationale Selbstorganisation an der Peripherie des Zarenreiches, Stuttgart 1998.
ID., Gesellschaft als lokale Veranstaltung. Selbstverwaltung, Assoziierung und Geselligkeit in den Städten des ausgehenden Zarenreiches, Göttingen 2002.
HERLIHY, PATRICIA, Odessa: A History, 1794-1914, Cambridge 1986.
ZVERSKOE IZBIENIE, in: Novaia Odesskaia gazeta, No. 45, 21.09.1908), p. 2f.
KÜNTZEL, KRISTINA, Von Niznij Novgorod zu Gor'kij: Metamorphosen einer russischen Provinzstadt. Die Entwicklung der Stadt von den 1890er bis zu den 1930er Jahren, Stuttgart 2001.
LAFI, NORA, The Ottoman Urban Governance of Migrations and the Stakes of Modernity, in: The City in the Ottoman Empire: Migration and the Making of Urban Modernity, ed. by ULRIKE FREITAG et al., London 2011, p. 8-25.
VOLZHSKII LISTOK, No. 564, 22.12.1907, p. 3.
ID., No. 653, 17.04.1908, p. 3.
MINCZELES, HENRI, Vilna, Wilno, Vilnius: La Jérusalem de Lituanie, Paris 2000.
PANDEY, GYANENDRA, Notions of Community: Popular and Subaltern, in: Postcolonial Studies 8, 4 (2005), p. 409-419.

PRAKASH, GYAN, The Impossibility of Subaltern History, in: Nepantla: Views from South 1, 2 (2000), p. 287-294.

QUATAERT, DONALD, Pensee 2: Doing Subaltern Studies in Ottoman History, in: International Journal of Middle East Studies 40, 3 (2008), p. 379-381.

RETISH, AARON B., Russia's Peasants in Revolution and Civil War. Citizenship, identity, and the creation of the Soviet state, 1914-1922, Cambridge 2008.

ROCKAWAY, ROBERT A., But He Was Good to His Mother: The Lives and Crimes of Jewish Gangsters, Jerusalem 1993.

SCHULZE WESSEL, MARTIN et al. (eds.), Vilnius. Geschichte und Gedächtnis einer Stadt zwischen den Kulturen, Frankfurt/Main 2010.

SHAIDULLINA, RIMMA RIFKHATEVNA, Torgovo-predprinimatel'skaia i blagotvoritel'naia deiatel'nost' brat'ev Khusainovykh (vtoraia polovina XIX-nachalo XX vv.), Candidate of Sciences in History Dissertation, Kazan University 2010.

SHANIN, TEODOR, The Awkward Class: Political Sociology of Peasantry in a Developing Society. Russia 1910–1925, London 1972.

SMIRNOV, DMITRII, Nizhegorodskaia starina, Nizhny Novgorod 2007.

SPIVAK, GAYATRI CHAKRAVORTY, In Other Worlds: Essays in Cultural Politics, London 1987.

ID., Scattered Speculations on the Subaltern and the Popular, in: Postcolonial Studies 8, 4 (2005), p. 475-486.

STALIUNAS, DARIUS, An Awkward City: Vilnius as a Regional Centre in Russian Nationality Policy (ca. 1860-1914), in: Russia and Eastern Europe: Applied "Imperiology,", ed. by ANDRZEJ NOWAK, Krakow 2006, p. 222-243;

STEINBERG, MARK D., Moral Communities: The Culture of Class Relations in the Russian Printing Industry, Berkeley 1992.

ID., Proletarian Imagination: Self, Modernity, and the Sacred in Russia, 1910–1925, Ithaca 2002.

SYLVESTER, ROSHANNA PATRICIA, Tales of Old Odessa: Crime and Civility in a City of Thieves, Northern Illinois 2005.

TANNY, JARROD MITCHELL, City of Rogues and Schnorrers: Russia's Jews and the Myth of Old Odessa, Bloomington 2011.

KAZANSKII TELEGRAF, No. 4452, 01.01.1908, p. 3 3.

ID., No. 4453, 03.01.1908, p. 3.

THOMPSON, EDWARD P., The Making of the English Working Class, 2nd ed., Harmondsworth 1968.

TROINITSKII, N. A. (ed.), Pervaia vseobshchaia perepis' naseleniia Rossiiskoi imperii 1897 goda, vol. 14, Kazanskaia guberniia, St. Petersburg 1904.

VISHLENKOVA, ELENA et al., Kazanskoe zhit'e, in: Kazan i ee zhiteli. Kazanskoe zhit'e, Kazan 2007, p. 787-1183.
ID. et al., Kultura povsednevnosti provintsialnogo goroda: Kazan i kazantsy v XIX-XX vv., Kazan 2008.
WEEKS, THEODORE R., From 'Russian' to 'Polish:' Vilna-Wilno 1900-1925. NCEEER Research Report, Washington, DC, 2006.
WEINBERG, ROBERT, Blood on the Steps: The Revolution of 1905 in Odessa, Bloomington 1993.
WHITE, LYNN, The Life of the Silent Majority, in: Life and Thought in the Middle Ages, ed. by ROBERT S. HOYT, Minneapolis 1967, p. 85-100.
WHITE, RICHARD, The Middle Ground: Indians, Empires and Republics in the Great Lakes Region, 1650-1815, Cambridge 1991.
WOLF, ERIC R., Europe and the People Without History, Berkeley 1982.
A RADICAL WORKER IN TSARIST RUSSIA: The Autobiography of Semen Ivanovich Kanatchikov, transl. and ed. by REGINALD E. ZELNIK, Stanford 1986.
ZIPPERSTEIN, STEVEN, The Jews of Odessa: A Cultural History, 1794-1881, Stanford, California 1985.

NATIONAL ARCHIVE OF THE REPUBLIC OF TATARSTAN (NART):
- f. 79: op. 1, vol. 2, del. 805.

DEHAAN, HEATHER, Nizhnii Novgorod: History in the Landscape: http://www.opentextnn.ru/space/nn/?id=542, 07.05.2013.

"... not intended for the Rich"
Public Places as Points of Identification for the Urban Poor – St. Petersburg (1850-1914)

Hans-Christian Petersen

"Very many people of Petrograd have heard that somewhere in their city there is a place called 'Vasia's Village'. But do many of them know its location and its functions?"[1] This rhetorical question is put at the beginning of a series of articles published in the "Little Gazette" (*Malen'kaia Gazeta*) in 1915, which dealt with one of the biggest slums of the Russian capital St. Petersburg which was renamed Petrograd at the beginning of World War I.[2] The author of these reports took the ignorance of the population he had noticed as an impetus to write in great detail about the co-existence of roughly 5000 inhabitants of "Vasia's Village". As is typical of 'uncovering stories' at that time (and even often of today) he added to his report numerous drastic details, introduced specific characters and, in order to verify the authenticity of his descriptions, he put words into their mouths for the dialogues which included their slang expressions. Like in West and Central European major cities, gruesome and obscene tales about the 'dark' sides of the city had become a worthwhile undertaking in Petrograd. They were a part of *slumming*[3] which included the 'discovery', marketing and presentation of the 'poor' to the 'better' part of the population for their amusement.

---

1   Iashkov, 03.01.1915, p. 3.
2   Ibid., 03.-04., 06. and 08.01.1915.
3   This expression was first used in Victorian England. Cf. Koven, 2006; Schwarz et al., 2007; Lindner, 2004. Hubertus Jahn has retraced this process of 'discovering' the urban poor for St. Petersburg: Jahn, 2010. The following work on the still valid relevance of slumming is now at hand: Frenzel et al., 2012.

In view of these circumstances it is obvious to analyse such a report first of all as a part of a discourse and to ask in the sense of postcolonial studies what we can learn from the text about the mental map of its author and the society. It was part of a process which presented images of the urban poor as the 'others', the 'dark' and the 'strange' and where the remaining inhabitants of the city assured themselves that they led better, 'brighter' lives. There is no doubt that such an approach is important, but does it cover everything? This question will be discussed in the following text. Is it true that we cannot gain any knowledge about the 'poor' from the reports about them? Is it only possible to write about poverty in Russian history as an object of "social imagination"[4], public welfare or control, as "beggars and the poor had no historical voices of their own until the end of the 19th century" and that we can only rely on "descriptions from outside"? Or do such sources – besides their discursive aspect – also provide information about those who, as in case of the report on "Vasia's Village", had unintentionally become objects of journalistic curiosity? In other words, to which extent is it possible for us to look behind the facade of urban poverty?

This question shall now be discussed by looking at two types of sources that present a totally different degree of 'authenticity' at first glance: on one hand we have the above-mentioned series of articles on "Vasia's Village" as an example of reports in connection with slumming and on the other we have several petitions submitted by traders from Petersburg's Haymarket, kept in the files of the tsarist Ministry of the Interior. The key aspect will be the question whether we will be able to gain information about the importance these locations had for the urban poor. Can they be regarded as points of identification which were important to them and which they regarded as their 'own'? In addition to a discussion on the epistemic possibilities and limitations of both types of sources it is thus my intention to challenge the still dominating narrative that the habitats of the urban lower class were solely places of dull backwardness characterised by cramped quarters and a narrowness of mind. This description does not take into account what this 'narrow world' meant for its inhabitants. The view from outside ignores the perspective from the inside. The following exposition will focus on this.

Let me first explain some terms. Places like "Vasia's Village" or "Viazemskaia Lavra" adjacent to Petersburg's Haymarket will be called *slums* – here defined as places of urban blight and utmost poverty. In doing so, I will follow Loïc Wacquants' differentiation between "slum" and "ghetto". He defines the "ghetto" "as a spatially based implement of ethnoracial closure" and points

---

4   This and the two following quotations were taken from JAHN, 2010, p. 16.

out "that not all ghettos are poor and not all poor areas are (inside) ghettos."[5] Such a differentiation solves the problem defined by Ilya Gerasimov. He said that the idea of an exclusive and socially homogeneous neighbourhood does not comply with the reality of Russian imperial society as "people of low socioeconomic status resided all over the city, while certain categories of the modernized could live in the slums (for example, poor students, teachers, or 'conscious' factory workers)."[6] This is undoubtedly true, especially in case of a city like St. Petersburg with its low degree of sociospatial segregation in comparison with other major cities.[7] Rich and poor were found close together in the town on the Neva River. However, you could also find more prosperous and poorer districts as well as clearly defined areas which were already at that time called *trushchoby* (impoverished areas, slums) by their contemporaries. Works such as the voluminous writings "Petersburg Slums (*Peterburgskie trushchoby*) by Vsevolod Krestovskii[8], "World of Slums" (*Mir trushchobnyi*) by Aleksei Svirskii[9] or "New Petersburg Slums" (*Novye Peterburgskie trushchoby*) by Iurii Angarov and M. Semenov'[10] made this term popular and marketed it as well, referring at the same time, however, to real existing places which were surely appropriately characterized by the term *trushchoba* (slum).

I. "Mud hole" and "anthill"? "Vasia's village"

"Vasia's Village" was situated between lines 17 and 18 on Vasil'evskii Island at the location of a former waste dump. Being the largest of the islands in the Neva Delta, Vasil'evskii Island was originally chosen as the centre of the new capital by Peter I after the foundation of St. Petersburg, before the site around the Admiralty was later favoured as the place for the city centre.[11] Correspondingly, many

---

5 Cf. the contribution by Loïc Wacquant in this book.
6 Cf. the contribution by Ilia V. Gerasimov in this book.
7 A comparative perspective is offered by PETERSEN.
8 This work has first been published as a series since 1864 in the journal "Otechestvennye zapiski". At the same time it was repeatedly published as a monograph, most recently a few years ago: KRESTOVSKII, 2011.
9 SVIRSKII, 1898.
10 ANGAROVI/SEMENOV', 1909-1910
11 Cf. SEMENCOV, 2007, on the building history of St. Petersburg. KUSBER, 2009, can be recommended as a recent introduction to the history of St. Petersburg

central buildings were erected on the East Bank of Vasil'evskii Island, among others the Arts House, the Twelve Collegia as well as the Academy of Sciences. The geometric design of the network of canals and streets demonstrated the ruler's ideas of rationalization and order.[12] The side of a street was called a line so that lines 16 and 17 as well as lines 18 and 19 made up one street each. "Vasia's Village" was situated in House No. 18 on line 17, only few houses away from the main boulevard of the island, the Bol'shoi Prospect.[13] Until the 20th century, the Bol'shoi Prospect was the border between that part of Vasil'evskii Island where streets which started at the prestigious bank of the Neva were lined on both sides by multi-storied stone houses and the markedly bigger part of the island on the other side of the prospect, which had no buildings at all or was the site of flat wooden buildings.[14] Accordingly, "Vasia's Village" consisted of several wooden houses, but was at the same time only a stone's throw away from the 'better-off' residential areas of Vasil'evskii Island. This is a typical example for the close proximity of rich and poor in the Russian capital. The well-known meteorologist Mikhail Tikachev, member of the Academy of Sciences, lived in House No. 20 for some time, directly adjacent to the slum. At the same time, lines 17 and 18 did not only belong to "Vasia's Village", but were also the location of orphanages and institutions for the poor.[15]

In the second half of the 19th century, several big industrial plants were erected on Vasil'evskii Island. This changed the social structure of the district. Dwellings for workers were built in the vicinity of the factories. Living conditions were similarly cramped and precarious as in other parts of the metropolis on the Neva River.[16] The island experienced a "densification process"[17]. Hitherto open areas or areas which had been used as vegetable gardens were turned into

---

12   Cf. NIKITENKO/SOBOL', 2008, for a recent encyclopaedic account of the history of Vasil'evskii Island (first edition: IBID., Vasileostrovskii raion. Enciklopediia ulic Sankt-Peterburga, St. Petersburg 1999). Cf. PIROGOV, 1996, for a survey from Soviet times.
13   Cf. NIKITENKO/SOBOL', 2008, p. 423 and 432, as well as the map of the Vasil'evskii Island, including the house numbers: PLANY POLICEISKIKH CHASTEI GORODA S.-PETERBURGA S POKAZANIEM DOMOV, VKHODIASCIKH V SOSTAVE ULIC I PRISVOENNYKH IM NOMEROM, 1902.
14   Cf. NIKITENKO/SOBOL', 2008, p. 16 and 413.
15   Cf. IBID., p. 423; ENCIKLOPEDIA BLAGOTVORITEL'NOSTI. Sankt-Peterburg: http://encblago.lfond.spb.ru/search.do?objectType=2805596371, 07.05.2013.
16   Cf. PIROGOV, 1996, p. 30-32.
17   Cf. NIKITENKO/SOBOL', 2008, p. 18.

building sites, and it is really not at all surprising that one of the biggest slums of the city developed in the wake of these changes. However, when looking at respective descriptions of the history of Vasil'evskii Island, "Vasia's Village" is either not mentioned at all or we find just a very cursory account.[18] This can be explained on one hand by the fact that this settlement was not in the centre of Petersburg contrary to the Haymarket and, on the other that it was largely unknown as we have seen from the citation at the beginning of this text. To write about it was in no way as profitable as the tales about the notorious "Viazemskaia lavra", the slum situated between Haymarket and Fontanka which were turned into literature in the works of Dostoevskii and Krestovskii. On the other hand, the fact that the image that should be conveyed for Vasil'evskii Island did not include the existence of a slum explains why "Vasia's Village" was largely neglected in the stories about urban districts: Under Soviet rule the poorest of the poor, the "lumpenproletariat" as they were derogatory termed already by Marx and Engels, did not fit into the teleological narrative about the class of 'conscious' workers eager for a revolution.[19] In post-Soviet Russia we see rather a concentration of high-culture and representative aspects of history, neither of which meshes with a closer look at a slum and its inhabitants.[20]

Now, what can we learn from the series of articles published on "Vasia's Village" in "Malen'kaia gazeta? According to the descriptions, the inhabitants were uncouth in their speech, were extremely prone to violence, addicted to alcohol and very good at surviving without 'honest work'. Garbage was simply thrown out of the windows and rows of toilettes without any doors were placed outside so that their users were in no way protected from the looks of neighbours (*vo*

---

18 The latter is only true for the encyclopaedia by NIKITENKO/SOBOL', 2008.

19 In addition to the work by Pirogov this narrative can also be found in: NIKITENKO/ SOBOL', 1981. In spite of its proximity to the Bol'shoi prospect "Vasia's Village" is not mentioned.

20 This is also shown by the popular scientific account of BUZINOV, 2006. In respect of the different narratives a comparative reading of the entries dealing with Vasil'evskii Island in the following encyclopedias is instructive: SANKT-PETERBURG – PETROGRAD – LENINGRAD. 1992; ENCIKLOPEDIA SANKT-PETERBURGA: http://encspb.ru/object/2803998688?lc=ru, 07.05.2013. Vasya's Village" is mentioned in neither of them, just as little as in the multi-volume encyclopedia which was published to mark the 300-anniversary of the city: Tri veka Sankt-Peterburga, 2005-2011. In contrast, for the "Viazemskaia lavra"can be found a single entry, supplementary to the already detailed article on the Haymarket: TERESHCHIK, 2005, p. 667f.

*vsei 'nature'*²¹), but had the opportunity of having long conversations during that time. By no means did the author say that all inhabitants were unwilling to work and corrupt. In addition to people like the "soothsayer"²², who had gained a relatively satisfactory fortune by making obscure prophesies and who lived in three numbers of the "village", we read here about the "honest worker"²³, who came to this settlement while looking for cheap living quarters or the "old single man"²⁴ who lived on alms. They were introduced as "humiliated people"²⁵, as victims just like the children who had names like "wolf" and whose fate "depended totally on the street"²⁶ (*ulica derzhit detei v polnoi svoei vlasti*). However, this differentiation between 'corrupt' and 'innocent' inhabitants served as a typical stylistic device for reports about the slums in order to evoke both revulsion and compassion and to satisfy the (assumed) lust of people for the spectacular.²⁷ The introduction of specific literary characters was meant to help readers to identify them again. In this respect it was above all "Krestovskiis' "Petersburg Slums" which exerted an influence on the style of others.²⁸

These passages were above all of a literary nature and can hardly be used as a historical source for the inner life of a slum. Are there – apart from this narrative level – descriptions which tell us about the actual geography of "Vasia's Village"? When we return to the beginning of the report, we find - together with the information about the location of lines 17 and 18 - markedly more details about the history of the settlement in comparison with the little information we find at other places. The encyclopaedia of Galina Nikitenko and Vitalii Sobol' states that "Vasia's Village" was founded on a large free space by a businessman from the peasant population named Egor Vasil'ev. It was his aim to let dwellings of this settlement named after him at low prices.²⁹ We find the same information in the "Malen'kaia gazeta". However, in addition we learn that Ego Vasil'ev came to St. Petersburg as an adolescent, made a living from collecting garbage for many years and through this was finally able to buy a piece of land

---

21 IASHKOV, 04.01.1915, p. 3.
22 This and the following quotation from IBID., 08.01.1915, p. 3.
23 IBID., 06.01.1915, p. 3.
24 IBID., 07.01.1915, p. 3.
25 IBID.
26 This and the following quotation from IBID.
27 Cf. for the perception of the street as a place of ‚the crowd' and of immorality STEINBERG, 2011 (especially chapter two).
28 Cf. JAHN, 2010, p. 123-128.
29 Cf. NIKITENKO/SOBOL', 2008, p. 423.

on Vasil'evskii Island.³⁰ Here he founded his own waste dump, and when he had collected a sufficient number of materials he built a first house on his estate with the assistance of some mates and the carpenter Klimentii. However, this house fell prey to the wind. He erected a second building which remained and was soon enlarged by further annexes. The first lodgers arrived whom Egor Vasil'ev allowed to stay upon payment of 5 copper kopeks per day. When the series of articles in the "Malen'kaia gazeta" was published in 1915, the settlement had grown to 247 flats with 5,000 inhabitants.³¹ According to the author, their names would fill "three books with a weight of several tons"³², and he met people who had already lived there for 20 years.

On one hand, this means that "Vasia's Village" had existed at least since the mid-1890s³³, hence since the time when the permanently notorious "housing problem" (*kvartirnyi vopros/zhilishchnyi vopros*) of St. Petersburg had increased even further.³⁴ There is no clear indication whether there is a correlation between the rise in prices of living space and the emergence of slums in the case of "Vasia's" Village as well as the other slums of St. Petersburg. Some facts in the newspaper report let us assume, however, that there is such a connection. Under the heading "inhabitants" (*zhil'cy*) we find the above-mentioned "honest worker"³⁵, but also quite a number of persons who could not afford another dwelling due to their low income, among others "the retired city clerk with 7,40 a month"³⁶ and the "widow with many children" who earned 30 kopeks per day for gluing cigarette packets together. According to the newspaper report they all lived in the slum because it offered "cheap flats and rooms".

The growth of "Vasia's Village" to more than several thousand inhabitants and the long stay of part of them make us wonder, however, whether there were more motives than the material necessity that made the people stay in spite of the undoubtedly minimal comfort the settlement offered. An answer to this cannot be found easily in this newspaper report owing to the author's scornful and condescending tone when, for example, telling us about the foundation of the set-

---

30 Cf. IASHKOV, 03.01.1915, p. 3.
31 Cf. IBID., 06.01.1915, p. 3.
32 IBID.
33 This corresponds roughly to the date stated in the encyclopaedia by Nikitenko and Sobol'. It says there that Egor Vasil'ev founded the "village" at the beginning of the 20ᵗʰ century. Cf. NIKITENKO;SOBOL', 2008, p. 423.
34 Cf. PETERSEN; SUKHORUKOVA, 2002; SVIATLOVSKII, 2012.
35 Cf. IASHKOV, 08.01.1915, p. 3.
36 This and the following two quotations from IBID., 04.01.1915, p. 3.

tlement by Egor Vasil'ev that he "looked for his fortune right there where every person born under a lucky star would look – among garbage."[37] Nevertheless, it becomes visible to some degree 'behind' this complacent attitude what "Vasia's Village" meant for its inhabitants in addition to being their refuge. Thus, the development of the slum can be interpreted also quite differently: As a 'wild' adoption of a hitherto unused area beyond the control from the government and with structures of its own. When we read in the newspaper report: "Above all I want to draw the attention of the reader to the lines in these buildings. What kind of lines are they? They could only be drawn by the highly talented heel of Egor Vasil'evs: One of the corners of a building is directed towards the onlooker, the other to the Caucasus Mountains [...]"[38] – then this demonstrates the author's aloofness in these surroundings. In spite of his assumed 'crossing the lines' and the supposed authenticity of his reports, he still remained a slum tourist who missed the straight lines so characteristic for the rest of Vasil'evskii Island.[39] At the same time it is shown that "Vasia's Village" lived by different, namely its own rules as we can learn from the following passage: "To enter a flat in 'Vasia's Village' is not as easy as is usually the case when we enter other buildings. Before you are able to enter, you have to look for the flat for roughly half a day, as annexes, staircases and numbers of flats are legion. Each of their inhabitants knows only his main entrance hole through which he creeps every day; he knows only the number of his own flat to which he is driven by the darkness of night and the cold. Even the guards in the yards of 'Vasia's Village' get lost in this impenetrable mud hole [*v étom neprokhodimom omute*]. When asked about the flats, they only wave their hand indifferently: 'Don't know..., climb the staircases, somewhere you will find it, but we have no idea [...]."[40]

What the reporter saw as a chaotic "impenetrable mud-hole", was for the inhabitants of "Vasia's Village" a place with which they could identify in so far as they marked it as 'their own'. The house numbers which were mentioned in the above passages were installed by the owner Egor Vasil'ev and were not only used for numbering purposes, but included some guidelines as follows: "Flat no. XY. 7 cubic Sazhen air. Not more than seven lodgers. Lodging is not permitted

---

37 IASHKOV, 03.01.1915, p. 3.
38 IBID., 04.01.1915, p. 3.
39 A brilliant description of this fear of the 'wilderness' of Vasil'evskii Island can be found in the character of the Tsarist bureaucrat Apollon Apollonovich in BELYI, 2004.
40 IASHKOV, 04.01.1915, p. 3.

in the corridors and in the kitchen."⁴¹ In correspondence with the tenor in the newspaper report, these instructions had in fact lost touch with reality – people lived in every corner of a room and in every dingy cellar in "Vasia's Village" just like in many other places of Petersburg. However, in addition to this they put inscriptions above the doors at the entrances which, for example, read "Fyodka-Ovchuch, thief".⁴² Such labels are certainly no reason to romanticize people's relationships in retrospect (I will deal with this later on); in the sense of the questions asked by this investigation they express the intentional overwriting of the original spatial order of a place, irrespective of moral assessment. Here we even find a certain amount of self-mockery.

The identification of the inhabitants with 'their village' was shown most prominently on the walls of the settlement. They were covered with numerous of their writings and drawings. One of the wall paintings showed the owner, Egor Vasil'ev as he approached on the back "of his cropped male dog with his fist raised and smoke coming out of his mouth while he called out: 'Have your dough ready, damned inhabitants of Vasia's Village (*Gotov'te gamzu, okaiannye vasinoderevency*)."⁴³

This graffiti is in two respects proof of an ongoing process of identification with that area, which is regarded as one's own possession threatened by the owner. On one hand, such marks on the wall are expressions of a process of adopting the respective space. It corresponds with Richard Sennett's definition of graffiti being "a writing of the underclass" – an openly shown sign of their presence: 'We exist, and we are everywhere. Moreover, you others are nothing; we write all over you.'"⁴⁴

On the other hand, the fact that they called themselves "damned inhabitants of Vasia's Village" tells us about their relationship to this place as well as to each other. The notion *Vasinoderevency* refutes the assumption stated in the newspaper report that the inhabitants of the 'village' do not care for each other but are merely interested in their own "dingy dwelling". Instead, the people had evidently found a joint identity just like it was reported from other places of poverty in Petersburg.⁴⁵

---

41 IBID.
42 IBID.
43 IBID. "Gamza" is an underworld slang expression and stands for "money, wallet". Cf. SNAPSKAIA, 2000, p. 121; GRACHEV, 2003, p. 187.
44 SENNETT, 1990, p. 207.
45 Aleksei Svirskii writes that the inhabitants of the slum called each other "slum brothers" (*truscobnye bratii*) and used the ironic nickname "slum yacht club"

This conclusion does not imply a retrospective romanticism of life in "Vasia's Village. Like other places of society in general and of urban underclass in particular, the slum on Vasil'evskii Island was penetrated by various power structures and inequalities. The wall painting described above is evidence of one of these confrontations – the opposition between owner and lodgers. The joint identity of the inhabitants described as *vasinoderevency* originated not least from the joint feeling of "we" against "him". At the same time, this "we" did not exist in the sense of an egalitarian co-existence, although the newspaper report conveys the idea of such an idyll in some instances, e.g. when we read about the numerous 'characters' found in the 'village' as follows: "Everything finds its place in the anthill of 'Vasia's Village'. It accommodates everybody, nobody is left outside."[46] The picture of an "anthill" is certainly true in so far as the slum was a place of refuge for those on the margins of society who were rejected at other places. However, we also find numerous examples in the newspaper report which show how strongly gender hierarchies moulded the structure of the social space "Vasia's Village". As an example may serve the omnipresent violence practised on the streets of the 'village' by men and juvenile gangs which caused women to keep away from these places in the evenings and at night.[47] These inequalities made the 'anthill' a contested area.

II. "... for poor people": The Haymarket seen from the viewpoint of 'itinerant peddlers'

A find from the archive will serve as a second source of information for a look behind the facade of urban slum areas. It comprises three petitions submitted by traders of the Petersburg Haymarket to the Minister of the Interior as well as to

---

(*truscobnyi iakhtklub*) for the night asylum on Izmail Field located between Fontanka and Obvodnyi Canal, cf. SVIRSKII, 1898. As another example can serve the "Viazemskaia lavra", in which lived among others the so-called "Viazemskie's cadets" (*Viazemskie kadety*), cf. SKORODUMOV, 1866.

46 IASHKOV, 06.01.1915, p. 3.
47 IBID. A fundamental treatise of this topic is to be found in NEUBERGER, 1993. Cf. also the contribution by Mark Steinberg in this book.

the Tsar personally in the mid-1860s. They are kept in the files of the finance department of the Tsarist Ministry of the Interior.[48]

The Haymarket, strictly speaking the Hay Square (*Sennaia ploshchad'*), was a place which was originally located on the outskirts of the city where farmers from the vicinity of St. Petersburg were allowed to sell hay and firewood at certain times.[49] When the city expanded, it was no longer situated on the periphery, but had finally moved to the centre of the capital by the 19th century, only a few minutes' walk away from the grand boulevard of St. Petersburg, the Nevskii prospect. Moreover, its functions changed from being a temporary trading place for specific goods to becoming the permanent marketplace with a markedly broader range of products where mainly the poor population of Petersburg bought their basic food.

In the second half of the 19th century the Haymarket became the epitome of the 'other', unknown and dangerous St. Petersburg in the minds of the inhabitants of the Russian capital. On one hand, this was to be attributed to increasing marketing efforts in connection with slumming, which was already mentioned above. Literary works even created the character of a typical lodger of the Haymarket (*Sennovskii obitatel'*).[50] On the other hand there was some reason for these projections and anxieties. The *Sennaia* as well as its market presented sanitation problems affecting – beyond its own boundaries – adjacent districts as well as the entire city. Already in its first year the "sanitary commission" which was set up by the municipal duma after the severe cholera outbreak in 1867 arranged for an inspection of the Haymarket. It reported alarming hygienic conditions. The ground of the place was covered by a thick layer of garbage, food leftovers and other debris from the market.[51] Moreover, there were several slums in the vicinity of the Haymarket, among others the above-mentioned "Viazemskaia

---

48 RUSSIAN STATE HISTORICAL ARCHIVE/ROSSIISKII GOSUDARSTVENNYI ISTORICHESKII ARKHIV (RGIA), f. 1287, op. 29, del. 1600.

49 A survey of the varying history of this place which is probably the most prominent square of St. Petersburg besides the Palace Square is presented by IURKOVA, 2011. Further titles are JAHN, 1996, as well as BAUER.

50 Cf. TSEITLIN, 1998, p. 3, as well as on the development of the myth "Haymarket" as a whole JAHN, 2010, p. 113-128.

51 O DEIATEL'NOSTI GORODSKOI SANITARNOI KOMISSII, 1868, p. 48f. When the medical doctors of the sanitary commission examined the place in the middle of March this layer was still mixed with snow and ice. Severe problems arose at the end of the freezing season. Cf. the report of the German travel writer KOHL, Vol. 1, p. 200f.

lavra" now housing up to 20,000 people.[52] In the eyes of the authorities the name "Haymarket" was associated with a constant potential threat to public order – at the latest since the time when it became the stage for the so-called "cholera revolt" (*kholernyi bunt*) in 1831 in the wake of the first cholera epidemic. This was the first people's revolt in the history of the city.[53]

This combination of real and imagined threats led to various efforts of the government to impose regulations on this 'wild' place. After the erection of a central police station (*Hauptwache*) in 1820, it was above all the project to build permanent market halls instead of the hitherto open place which had been on the agenda for more than 20 years.[54] There were three opposing parties: The first was represented by the Governor or Gradonachal'nik of St. Petersburg, Count Nikolay Levashov. He wanted the Haymarket to become a representative marketplace appropriate for the image of the Russian capital. He promoted projects which intended to turn the entire Haymarket into one big covered marketplace. As such schemes were expensive and did not fit into the budget of the duma, Levashov advocated payment by private persons who should, at the same time, be in charge of the Haymarket. This means that it was the governor's aim to privatize the Haymarket which had so far been in possession of the municipality.[55]

Just as the Governor, the municipal duma was also in favour of a solid covered market. Last but not least, its interest was of a concrete economic nature. Income from the rents of market stalls amounted to up to 50,000 roubles a year. However, unlike Levashov, the majority of delegates of the duma emphasized the importance of the Haymarket as a market for the 'common people'. It was said that the nature of this location was to be preserved. That was why the re-construction should be "as simple as possible"[56] including roofing for only half of the market, whereas the other half should be used for the traditional sales by peasants directly from their carriages (*vozy*) also in the future.

---

52 In addition to the above-mentioned literature cf. CHARITONOVA, 1996. Cf. for a contemporary report by a commission founded by the city council on the interior of the "Viazemskaia lavra" O SANITARNYKH MERAKH PO DOMU KNIAZA VIAZEMSKAGO, 1883, p. 872-885.

53 Cf. the report of an officer on duty on this event FON-DER-KHOVEN, 1885, as well as the account by KOHL, Vol. 1, p. 194-196.

54 Cf. besides IURKOVA, 2011, also VEKSLER, 2008. A detailed analysis of this re-organization of the Haymarket is in preparation.

55 Cf. amongst others: OB USTROISTVE NA SENNOI PLOSHCHADI RYNOCHNAGO ZDANIIA DLIA PROIZVODIASHCHEISIA TAM TORGOVLIA, 1865, p. 450-464.

56 OB USTROISTVE SENNOI PLOSHCHADI, 1866, p. 401.

A third opinion was held by the municipal sanitary commission and the Chief Police Officer of Petersburg. The chairman of the sanitary commission, Petr Zhukovskii, emphasised repeatedly that the Haymarket was above all a source of epidemics which should be demolished altogether and reconstructed from scratch. In addition, the nature of the market would have changed fundamentally. Today the queues in front of the food concourse (*obzhornyi riad*) would scarcely consist of workers, but instead of many "useless people"[57] from surrounding houses. This argument was supported by the Chief Police Officer in a similar way. He felt that the continued existence of the market was dangerous from the point of view of the police as it would attract a large number of criminals and prostitutes in addition to the buyers. This "enormous number of dangerous people of our society"[58] would find ideal conditions at the Haymarket where they could hide and gather in the adjacent houses. This development could only be stopped by a "complete cleanup of the place" and the removal of the market to the outskirts of the city.

The debate on the reconstruction of the Haymarket went on for well over 20 years before it resulted in the construction of four large metal pavilions which opened in 1886. After this there was no room for the traditional sales of peasants from their carriages which were originally deemed important by the duma. Trade was now conducted at fixed and equally large stalls in the market halls.[59] Hence the transformation of the Haymarket was an example of the city's endeavours to organize public space in a 'better way', i.e. to regulate it. During this time, numerous reconstruction projects were carried out on the markets of Petersburg among which the Haymarket was merely the most prominent example.[60]

The three petitions, which shall now be looked at in detail, are part of this controversial constellation. They were filed by traders who offered their goods on the Haymarket and who had come into conflict with the new regulations. The petitions belong to the very few statements we have from inhabitants and traders of the Haymarket. As much as has been written about this place, a history of the

---

57   OB USTROISTVE KRYTAGO RYNKA NA SENNOI PLOSHCHADI, 1870, p. 142.
58   This and the following quotation were taken from the letter of Chief Police Officer of St. Petersburg to the Ministry of the Interior 29.06.1869, RGIA, f. 1287, op. 40, del. 310, l. 114.
59   Insights into the interior of the market halls can be found in ZASOSOV/PYZIN, 1999, p. 110-112; BAKHTIAROV, 1994, p. 138-148.
60   A comparative treatise of this process is still missing. A first survey is presented by PROCAI, 2005.

Haymarket 'from below' is still missing. We get an idea from these petitions how these regulations of public space were perceived by the people concerned.

When we look at the epistemic value of these sources, the petitions seem to show a markedly higher degree of 'authenticity' than the reports published in the "Malen'kaia gazeta". In fact, the categorical difference is – as may be readily concluded – that here we have the voices of the 'common people' themselves and not an account by a third person wanting to sell a 'story'. In this context Keith Snell, the author of fundamental studies on the self-conception of the English poor, defines letters and petitions as "alongside oral history [...] *the* most authentic sources for 'history from below' and historical questions of identity among the poor"[61] we have.

On the other hand, we have narrative conventions observed by such sources. Russian history has known petitions since the Middle Ages which means that they follow a certain tradition as regards contents and formal layout.[62] Hence, this leads to the conclusion that an overoptimistic interpretation of these sources as 'authentic' may be questionable.[63] First of all, it has to be considered who wrote the petitions, the undersigned himself or the undersigned parties themselves or rather a scribe? This was not unusual in view of the widely spread illiteracy of the urban poor. In addition we have to ask how the wording of the petitions which we see on paper was actually composed. Who took part and how big was the contribution of a possible scribe in the final text? And, last but not least, it has to be considered that petitions were a performative act which served to let one's request appear in the most favourable light in order to convince the addressee who, as a rule, was in a much higher position. Are they really the utterances of the poor 'themselves'? To find an answer to this question, let us look at the petitions of the traders and consider at the same time whether they offer information about the Haymarket as a place of 'their own'.

As to the formal characteristics of the petitions it can be stated that all three were written down between February 1865 and June 1866. In February 1865 as

---

61 SNELL, 2012, p. 2.
62 In this connection, I refer to the paper submitted by Hubertus Jahn on the occasion of the conference "Poverty in Modern Europe. Micro-perspectives on the Formation of the Welfare State in the 19th and 20th Centuries" at the German Historical Institute in London in May 2012: Voices from the Lower Depths: Russian Poor in Their Own Words, presenting an analysis of petitions for the time from the 17th to the 20th centuries. A publication of the contributions to this conference is under way.
63 Cf. on the following also KING, 2008, p. 252f.

well as in May 1866 they were addressed to the Ministry of the Interior. On June 6, 1866 they were addressed to the Tsar himself. In each case the handwritings do not correspond to the signatures of the applicants so that it may be assumed that the petitions were written down by scribes. How the final wording came about cannot be said for lack of further sources for these petitions. It is possible that the applicant narrated the case to the scribe. In all three cases about 90 % of the signatures were those of peasants as well as of petty commoners (*meshchane*) in a few cases. While the petitions of February 1865 as well of June 1866 bore signatures of about 100 names, they numbered only 15 on the petition of May 1866. Obviously as many signatures as possible were collected for the last petition which was the only one addressed to the Tsar himself. It can be noticed that some of the people who had already signed the petition of February 1865 put their signature under this document as well. It may hence be concluded that these people knew each other or were at least in touch so that contacts could be established quickly. Moreover, they must have had similar interests. This leads us to the question of the contents of the petitions.

A central concern of the petition of February 1865 was the right to sell meat at the Haymarket also during the summer, a right that was threatened from the viewpoint of the undersigned parties. The two petitions of the following year asked for the permission to continue the sale of goods along the edges of the Haymarket close to public and private buildings. The origin of both requests was very similar, which explains the existence of overlapping signatures: They were 'itinerant peddlers' (*torgovcy v raznos*) without any permanent place who expressed their concern and fought a treatment considered unfair in their opinion. The composition of the signatories of the petition shows that they were for the most part peasants who sold their goods directly from their carriages (*vozy*) contrary to those stationary traders who had permanent stalls (*lavka*).

Correspondingly, the petitions are very similar in respect of set-up and argumentation.[64] Each of them was caused by actions of the commercial police to enforce resolutions of the municipal duma: on one hand, the prohibition of meat sales by 'itinerant peddlers' at the Haymarket between April and November and on the other a decree forbidding sales of 'itinerant peddlers' close to public and private buildings. The decrees passed by the duma in connection with meat sales were preceded by requests of stationary traders asking the commercial police

---

64 In addition, the two petitions of May and June 1866 show partly identical passages. However, this is not surprising as their concerns were the same and they were written down within a short period of time.

to take steps against the competition from 'itinerant peddlers'.[65] The petitions opposed these measures by arguing in two ways: by referring to the law and by emphasising that the Haymarket was a traditional place of the 'common people'.

As to the legal aspect of this dispute, it has to be said that it was the duma's principal right to enact trade regulations at the Haymarket as this place was part of the municipal property. However, its resolutions could be overturned by the Ministry of the Interior. In the case of meat sales by 'itinerant peddlers' during the summer months the legal position was undisputed: Since 1842 sales of fresh meat had only been allowed at the Haymarket during the summer at permanent stalls where it was possible to keep goods cool.[66] The general ban on trade in the vicinity of public and private buildings was more controversial in some respects. It was not without reason that the signatories of the petition argued that the decree passed by the duma was above all directed at sales conducted in front of houses adjacent to the Haymarket or in their courtyards. These houses were not part of the property of the duma, but belonged to individual owners. Correspondingly, the signatories emphasized that such a ban would violate the "right to private ownership"[67] (*prava chastnoj sobstvennosti*). However, this point was not undisputed. In the end it was a matter of political decisions. Already at former instances the duma had passed decrees entitling it to decide about the allocation of trading places. However, these resolutions were met by opposition from private house-owners as well as the Ministry of the Interior. In 1842, the latter had decreed that peasants coming from the urban hinterland had the principal right to sell their products at the city's trading places.[68] However, in 1854 the Ministry made it clear that private persons were not entitled to allocate

---

65   Cf. Proshenie krest'ian, torguiuvshchikh miasom na Sennoi ploshchadi, 09.02.1865, RGIA, f. 1287, op. 29, del. 1600, l. 21. The complaint is also mentioned in O VOSPROSHCHENII TORGOVLIA MIASOM NA SENNOI PLOSHCHADI, A TAKZHE MELOCHNAGO TORGA S POSTOIANNYKH MEST OKOLO CHASTNYKH I KAZENNYKH ZDANII, 1867, p. 373.

66   Cf. O VOSPROSHCHENII TORGOVLIA MIASOM NA SENNOI PLOSHCHADI, A TAKZHE MELOCHNAGO TORGA S POSTOIANNYKH MEST OKOLO CHASTNYKH I KAZENNYKH ZDANII, 1867, p. 373.

67   Proshenie s Peterburgskikh torgovcev v raznos, 21.05.1866, RGIA, f. 1287, op. 29, del. 1600, l. 28.

68   The respective decree of the Ministry of the Interior of November 29, 1842 was published in: OB OTVODE MESTA DLIA BAZARNOI VOZOVOI TORGOVLI I OB IZDANII OBIAZATEL'NAGO POSTANOVLENIIA O PORIADKE TORGOVLI Z VOZOV V S.-PETERBURGE, 1885, p. 315. This included fish and meat, however, only as frozen goods.

trading places by passing a new resolution. This would impair municipal finances.[69] Because of this rather unclear legal situation the sales by peddlers without a permanent stall were ultimately tolerated around public and private houses, until the commercial police tried to stop them in 1864. Last but not least it was the decree of 1842, which the signatories used as a reference when applying directly to the Ministry of the Interior.

However, the passages of the petitions referring to the nature of the Haymarket as a place of the 'common people' are of a greater relevance to the context in this essay than the legal aspects of the dispute. One of the arguments pointed out by the undersigned parties was that the "wellbeing of the people"[70] (*narodnoe blagosostoianie*) would be jeopardized if extensive restrictions were imposed on 'itinerant trade'. So far "a large proportion of the capital's poor population who shopped at the Haymarket" had bought fresh meat from them which was of equal quality as that offered at the stalls, but their prices were much lower. If their sales were stopped, permanent traders could fix prices "arbitrarily"[71]. This would lead to the establishment of a "monopoly"[72] which would above all affect the poor population of Petersburg.

At the same time the undersigned parties argued that there existed a kind of customary right. They pointed out that they would conduct their sales in the same way as had been practised already "for a long time"[73]. They would ask for nothing more but the right to return to their customary places at which they had conducted their sales "up to today"[74] (*ponyne*). Consequently they rejected the allegation of the duma that they had usurped these places "unauthorized"[75]

---

69 Cf. O VOSPROSHCHENII TORGOVLIA MIASOM NA SENNOI PLOSHCHADI, A TAKZHE MELOCHNAGO TORGA S POSTOIANNYKH MEST OKOLO CHASTNYKH I KAZENNYKH ZDANII, 1867, p. 373. A possible economic damage refers to the fact that itinerant peddlers had to buy a tin token from the municipal authorities at 2 roubles and 86 kopeks.

70 This and the following quotation: Proshenie krest'ian, torguiuvshchikh miasom na Sennoi ploshchadi, 09.02.1865, RGIA, f. 1287, op. 29, del. 1600, l. 22.

71 IBID., l. 21 ob.

72 IBID., l. 22.

73 Proshenie s Peterburgskikh torgovcev v raznos, 21.05.1866, RGIA, f. 1287, op. 29, del. 1600, l. 27.

74 Proshenie, 06.06.1866, RGIA, f. 1287, op. 29, del. 1600, l. 32.

75 O VOSPROSHCHENII TORGOVLIA MIASOM NA SENNOI PLOSHCHADI, A TAKZHE MELOCHNAGO TORGA S POSTOIANNYKH MEST OKOLO CHASTNYKH I KAZENNYKH ZDANII, 1867, p. 374.

(*samovol'no*): "We cannot accept the seizure of our places by the duma as it does not own them and therefore has no right to allocate them."[76] Instead, they would have obtained the places "in accordance with an agreement with the house-owners in the same way as practised by the duma". If, however, the house-owners would not have the right to do so "we will accept the trading places also from the duma and [...] and pay the customary fee." In any case, stop the "unsubstantiated prosecution" by the police that "has driven so many of us into poverty".

The background for these arguments was the traditional sale of goods by peasants who came to town.[77] This situation could still be seen at the Haymarket at the time of the formulation of the petitions in so far as the place had been divided into two halves since the beginning of the 19th century: on one side, the open "green" area where products were sold directly from the carriages of incoming traders (during the wintertime timber and hay, in the summer agricultural produce such as vegetables, cabbage and milk)[78], on the other half the sale of mainly meat, fish, fruit and vegetables at permanent stalls. The undersigned parties of the petitions quoted as a precedent that they had sold their meat products directly in the "green area" until the interference of the commercial police. The permanent traders at this place would have taken no offence up to then.

Whether these arguments were sound, was disputed in the duma. Supporters of a general "clean-up" of the total Haymarket, such as the above-mentioned Petr Zhukovskii or the delegate Ivan Glazunow, denied the existence of such a customary law. They pointed out that the majority of traders had stopped being farmers long ago and that they acted as intermediaries. Through this the market had fundamentally changed its nature and no longer followed the tradition of the former trading place on the outskirts of the city.[79] They considered open sales

---

76 This and the following quotations up to the end of the paragraph Proshenie, 06.06.1866, RGIA, f. 1287, op. 29, del. 1600, l. 31 ob-32 ob.

77 Cf. the comprehensive account by BAUER. During the winter, the sale was carried out from sledges, cf. KOHL, Vol. 1, p. 198.

78 Cf. on the range of products offered the report of the commission for public interests and necessities of January 28, 1868, in: IZVESTIIA SANKT-PETERBURGSKOI GORODSKOI OBSHCHEI DUMY, 1868, No. 2, p. 75; ISTORICHESKIE TRUDY ALEKSANDRA TOMILINA, 1854, p. 66-69; KOHL, Vol. 1, p. 196f.

79 An example of this argument can be found in the contribution by Glazunov in the debate in the duma of February 15, 1868, in: IZVESTIIA SANKT-PETERBURGSKOI GORODSKOI OBSHCHEI DUMY, 1868, No. 5, p. 226-243.

as well as the adjacent food concourse a "disgrace"[80] (*bezobrazie*) which had to be abolished. This was vigorously denied by other delegates. Aleksandr Iakovlev emphasized that besides the repeatedly appearing images of the Haymarket there were also traders who were no criminals. Moreover, the constant demonization of intermediaries who were said to have destroied the 'original' bazaar would not at all be convincing in view of the growth of the Haymarket as well as the entire city: "The answer could be that indeed every merchant could be regarded as an intermediary. He buys goods first hand and sells them immediately afterwards. I cannot see that this is condemnable or unethical."[81] He went on saying that the social function of the Haymarket and its 'itinerant peddlers" had to be taken into consideration as well and that the Haymarket is the only "market of the people"[82] (*narodnyi rynok*) in St. Petersburg. He continued: What would it mean to close down such an institution as the 'food concourse' which was called "kitchen of the nobility" (*dvorianskaia kuchnia*) by the man in the street: "It is said that among others you will find people eating there who do not deserve any attention according to an expression used by the sanitary commission: among others homeless people, thieves, fraudsters, illegal persons without any documents [*bezpasportnye*]; this may be true, but they still have to eat. They will not go to the permanent food stalls for fear that their passports be checked."[83]

Eventually the majority of the delegates of the duma adopted Iakovlev's point of view and voted in favour of continuing open sales as well as keeping the 'food concourse'.[84] As regards the three petitions, it had already been decided beforehand that the sale of meat in tents would be allowed for a year under the same sanitary conditions as those applying to permanent sale stalls.[85] As regards trading in front of private and public buildings the duma made it clear that the right of the house-owner would end at the facade of the house and that everybody offering his goods could only do so by asking permission of the duma and

---

80   Amongst others the expression used by the governor-general in a letter to the head office for traffic infrastructure and public buildings of August 16, 1855: RGIA, f. 218, op. 3, del. 1288, l. 3.
81   IZVESTIIA SANKT-PETERBURGSKOI GORODSKOI OBSHCHEI DUMY, 1868, No. 5, p. 233.
82   IBID., p. 235.
83   IBID., p. 240.
84   Cf. IBID., p. 241-243.
85   Cf. the protocol of the debate in the duma of July 7, 1867, in: IZVESTIIA SANKT-PETERBURGSKOI GORODSKOI OBSHCHEI DUMY, 1867, No. 16, p. 856.

by paying a corresponding fee. Basically, it was endeavoured to keep trading to locations of the city which were intended for this purpose.[86]

Thereby a preliminary arrangement was found for the Haymarket before the inauguration of the four market halls stopped any open trading whatsoever on the market – at least officially. However, the matter of 'itinerant peddlers' was still a topic. This is not only true for the vicinity of the Haymarket where peddlers moved to other places such as the Obuchovskii Square on the Fontanka.[87] Also at other places the municipal authorities did not manage to stop this type of trading. In the same year when the halls at the Haymarket were inaugurated, the gradonachal'nik of Petersburg felt impelled to issue a regulation in which he complained that open trading was still conducted at "certain places"[88]. He continued his appeal to observe the respective decrees of the duma, but this did not bring about any significant changes. Even at the beginning of the 20th century the 'itinerant peddlers' were still the object of controversial discussions about the farmer's market *(Sytnyi rynok)*[89] located at the Petersburg side as well as in connection with the project to establish a central market at the Vyborg side.[90]

This shows that the petitions discussed in this paper do not represent isolated cases. The topic concerned the entire the city. At the core of the matter we find the question as to who had the right to organize day-to-day activities at places like the Haymarket. Or to be more precise: Who owned the markets of the city?[91] Irrespective of the conclusive answer to this question, the above-mentioned passages make it clear that the 'common people' regarded places such as the Haymarket as places of their own where they had conducted trading for a long time. Of course, reverting to the argument of the "wellbeing of the people" was also part of their discursive strategy, which intended to present the problem as a matter of general interest. As stated by Steven King, petitions were in fact "multi-functional documents, combining reportage, fact, posturing, rhetoric and circumstance".[92] But, King goes on, the narrative and strategic formation of such

---

86 IBID.
87 Cf. ZASOSOV/PYZIN, 1999, p. 112.
88 Decree of the gradonachal'nik as well as of the police of August 1886, in: IZVESTIIA SANKT-PETERBURGSKOI GORODSKOI OBSHCHEI DUMY, 1886, No. 35, p. 663.
89 Cf. the report of the municipality of May 23, 1904, in: IZVESTIIA SANKT-PETERBURGSKOI GORODSKOI OBSHCHEI DUMY, 1904, No. 13, p. 1205-1214. Just like 30 years ago the basis for this was again the complaint of the stationary traders.
90 Cf. RGIA, f. 1293, op. 137, del. 91.
91 Cf. for the concept of a "Right to the City" LEFÈBVRE, 1968.
92 KING, 2008, p. 253.

sources does not mean that we cannot see them as part of an agency that tried to exert an influence on real existing processes.[93] This is also true for the examples analysed in this paper. By submitting a petition, the signatories articulated their claim to the Haymarket and tried at the same time to make their position public. The fact that they themselves did not write them does not mean that they do not reflect the interests of the subjects. The reference to the Haymarket as a place of the poor did not only fulfil a rhetorical function but was also part of their self-positioning in contrast to the places of the rich. This is demonstrated by another petition mentioned in the book by Zoia Iurkova which also dealt with retail trading: "It is a well-known fact [...] that the duma harasses the poor people (*bednyi narod*) and keeps on supporting the rich, but the Haymarket was not intended for the rich, but for rural, for poor people and today they are not even provided with a slice of bread."[94] The self-positioning of the poor people was attached to certain locations in the city – in this case to Petersburg's Haymarket.

III. Summary

Let us revert to the question asked at the beginning of this article. In how far is it possible to look behind the facade of urban poverty? An interpretation of both types of sources which were discussed as examples is faced with many difficulties when we try to answer this question. This is also true for the allegedly 'more authentic' petitions which are indeed also "multi-functional documents". On other hand, however, differences should not be completely equalized. Both for the acting persons of that time as well as for our interpretation of today it was and is certainly not irrelevant whether you could support a petition by signing it yourself or whether you were able to refrain from putting your name under this paper. The inhabitants of "Vasia's Village" did not have such an opportunity of authorising a text which we find as a source in the archives today.

As difficult as newspaper reports such as those published in the "Malen'kaia gazeta" may be, they are frequently and also in this case nearly the only reports on the inner life of a slum like "Vasia's Village". The method suggested by this article was an approach to the world of the urban poor by looking at concrete places. Beyond stylistic devices, both types of sources provide us with information about places which were important to their inhabitants and which they regarded as 'their own'. In this way, it may be possible to confine an investiga-

---

93 Ibid., p. 271. In respect of petitions, this view is also shared by Jahn (cf. note 62).
94 IURKOVA, 2011, p. 89.

tion not just to an analysis from the outside, but to outline perspectives from the inside as well and to demonstrate the importance attached to such places by their inhabitants in spite of their social marginalization.

At the same time such an approach by means of places makes it possible to show internal heterogeneities and inequalities. The analysis has revealed the existence of inner power structures between owner and inhabitants, men and women as well as between 'itinerant' and stationary traders. Not only does this fact prevent a subsequent well-meaning romanticization of the everyday life of the urban poor but above all it allows us to have an amplified and differentiated look at the 'Russian poor" which were in fact more than the "black people" (*chernyi narod*) as they are usually called in Russian. In contrast to such generalising opinions the examples outlined in this investigation present the poor inhabitants of the city as people who were actively engaged in dealing with the precarious conditions they faced.

Literature

ANGAROV, IURII/SEMENOV', M., Novye peterburgskie trushchoby: Ocherki stolichnoi zhizni. Vys. 1-4, St. Petersburg 1909-1910.

BAKHTIAROV, ANATOLII A., Briukho Peterburga. Ocherki stolichnoi zhizni, St. Petersburg 1994.

BAUER, ALEXANDER, Platz – Herrschaft – Kaufleute. Regulierung des öffentlichen Raums am Beispiel des Heuplatzes, in: Räume der Macht. Metamorphosen von Stadt und Garten im Europa der Frühen Neuzeit, ed. by ANNA ANANIEVA et al., Bielefeld (forthcoming).

BELYJ, ANDREI, Petersburg, St. Petersburg 2004 (first published 1912-1913).

BUZINOV, VIKTOR, Desiat' progulok po Vasil'evskomu. Izdanie tret'e, dopolnennoe, St. Petersburg 2006.

O DEIATEL'NOSTI GORODSKOI SANITARNOI KOMISSII, in: Arkhiv sudebnoi mediciny i obshchestvennoi gigieny 4, 1 (1868), p. 48-50.

FON-DER-KHOVEN, I. R., Bunt na Sennoi ploshchadi v Sankt-Peterburge, Iiun 1831 g., in: Russkaia starina 47 (1885), p. 61-68.

FRENZEL, FABIAN et al. (eds.), Slum Tourism. Poverty, power and ethics, Abingdon, New York 2012.

GRAKHEV, M. A. (ed.), Slovar' tysiacheletnego russkogo argo: 27.000 slov i vyrazheniy, Moskva 2003.

IASHKOV, V., "Vasina derevnia", in: Malen'kaia gazeta, 03., 04., 06. and 08.01.1915, respectively p. 3.

IURKOVA, ZOIA, Sennaia ploshchad'. Vchera, segodnia, zavtra, Moscow, St. Petersburg 2011.
IZVESTIIA SANKT-PETERBURGSKOI GORODSKOI OBSHCHEI DUMY, 1868, No. 2, p. 72-77.
ID., 1868, No. 5, p. 226-243.
ID., 1867, No. 16, p. 854-857.
ID., 1886, No. 35, p. 663.
ID., 1904, No. 13, p. 1205-1214.
JAHN, HUBERTUS F., Der St. Petersburger Heumarkt im 19. Jahrhundert. Metamorphosen eines Stadtviertels, in: Jahrbücher für Geschichte Osteuropas 44, 1 (1996), p. 162-177.
ID., Armes Russland. Bettler und Notleidende in der russischen Geschichte vom Mittelalter bis in die Gegenwart, Paderborn et al. 2010.
KHARITONOVA, EKATERINA, Sennaia ploshchad' - Centr Peterburgskikh trushchob, in: Nasledniki velikogo goroda. Vys. 5, St. Petersburg 1996, p. 127-131.
KING, STEVEN, Friendship, Kinship and Belonging in the Letters of Urban Paupers 1800-1840, in: Historical Social Research 33, 3 (2008), p. 249-277.
KOHL, JOHANN GEORG, Petersburg in Bildern und Skizzen, 3 Bde, zweite vermehrte und bessere Auflage, Dresden, Leipzig 1841-46.
KOVEN, SETH, Slumming. Sexual and Social Politics in Victorian London, Princeton 2006.
SCHWARZ, WERNER et al. (eds.), Ganz unten. Die Entdeckung des Elends. Wien, Berlin, London, Paris, New York. 338. Sonderausstellung des Wien Museums, Wien 2007.
KRESTOVSKII, VSEVOLOD, Peterburgskie trushchoby. Kniga o sytykh i golodnykh. Polnoe izdanie v odnom tome, Moscow 2011.
KUSBER, JAN, Kleine Geschichte St. Petersburgs, Regensburg 2009.
LEFÈBVRE, HENRI, Le droit à la ville, Paris 1968.
LINDNER, ROLF, Walks on the Wild Side. Eine Geschichte der Stadtforschung, Frankfurt a. M. 2004.
O SANITARNYKH MERAKH PO DOMU KNIAZA VIAZEMSKAGO, in: Izvestiia Sankt-Peterburgskoi Gorodskoi Obshchei Dumy, 1883, No. 14, p. 872-885.
NEUBERGER, JOAN, Hooliganism. Crime, culture, und power in St. Petersburg, 1900-1904, Berkeley 1993,
NIKITENKO, GALINA/SOBOL', VITALII, Bol'shoi prospect Vasil'evskogo ostrova, Leningrad 1981.
ID., Doma i liudi. Vasil'evskogo ostrova, St. Petersburg 2008.

OB OTVODE MESTA DLIA BAZARNOI VOZOVOI TORGOVLI I OB IZDANII OBIAZATEL'NA-
GO POSTANOVLENIIA O PORIADKE TORGOVLI Z VOZOV V S.-PETERBURGE, in: Izvestiia Sankt-Peterburgskoi Gorodskoi Obshchei Dumy, 1885, No. 35, p. 313-318.

PETERSEN, HANS-CHRISTIAN, Gentrifizierung in historischer Perspektive? Aufwertung und Verdrängung in St. Petersburg, Wien und London (1850-1914), in: VSWG-Beihefte, Nummer 209: Arm und Reich (24. Arbeitstagung der GSWG 2011 in Bonn), ed. by GÜNTHER SCHULZ et al. (accepted for printing).

PIROGOV, PETR, Vasil'evskii ostrov, Leningrad 1966.

PLANY POLICEISKIKH CHASTEI GORODA S.-PETERBURGA S POKAZANIEM DOMOV, VKHODIASCIKH V SOSTAVE ULIC I PRISVOENNYKH IM NOMEROM, in: Adresnaia kniga goroda S.-Peterburga za 1902 god, St. Petersburg 1902 (without page numbers).

PROCAI, LIUDMILA A., Rynki Peterburga. Konec XIX-nachalo XX veka: Al'bom, St. Petersburg 2005.

SANKT-PETERBURG – PETROGRAD – LENINGRAD. Enciklopedicheskii spravochnik, Moscow 1992.

SEMENCOV, SERGEJ V., Gradostroitel'noe razvitie Sankt-Peterburga v 1703-2000-e gody. Unpublished dissertation, 2 volumes, St. Petersburg 2007.

SENNETT, RICHARD, The Conscience of the Eye. The design and social life of cities, New York 1990.

SKORODUMOV, PETR, Vjazemskie kadety, in: Peterburgskii listok, 02.07.1866, p. 4.

SNAPSKAIA, S. M. (ed.), Bol'shoi slovar' russkogo zhargona, St. Petersburg 2000.

SNELL D., KEITH, Belonging and Community: Understandings of 'Home' and 'Friends' among the English Poor, 1750-1850, in: The Economic Historical Review 65, 1 (2012), p. 1-25.

STEINBERG, MARK D., Petersburg. Fin de Siècle, New Haven, London 2011.

SUKHORUKOVA, ANNA, Peterburgskaia gorodskaia duma i problemy gradostroitel'stva v konce XIX-nachale XX veka. Unpublished dissertation, St. Petersburg 2000.

SVIATLOVSKII, VLADIMIR, Zhilishchnyi i kvartirnyi vopros v Rossii. Izbrannye stat'i, Moscow 2012.

SVIRSKII, A[LEKSEI] I., Pogibshie liudi. 3 volumes, here vol. 1: Mir trushchobnyy, St. Petersburg 1898.

TERESHCHIK, A. V., Viazemskaia lavra, in: Tri veka Sankt-Peterburga, Vol. 2.1, St. Petersburg 2005, p. 667f.

ISTORICHESKIE TRUDY ALEKSANDRA TOMILINA, St. Peterbsurg 1854.

TSEITLIN, E. I., "Sennovskii obitatel'" v Peterburgskoi istorii i kul'ture, in: Piatye otkrytye slushaniia "Instituta Peterburga", St. Petersburg 1998, p. 1-6: http://www.institute-spb.standardsite.ru/userdata/files/05-17_Tseytlin.pdf, 12.04.1013.

OB USTROISTVE KRYTAGO RYNKA NA SENNOI PLOSHCHADI, in: Arkhiv sudebnoi mediciny i obshchestvennoi gigieny 6, 2 (1870), p. 140-147.

OB USTROISTVE NA SENNOI PLOSHCHADI RYNOCHNAGO ZDANIIA DLIA PROIZVODIASHCHEISIA TAM TORGOVLIA, in: Izvestiia Sankt-Peterburgskoi Gorodskoi Obshchei Dumy, 1865, No. 9, p. 450-464.

OB USTROISTVE SENNOI PLOSHCHADI, in: Izvestiia Sankt-Peterburgskoi Gorodskoi Obshchei Dumy, 1866, No. 8, p. 399-405.

VEKSLER, A. F., Sennaia ploshchad', in: Tri veka Sankt-Peterburga, Vol. 2.6, St. Petersburg 2008, p. 206-210.

ID., Sennoi rynok, in: Tri veka Sankt-Peterburga, Vol. 2.6, St. Petersburg 2008, p. 210-213.

O VOSPROSHCHENII TORGOVLIA MIASOM NA SENNOI PLOSHCHADI, A TAKZHE MELOCHNAGO TORGA S POSTOIANNYKH MEST OKOLO KHASTNYKH I KAZENNYKH ZDANII, in: Izvestiia Sankt-Peterburgskoi Gorodskoi Obshchei Dumy, 1867, No. 7, p. 372-377.

ZASOSOV, DMITRII A./PYZIN, VLADIMIR I., Iz zhizni Peterburga 1890-1910-x godov. Zapiski ochevidcev, 2-e izd., dos., St. Petersburg 1999.

RUSSIAN STATE HISTORICAL ARCHIVE/ROSSIISKII GOSUDARSTVENNYI ISTORICHESKII ARKHIVE (RGIA):
- f. 218: op. 3, del. 1288.
- f. 1287: op. 29, del. 1600; op. 40, del. 310.
- f. 1293: op. 137, del. 91.

ENCIKLOPEDIA BLAGOTVORITEL'NOSTI. Sankt-Peterburg: http://encblago.lfond.spb.ru/search.do?objectType=2805596371 , 07.05.2013.

ENCIKLOPEDIA SANKT-PETERBURGA: http://encspb.ru/object/2803998688?lc=ru, 07.05.2013.

Blood in the Air

Everyday Violence in the Experience of the Petersburg Poor, 1905-1917

MARK D. STEINBERG

> The object of force is to impose a certain social order in which the minority governs, while violence tends to the destruction of that order.
>
> (Georges Sorel, Reflections on Violence, 1908)

In 1913, a popular newspaper columnist in the Russian capital observed with dismay that "newspapers are printed on white paper, but, really, in our times its pages seem covered with blood"[1]. Many commentators shared this view, often emphasizing the point with dramatic metaphors. Both typical and often repeated was a phrase that the physician and public health activist Dmitrii Zhbankov often used in talks, reports, and newspaper columns: a "traumatic epidemic of blood and violence" was raging in everyday city life, especially in the capital city St. Petersburg.[2] For newspapers, it was "everyday" violence that was the main concern. Certainly, there was a great deal of political violence in the years between 1905 and 1914 – ranging from government repression to revolutionary terrorism, not to mention the wars and revolutions that bookend these years.[3] But this story has a different focus, at least ostensibly: more local, more ubiquitous, and more troubling in both its everydayness and its seeming absence of

---

1 SKITALETS, 1913(2), p. 3.
2 He used this phrase in many of his writings, for example, ZHBANKOV, 1910(1), p. 2.
3 Cf., for example, HOLQUIST, 2003, p. 627–652.

purpose. Such everyday violence included bloody "epidemics" of street knifings, robberies with weapons, rape, bar-room fights ending in bloodshed, and suicide.[4] These stories unfolded mainly in the neighborhoods and lives of the city's poor.

Like all stories, these were told as embodying larger meaning. Perhaps precisely because they were so disturbing, they became powerful signs to interpret and to interpret with, especially about the "spirit of the age" and the meaning of "these times" (both frequent phrases in these discussions). These were city stories – present throughout the empire but most widespread, and worrisome, in the imperial capital, St. Petersburg. Cities are often viewed as symbols in European cultures, not least because they are the biggest and most enduring creations of human society. St. Petersburg has been a symbol, from the time of its foundation on newly conquered land, of Russia's forceful turn away from its past and toward the modernity of the West. Stories of ubiquitous and growing city violence ran counter to the civilizing march of modern progress. So, too, did other ubiquitous stories of urban degeneration and moral disorder, to which the epidemic of violence was often linked, especially the sexual "bacchanalia" (a metaphor of debauchery used, in turn, to speak of a "bacchanalia"[5] of violence) and suicide. Together, these stories were interpreted as signs of a "monstrously ugly" "spirit of evil"[6] in the air, the presence of "something fatal"[7] in contemporary life, some deep and ubiquitous "sickness"[8]. And the interpreting did not stop there. Numerous commentators read this evidence, especially the stories that "covered" the newspapers with so much "blood," as defining the experience of modernity as heavily marked by "tragedy," "catastrophe," and "trauma," producing dark feelings ranging from "melancholy" to "despondency".[9]

The question is, can we do more to understand urban violence in Russia than describe how these stories were narrated and interpreted by contemporaries? Can we understand the actual experience of violence, especially from the perspective of the perpetrators themselves? We know the difficulties. That it is impossible to disentangle the experiences and meanings of the most excluded from the narrating language of those with the power to most shape public dis-

---

4   Cf. among the few historians who have emphasized this everyday violence, especially MORRISSEY, 2006; STEINBERG, 2011; MCREYNOLDS, 2012.
5   For example, SKITALETS, 1913(2), p. 3.
6   VADIM, 1913, p. 3.
7   PODPISCHIK ZHURNALA ZHIZN' DLIA VSEKH, 1913, p. 1289f.
8   AZ., 1908, p. 4.
9   Cf. STEINBERG, 2011.

course and thus the very vocabulary of available interpretation. That we have little access to unmediated experience in the past, for the only *evidence* of experience we have is so imbricated with language and culture and desire that it is (as the historian Joan Scott famously argued) "always already an interpretation"[10]. In other words, to adapt a famous question, "can the knife-wielding subaltern speak" outside the construction of their voice by others?

One solution is suggested by the recent "descriptive turn" among literary scholars who have warned against overriding and overwriting past texts with our own voices, whether through critical readings shaped by the "arrogance" of heavy theory or forcing everything into the box of "context": what is needed, they argue, is more "intimacy" with texts, readings that are more "susceptible" and "attentive," reading more "with the grain" than "against" it.[11] For historians, this is a welcome methodological critique: we love to revel in the archive, to wander through past texts listening for past lives. And a particularly good text for this is the daily press. I will travel a way down this path myself, with newspapers as my main source. But I also find this path to be too seductive. To understand the past, we also need to escape its interpreting grip and view the past from outside its own perspectives. Attentively, yes, with receptivity to possibilities. But also with critical questions and suspicions. In other words, through the voices of theory – in this case, theories of violence and theories of emotion – not constrained by the mediation of interpreting contemporaries.

In thinking about newspapers and other periodicals as evidence of "experience," I find suggestive Walter Benjamin's remark in 1939, in his attempt to explain his own effort to make sense of city stories in the *Arcades Project*, that "to seize the essence of history, it suffices to compare Herodotus and the morning newspaper"[12]. One way to understand this is to view the newspaper as *Erlebnis*-history, using the distinction, explored by Benjamin among others, between the two German words for "experience," *Erlebnis* and *Erfahrung*. The newspaper points toward the immediate, particular, personal, and discontinuous – in other words, it is grounded in "life" (*Leben*), it is "lived experience." This stands in apparent contrast to a history that is narratively integrated, whole, continuous, shared, and directional – the "journey" at the etymological heart of *Erfahrung*.[13] The problem, and necessity, is how to bring into dialogue the daily news and

---

10   SCOTT, 1991, p. 797. Cf. also JAY, 2005.
11   Cf. FELSKI, 2011, p. 573-91; BEST AND MARCUS, 2009, p. 1-21; LOVE, 2010, p. 371-391.
12   BENJAMIN (1939), 1999, p. 14.
13   Cf. especially JAY, 2005.

the long narration, the discontinuous present of experience and the coherent experience of living in meaningful time. This requires a perspective from both inside and outside the local and the particular. This shifting dialogue between perspectives – between the rawness of described violence, interpretations by contemporaries, and a critical reading of both – is my aim in this paper, hoping to open up the possibility of deeper interpretation.

Describing violence

We begin with these stories in their first narrating drafts – echoing the popular self-description of American journalists as writing "the first draft of history." A great many stories of urban public life in Russia between 1905 and 1917 did indeed cover the pages of newspapers with "blood." News reports of accidents, ranging from fires to workplace deaths (both of which earned the headline of "epidemics") were an almost daily accompaniment of urban life and a reminder of its precarity. Especially disturbing were accidental deaths of unsupervised children (mostly working-class children, of course), which, according to a reporter for the mass-circulation paper *Peterburgskii listok* (Petersburg Sheet) in 1913, had "in recent years become an epidemic phenomenon in the capital." On a single day in May of that year, for example, he counted unsupervised children drowning in a canal, toppling off an apartment balcony, falling under the wheels of a cart, being run over by an automobile, and being crushed by a tram.[14]

But by far the greatest dangers to life came from the deliberate actions of other people, often strangers. Most common were stabbings in the course of a robbery, mostly on the street and especially in rougher neighborhoods. The narratives were simple and similar: a perpetrator, individually or with a group, approached a victim and demanded money, becoming violent when rebuffed. Much of this violence, though, lacked the purposefulness of robbery. Newspapers reported numerous stories like that of the man at a café who quarreled for no clear reason with other customers and then stabbed several;[15] or the brawl in a bar that started with an argument among strangers after a professional wrestling match and ended in a knife fight;[16] or the man who chased down and repeatedly stabbed a woman who ignored his "degrading suggestions"[17] as she walked

---

14   Cf. Peterburgskii listok, 27.05.1913, p. 4.
15   Troinoe ubiistvo, in: Peterburgskij listok, 14.01.1913, p. 3.
16   Cf. Peterburgskii listok, 20.04.1909, p. 4; 09.05.1910, p. 5; 27.05.1913, p. 4.
17   Ibid., 13.01.1910, p. 5.

along a street. As a rule, both perpetrators and victims were young males. Lower-class men were more likely to carry knifes and to rob and quarrel violently. Women, we shall see, were more likely to kill themselves – or be victims of male violence, including sexual violence. Hans-Christian Petersen, in his chapter in this volume, identifies a subculture of male violence in the city's poorer neighborhoods. Indeed, these stories implied a violent masculinity that was a troubling story about both gender and class.

Beside violent attacks by strangers, public violence among friends seemed also to have become epidemic, often erupting at the slightest provocation, especially when alcohol loosened self-restraint (heavy drinking, of course, was viewed as a characteristically male). When weapons were at hand, and they often were, these fights could be lethal. Many men, it seems, carried concealed knives when out in public (although one could beat a man to death with fists and boots as well). The papers were full of accounts of degenerating arguments, often in bars or on the street, frequently over "trifles," often presumed insults, ending in spilled blood and sometimes death.[18] To give one example out of hundreds, a couple of working-class friends were sitting around drinking vodka when one decided he needed to go home to get some sleep before work the next morning; angry, his drinking buddy shouted "I will show you how to treat a friend"[19] and stabbed him in the side. Not all violence was so public, of course. But even the most private violence, notably domestic violence, was regularly turned into a public spectacle by the newspapers.[20]

Sexual violence was yet another "epidemic." The papers regularly reported women and girls raped (and then sometimes killed) by men, usually strangers, in dark streets or squares in the poorer parts of town.[21] This "bacchanalia" of sexual violence was said to have never before reached "such a colossal extent"[22], nor taken such exceedingly "disgusting and beastly forms."[23] Today, we recognize

---

18   Cf. GAZETA-KOPEIKA, 02.07.1908, p. 3; PETERBURGSKII LISTOK, 09.04.1909, p. 6; 04.02.1910, p. 5; 10.02.1910, p. 5; 08.08.1910, p. 7; SKITALETS, 1913(1), p. 3.
19   GAZETA-KOPEIKA, 26.06.1908, p. 2.
20   Cf. for example, ZHESTOKOE ISTIAZANIE REBENKA, 1910, p. 6; NOVOE VREMIA, 06.07.1909, p. 2.
21   GAZETA-KOPEIKA, 22.07.1908, p. 2; 07.03.1909, p. 3; 09.08.1908, p. 2f.; 28.09.1908, p. 2; 24.03.1909, p. 5; 27.06.1910, p. 4; 21.08.1911, p. 4; 31.07.1913, p. 3; PETERBURGSKII LISTOK, 09.08.1910, p. 3; 04.01.1913, p. 4; 25.01.1913, p. 4; SKITALETS, 1910, p. 3. Cf. also OBERLÄNDER, 2011.
22   D., 1909, p. 3.
23   ZHBANKOV, 1910(2), p. 69.

that all rape is violence. But at the time it seemed a sign of something new that, as Dr. Zhbankov wrote, "normal rape," which he believed reflected unrestrained sexual desire, was being replaced by "pathological" rape, which was nothing but "cold"[24] violence.

In reporting these "epidemics," the newspapers made a point of describing the precise location of incidents: mapping violence into a social and moral map of the city that distinguished certain urban spaces as dangerous and sick. The map of "bloody Petersburg," as it was called, covered most of the industrial outskirts (in Russian, *okrainy,* a term also used for the borderlands of the empire). Neighborhoods like Okhta, on the right bank of the Neva to the east of the city center, or the industrial district known as "Beyond the Nevskii Gate" (*za Nevskoi zastavoi*), along the left bank of the Neva below the Obvodnyi canal (the gate was already long gone, but its memory recalled that this district was outside the entrance to the city proper), or parts of the "Petersburg Side" across the Neva to the north of the city center were described as so rough as to seem to be located in a different time and place morally and culturally. Typically (not only in Russia, of course), class otherness was translated into moral and even racial otherness. Okhta, for example, was described as a "Petersburg Mexico or Peru," where the primary occupation for young people is "fist-fighting and bloodletting"[25]. A report on Donskoi Street, a particularly rough alley on Vasilevskii Island, observed that "mores there are such that you don't know whether you are in Petersburg or Babylon or among some North African savages"[26].

The map of "bloody Petersburg" also included social spaces closer to the center and less visibly marked as "other" by the physical boundaries of river or canal – especially the district known as "Ligovka" surrounding Ligovskaia Street, which ran from the main Nikolaevskii railroad station at Nevskii Prospect across the Obvodnyi canal (generally considered the boundary of the central city) into the southern margins of the city. This notoriously rough neighborhood, especially Ligovskaia Street itself, was the subject of regular and frequent press reports about both grizzly crimes and colorful characters (though often of a debauched and criminal sort). Even at high noon, one reporter observed, the people in this district, both men and women, seem to have stepped right out of the stories of Maxim Gorky, for this was a sort of "Petersburg lower depths" filled with down-and-out "former people" (both phrases Gorky made famous).[27] The

---

24   Ibid., p. 88f.
25   Okhtenskie 'rebiata', 1908, p. 5.
26   Zerkalo stolitsy, 1914, p. 3.
27   Cf. V. T., 1909, p. 3.

lowest depth of Ligovka was the neighborhood known by its old name Iamskaia sloboda (Coachmen's settlement), around the intersection of Ligovskaia Street and Chubarov Alley (close to the railroad tracks and the canal), a district known for its heavy concentration of brothels and criminal "dens"[28]. At night and well into the morning, journalists reported, it was impossible to walk on Ligovskaia Street near the Obvodnyi canal without risk of robbery and violence.[29]

Children were said to have been dehumanized by everyday life in poor districts – a life described in an editorial in *Peterburgskii listok* in 1910 as "chaotic disorder and ruin, abnormal family and social relationships, rising destitution, alcoholism, and degeneration [*vyrozhdenie* – a common term]"[30]. Because children in such neighborhoods, it was said, "grew up on the street," they were deformed by the street. "The street" was a keyword laden with as many interpretations as "the city." As a material and social space of public interaction, and as definably urban, the street was often a metaphor and symbol of the most worrisome aspects of human society and personality, including desire, spontaneity, disorder, danger, and violence.[31] It also often denoted spaces closest to the lives of the poor. Children and the street were viewed as a lethal combination.[32] Typical was the 1909 report about a twelve-year-old boy who fatally stabbed his mother with a kitchen knife when she refused to let him go play in the streets. "Who is to blame?" the reporter asked. He answered his own question: "the street" itself to which the boy was so passionately attracted and which had ruined him.[33]

The "hooligan" had a special place in these stories of the street and violence, for hooligans seemed to embody the sense that life among the urban poor was more and more a story of pathological excess. Joan Neuberger, in her important study of hooliganism in St. Petersburg, showed how this term was applied widely to all sorts of aggressive and transgressive behaviors in public spaces, ranging from stabbings in back streets to mocking harassment of respectable citizens in the center of the city (such as unscrewing park benches and laughing

---

28 SLEDOPYT, 1914, p. 4.
29 Cf. MASSOVYE BUIISTVA KHULIGANOV, 1905, p. 4.
30 DETSKII SUD, 1910, p, 1. Cf. also LIUBOSH, 1910, p. 2; KHOLMSKII, 1914, p. 4; FROMMET, 1914, p. 696-700.
31 Cf. for example BENJAMIN, 1928 and ÇELIK, et al., 1994.
32 Cf. for example, NOVIKOV, 1914, p. 526-532.
33 Cf. GAZETA-KOPEIKA, 02.01.1909, p. 3.

when someone fell, or pulling ribbons from women's hair).[34] Most hooligan acts, though, were violent.

As a form of violence, hooliganism was defined by the excess of its transgression: not just violating the bodies of others (with a knife, for example), but transgressing the presumed boundaries of reason itself. The press was full of stories like that of the young "hooligan" who demanded money for a beer from a nineteen-year-old man he came across and then stabbed the youth four times in the stomach when he refused,[35] or the story of a man stabbed in the neck and chest when he refused a demand for fourteen kopecks to buy vodka.[36] Worst of all were the hooligan knifers who, it was reported, skipped the preliminary demands and just attacked.[37] As an editorial in 1910 in the mass-circulation newspaper *Gazeta-kopeika* (Kopeck-gazette) concluded, "the hooligan knife [...] slashes and cuts without any reasons at all"[38]. And even when attacks had an ostensible purpose, especially money or sex, these goals seemed secondary.

Reports emphasized the connection of hooliganism to the neighborhoods and lives of the poor. The typical hooligan was described as young man from the slums. The newspapers linked hooliganism to the "dark Petersburg" of the urban underclass,[39] the lumpenproletariat of the homeless and unemployed,[40] "tramps [*bosiaki*], residents of flophouses, prostitutes [known often to associate with hooligans, who sometimes acted as pimps], and others of the Maxim Gorky type"[41]. The police agreed, organizing huge raids (800 people were rounded up in a raid in 1910, for example) on the places such types were believed to hole up: cheap teahouses and taverns, public parks on the city outskirts, and river barges, which housed a special lower-class subculture of its own.[42] No less important, hooligans were seen to embody the presumed connection between poverty and moral degeneracy. As an editorial in *Peterburgskii listok* in 1910 put it, poor

---

34 Cf. NEUBERGER, 1993.
35 Cf. PETERBURGSKII LISTOK, 10.05.1913, p. 4. Cf. also PETERBURGSKII LISTOK, 03.04.1909, p. 1.
36 Cf. ZHIZN' ZA 14 KOPEEK, 1912, p. 3.
37 Cf. for example, OMUT ZHIZNI: KHULIGANY, 1908, p. 3; PODVIGI ULICHNYKH GRABITELEI, 1910, p. 3.
38 GAZETA-KOPEIKA, 06.10.1910, p. 1.
39 Cf. PETERBURGSKII LISTOK, 12.05.1910, p. 4.
40 Cf. IBID., 05.05.1907, p. 4.
41 ULICHNAIA SEKTANTSKAIA MISSIIA, 1908, p. 2.
42 Cf. GRANDIOZNAIA OBLAVA NA KHULIGANOV I BEZDOMNIKOV, 1910, p. 2.

children were driven toward hooliganism by "destitution, alcoholism, and degeneration [*vyrozhdenie*]"[43].

Violence against self was treated as part of the same story. The press recorded the almost daily toll of suicides – many of which occurred in public places, especially cafes, taverns, and streets – during the suicide "epidemic" in Petersburg between 1906 and the war.[44] Official statistics on the reasons for suicide placed poverty at or near the top; if it yielded pride of place, it was to drunkenness, also linked to lower-class life.[45] Newspaper reports were often headlined "Due to Hunger"[46]. So common were these histories that the popular columnist Skitalets ("the wanderer"), writing in *Gazeta-kopeika*, observed that stories of "despairing" unemployed men committing suicide were so "ordinary" that they were often ignored by newspapers and readers looking for something more interesting and dramatic.[47] The essayist Vasilii Rozanov similarly concluded that the public found little of interest in suicides from poverty – or perhaps, we may elaborate, had grown morally numb to its traumatic ubiquity – for "of poor people there are always so many"[48].

Of particular interest to readers was the "epidemic" of suicide among prostitutes,[49] where stories of desperate poverty (the reason most often given for why women "fell" into prostitution) combined with experiences of subordination, humiliation, and physical abuse.[50] The archetypal report described prostitutes committing suicide together, perhaps in "some stifling and stagnant tavern amidst rowdiness and drunken intoxication," toasting their escape from life with glasses of poisonous vinegar essence.[51] That women were more likely to kill themselves, or be victims, than to assault others, reminds us of the intertwining of narratives of gender along with class in these histories of everyday violence.

---

43 DETSKII SUD, 1910, p. 1.
44 Cf. for other discussions of suicide in Russia in these years, MORRISSEY, 1995, p. 201-217; IBID., 2006, chaps. 10-11; PAPERNO, 1997, p. 94-104, 109f., 121f., 158f.; PINNOW, 2010, p. 25-42.
45 Cf. PREDVARITEL'NYI SVOD STATISTICHESKIKH DANNYKH PO G. S-PETERBURGU ZA 1909 GOD, p. 39.
46 For example, IZ-ZA GOLODA, 1909, p. 4; cf. also ZHBANKOV, 1910(1), p. 29.
47 GAZETA-KOPEIKA, 18.08.1910, p. 3.
48 ROZANOV, 1911, p. 50f.
49 Cf. OBYVATEL', 1909, p. 2; ZHBANKOV, 1910(2), p. 63; GORDON, 1910, p. 1f.
50 Cf. NE VYNESLI POZORA, 1909, p. 4. Cf. also V. T., 1909, p. 3; PETERBURGSKII LISTOK, 17.01.1913, p. 14; OMUT ZHIZNI, 1908, p. 3.
51 NEMIROVICH-DANCHENKO, 1910, p. 581-583. Cf. also BERNSTEIN, 1995, p. 78.

Interpreting violence

There is a naked reality to these stories: government statistics documented exceptionally high rates of violence and suicide in the Russian capital in these years.[52] However, as can already be seen, the factual reporting of such "incidents" was never far removed from interpreting them, starting with the view that they were part of a common phenomenon. A key interpreting theme was "excess." There was quantitative excess, emphasized by the metaphors used to frame and unite these different stories into one: a "bountiful harvest of death"[53], a "bacchanalia"[54] of death, an "atmosphere of death"[55], an environment where "pools of blood are on the floor, [and] the walls ooze pus"[56]. Most troubling, though, was the qualitative excess. The stabbing of a stranger "for 14 kopecks" was emblematic. And this was not only a view of such people as definable "others" threatening the norms of "civilized" public life from without (as Joan Neuberger argued about hooligans, who exemplified these behaviors[57]) but also something worse: a symptom of an ailing social body, of a sick self.[58]

"Sickness" was a master metaphor for contemporaries. One of its worst symptoms was said to be the loss of value of life itself. Newspapers regularly headlined reports of violence with phrases like "life today is cheap," "life has lost value!"[59] people today are "valued cheaper than trash"[60]. The hooligan seemed to embody this spirit to dark perfection. The hooligan philosophy of life was "everything existing on this earth is rot [*tlia*] and people are shits [*gnidy*— literally, lice eggs]"[61]. The debased value for life, a *Gazeta-kopeika* columnist concluded, was the dark heart of "our terrible times"[62], and made killing (and self-killing) easy.

---

52 Cf. N., 1909, p. 544-547.
53 N. V., 1908, p. 1.
54 SKITALETS, 1913(2), p. 3.
55 ARNOVA, 1911, p. 476.
56 ENGEL'GARDT, 1908, p. 1.
57 Cf. NEUBERGER, 1993.
58 Cf. STEINBERG, 2011.
59 DUKH BANKO [The Ghost of Banquo], 1907, p. 1; GAZETA-KOPEIKA, 19.10.1909, p. 3; NEMIROVICH-DANCHENKO, 1910, p. 581-590; FILENKIN, 1911, p. 3.
60 SKITALETS, 1911, p. 5.
61 SVIRSKII, 1914, p. 253, 258-269. On Svirskii, cf. MCREYNOLDS, 1991, p. 151f.
62 PODOL'SKII, 1909, p. 3.

But why? Some writers blamed the government for nurturing this atmosphere: the aftershocks of the Russo-Japanese war of 1904-5 and especially of widespread repression, including a great number of executions, following the 1905 revolution. "Days without a death sentence and execution have been the exception" over the past year, a journalist noted at the end of 1909, and so "human life has lost value"[63]. Other writers blamed the revolutionary movement, especially terrorist attacks on officials, which proliferated in these post-revolutionary years. In the wake of the execution of Prime Minister Petr Stolypin in September 1911, a liberal journalist offered a characteristic lament: "We are to blame, all of us, even the air we breathe and the thoughts and feelings we experience. For six years already we have been sowing seeds of violence, betrayal, and murder, and have been killing with knife, bullet, and bomb, and with soaped noose."[64]

But most writers, when looking for reasons and causes, blamed the modern city. If "these times" were sick, most journalists seemed to feel, the city was, as it were, the "epidemiological pump." Statistics were available to confirm this: as a chronicler of Petersburg crime summarized the numbers, "the more urban, the more crime [...] including the most terrible bloody acts"[65]. Explanations varied. Conservatives blamed modern secular individualism for eroding traditional values, especially respect for others and love of the good.[66] Liberals and socialists blamed the harsh conditions of social life (and, though they could not say this too loudly, the lack of political and civil rights and freedoms, which aggravated social hardships). But almost everyone agreed, in one way or another, that modern city life – indeed, modern progress itself, for which the city stood both socially and symbolically – had a paradoxical effect, especially on the lives of the poor: it made people into "savages," "beasts," and "animals" capable of the most "cruel" and "brutal" crimes – terms often used in newspaper crime reports.[67] Commentators wrote again and again of the harmful "atmosphere" of modern social life, especially in big cities and especially for those whose social lives were the most precarious.[68] To quote typical phrases from the press: the

---

63   BLANK, 1909, p. 1f.
64   TAN, 1911, p. 60f.
65   ABORIGEN, 1914, p. 43.
66   Cf. BRONZOV, 1912, p. 4-9.
67   Cf. TROFIMOV, 1909, p. 3; ZVERSKOE UBIISTVO, 1909, p. 3; POSSE, 1909, p. 83-85; NOVITSKII, 1909, p. 1; LIUDI-ZVERY, 1909, p. 3; DIKIE NRAVY, 1908, p. 3; ENGEL'GARDT, 1910, p. 3.
68   Cf. ARNOVA, 1911, p. 482.

modern big city was a murderous "trap"[69], a devouring "stone monster"[70], a fatal "mirage"[71]. The fact that so many new arrivals to the capital – from small towns or the countryside – took their own lives was a symbol easy to interpret with.[72]

So, to recall Walter Benjamin's remark, we can see the work of "Herodotus" already in the "morning newspaper," if "Herodotus" means a constructed narrative history of experience that explains and gives coherent meaning to the fragmentary and contradictory evidence of lived experience. These interpreting stories suggested solutions as well: for some, a revival of morality or religion; for others, social and political reform, perhaps revolution. Many worried, however, that there might be "no exit" (another frequent phrase in the press) from what one journalist gloomily called "the long, black, stinking corridor" of the present, its atmosphere "saturated with the exhalations of putrefying corpses"[73].

Theorizing violence

Can we do more to interpret this evidence? Can we see beyond a "susceptible" and "attentive" reading "*with* the grain," beyond contemporaries' own interpretations of their own lives? Most difficult, can we know anything of the experiences and motives, the subjectivities, of the subjects who enacted this violence? We have often been warned, especially by postcolonial theorists, of the danger of assuming transparency in voices from the past, of failing to recognize the inaccessibility and untranslatability of the discourses of others, of trusting our own constructions of (and desires for) the subaltern voice, of nostalgically recovering what seems lost – the danger of the "intellectual masquerading as the absent nonrepresenter who lets the oppressed speak for they themselves," as Gayatri Spivak wrote when suggesting that our knowledge that the "subaltern *cannot* speak" can serve as both a critical warning against epistemic violence and a path toward some understanding of social realities and experiences.[74] This warning must extend to local knowledge: contemporary interpreters, such as

---

69 GRIDINA, 1913, p. 3.
70 SHCHIGALEEV, 1912, p, 5.
71 GRIDINA, 1910, p. 3. Cf. also IBID., 1911, p. 3.
72 Cf., for example, ZHERTVA OBSHCHESTVENNOGO RAVNODUSHIIA, 1908, p. 4; IZ-ZA GOLODA, 1909, p. 4; V. T., 1909, p. 3.
73 ENGEL'GARDT, 1908, p. 1.
74 Cf. SPIVAK, 1988, though I am using her insights and arguments somewhat differently than she intended.

we find in the press, are not necessarily closer to social realities and experiences than our own interpretations from afar.

A point of entry into this problem is the place that seemed to contemporaries most resistant to interpretation: irrational violence for violence's sake, with no other end or purpose.[75] When contemporary interpreters did find meaning in this, we have seen, it was to see symptoms of moral and spiritual illness. Perhaps less parochial voices can help us see further than they could, or were willing to, and open up a field of alternative interpretation.

Consider, for example, the perspective of the psychiatrist and radical philosopher Frantz Fanon in his 1961 book *Les Damnés de la Terre* (The Wretched of the Earth). His arguments were not merely theoretical, of course. They grew from his work among colonized North Africans, whose violence, he concluded, was a response to the material conditions and psychological effects of colonialism. Fanon described the world of colonialism – in terms, I think, that have uncanny suitability to the world of entrenched but fearful Russian autocracy and rapidly developing capitalism – as a "hostile, oppressive and aggressive world," a world of "daily humiliations" and periodic repressive violence, that was simultaneously a "hell" from which the colonized dreamed of escape and a "paradise within arm's reach guarded by ferocious watchdogs"[76]. In such an environment, "the muscles of the colonized are always tensed" and "the colonized's affectivity is kept on edge, like a running sore flinching from a caustic agent." This produced what Fanon called "atmospheric violence": a violence "rippling under the skin," a tense "rage" ready to burst out in "periodic eruptions" of "bloody fighting" among themselves, including "the most brutal aggressiveness" and the most "impulsive violence." "It is not uncommon," Fanon wrote, "to see the colonized subject draw his knife at the slightest hostile or aggressive look from another colonized subject."[77] Other theorists of violence, examining other settings, have offered a similar perspective. Walter Benjamin, for example, in the wake of the terrible losses and brutalities of the Great War, described an "everyday" violence, where "man is impelled by anger" to the "outbursts of a violence that are not related as a means to a preconceived end" but are an expression of the conditions of "existence"[78], indeed, of experience.

Key to understanding this everyday, existential, atmospheric violence is what may be termed "blocked agency." Hannah Arendt, for example, though

---

75 Cf., for example, IVANOV, 1914, p. 48.
76 FANON (1961), 2004, p. 16, 219.
77 IBID., p. 16-19, 31.
78 BENJAMIN, 1921, p. 248.

hostile to Fanon's justification of the violence of resistance (and especially Jean-Paul Sartre's advocacy of Fanon's arguments), nonetheless recognized that such violence emerges from conditions of modern "progress" that suppress freedom and creativity. As she wrote in her 1969 essay "On Violence," "the present glorification of violence is caused by severe frustration of the faculty of action in the modern world," such that "riots in the ghettos" make "people feel they are acting together in a way they rarely can"[79]. More recently, James Scott similarly described a "latent sense of violence" produced when systems of domination block action and agency, when the "routine harvest of insults and injury to human dignity" cannot be answered with "reciprocal aggression," for these systems have the power to frustrate and deny the "natural impulse to rage, insult, anger, and the violence that such feelings prompt"[80].

It is important to emphasize the notion of self that is seen to drive the human desire for agency and become frustrated by its obstruction: a particular conception of human personhood as possessing natural human dignity and thus innate sensitivity to insult and humiliation and to constrictions of will. In Russia as in Europe, this notion has had a long and persistent history. An early and influential view of this is G. W. F. Hegel's notion of "recognition" (*Anerkennung*). Hegel defined "recognition" of "self," of "personhood," of "being," of "will," of one's "existence" as an individual, as essential human needs. Failure to be "recognized," "negation" of one's "self-expressive will," produces crime and violence, which can be understood to be an effort to "reinstate" one's "will to power," "to count for something, to be recognized"[81]. In Russia, arguments about harm to the natural "human personality" (the Russian keyword is *lichnost'*) caused by social conditions that degrade and injure the self were strongly developed among the nineteenth-century intelligentsia and became ubiquitous in public discourse, including in the daily press, by the start of the twentieth century.[82]

The idea that frustrated human agency can fuel violent rage has recently been developed by Slavoj Žižek (also a psychoanalyst and radical philosopher) in his 2008 book *Violence*. More than his predecessors, though, Žižek confronts head-on the epistemological and hermeneutic resistance of much violence to

---

79 ARENDT, 1969, p. 83 (the final quotation is Arendt quoting an essay by Herbert Gans on "ghetto rebellions").
80 SCOTT, 1992, p. 37-39.
81 HEGEL, 1805-1806, part II ("actual spirit"), section A ("recognition"), esp. section iii ("crime and punishment").
82 Cf. discussion and sources in STEINBERG, 2002, chap. 2; and STEINBERG, 2011, p. 151-153.

our desire and effort to read a meaningful message. He gives the example of the 2005 riots in the poor and immigrant *banlieues* of Paris: "what is most difficult to accept is precisely the riots' meaninglessness," that they are less "a form of protest" than "an impulsive movement into action which can't be translated into speech or thought." This meaninglessness, he argues, "bears witness" both to the "impotence of the perpetrators" and to their "inability to locate the experience of their situation within a meaningful whole." Such violence resists translation into familiar narratives, whether the backwardness of class and racial others or the heroic resistance of the oppressed. And yet, Žižek does see interpretable signs and even a type of politics in these acts. He sees violence as an effort to acquire denied "presence," to make oneself "visible," "to create a problem" – even while "neither offering a solution nor constituting a movement for providing a solution." In other words, these acts are a "sign" not a "meaning," a "means" not an "end"[83]. Or, as Arendt put it, drawing on Benjamin, violence is an "interruption" of processes in human history that otherwise seem "automatic," predictable, and unyielding.[84]

Recent work by theorists of affect and emotions reinforce such arguments. To be sure, most attention in recent scholarship on the relationship between violence and emotions has focused on collective and explicitly political violence, such as the role of emotions in stimulating nationalist and ethnic violence, or, closer to our case, the ways collective experiences of loss, moral hurt, resentment, and anger have fueled moral claims that produce defiant and retributional violence.[85] Some studies, however, notably the work of Sara Ahmed and Sianne Ngai, suggest an everyday and individual politics of emotion, especially in how people deal with social "pain," "injury," and "wounds." Key here is what Ngai calls a "state of obstructed agency," which means not only social and political oppression restricting collective action, but a deep incommensurability between the hurt and any available solution: what practical action, for example, is strong enough to undo the injuries of class subordination, poverty, or racism (the effects of symbolic violence, in Pierre Bourdieu's important term)? These conditions can stimulate vehement emotions, often embodied in violence, which become a "sign," a way to "speak out." Such violence tends toward excess and attachment to what Ngai calls "ugly feelings," such as envy, anxiety, paranoia, irritation, and disgust. But these vehement and sometimes violent emotions also contain "critical potential." Not as simple or adequate resistance, much less mechanisms

---

83 ŽIŽEK, 2008, esp. p. 76f., 179, 185, 200-202.
84 Cf. ARENDT, 1969, p. 30.
85 Cf. STEINBERG/SOBOL, 2011.

of change, nor even as adequate catharsis, but as strong signs of disenchantment, disaffection, and refusal.[86]

Returning to the evidence of the Russian press, these arguments resonate with the epidemics of excessive, "irrational," "meaningless" violence without "end" or "reason" beyond the act itself, exemplified by what one journalist described as the "hooligan" stance of being "the enemy of each and everyone"[87]. As this suggests, some contemporaries saw the hints of the political in this. The hooligan, a persona that had come to embody irrational and excessive violence among the poor, wanted to "outrage/offend/defile society" (*nadrugat'sia nad obshchestvom*), and if material damage could be added to this "moral harm," all the better. The hooligan acted "as if to avenge himself on society for something"[88]. More radical writers elaborated on this "as if" and "for something." In 1913, the worker writer Aleksei Gastev argued that "today in Russia people label as 'hooligans' anyone who does not perform 'cultured,' which is to say lackey, duties for the large and small parasite masters"[89]. Violence against the self could also be read as a sign of refusal, as a way to bear witness with one's own life to (and literally interrupt) the tragic conflict in modern life between heightened desires and "empty" "reality," as the regular *Gazeta-kopeika* columnist, Ol'ga Gridina, wrote in an essay titled "Death Answers"[90]. Some went further and described the suicide epidemic as "a mass bloody protest against life as it is"[91].

To translate this history through interpreting languages of other times, situations, and perspectives, we can argue that the "epidemic" of everyday violence among the urban poor in Russia – and here we can agree with contemporary commentators who treated robberies at knife point, barroom brawls, suicide, and domestic violence as a single phenomenon – reflected a psychological "affectivity" and "muscular tension" always on "edge," a vague "rage" and "latent" violence that could "erupt" at the slightest provocation. At its heart were "pain," "wounds," and "injuries" that denied dignity and recognition, made more painful by structures of domination that blocked action and agency. This violence contained "critical potential" by "bearing witness" to political "impotence," making oneself "visible" and "present" in the face of exclusion and marginaliza-

---

86   Cf. AHMED, 2004, esp. p. 33-34, 169, 193-194; NGAI, 2005, esp. p. 1-29, 161, 188.
87   IVANOV, 1914, p. 47-50.
88   IBID.
89   ZORIN, 1913, p. 1457.
90   GRIDINA, 1910, p. 3. Cf. also NEMIROVICH-DANCHENKO, 1910, p. 584.
91   ABRAMOVICH, 1911, p. 113. Cf. also ZHERTVA OBSHCHESTVENNOGO RAVNODUSHIIA, 1908, p. 4.

tion, "speaking out," "interrupting," and "creating a problem." True, it "served no means" or end. So perhaps it is too strong to speak of resistance. But we can speak of "vehement" "disaffection" and "rage" as a political "sign," as a form of refusal, even a form of "revenge" for so much wreckage. Differentiating between rational and irrational in these acts, as contemporaries did, helps little to understand them.

But how far should we go in viewing these acts as political? Can we find here the possibility, in Fanon's terms, of translating atmospheric violence into revolutionary "violence in motion," a violence that "cleanses," changes, and liberates?[92] Or, what Georges Sorel, writing at the same time as this Russian story, described as a violence that resists civilization's barbarity and authoritative force, that is ultimately a violence of life, will, creativity, and virtue?[93] Or what Benjamin called the "divine violence" that can destroy the violence of power and "deliver justice" "for the sake of the living"[94]? Or what Jean-Paul Sartre, in his preface to Fanon's book, called the "violence, like Achilles' spear, [that] can heal the wounds it has inflicted?"[95]

We may desire such transfiguration, for there is hope and the appealing promise of redemption in it. But this optimism, and the encouraging voices of authoritative theorists, may be more seductive than real. Fanon himself recognized how "melancholy" and "suicidal" everyday violence among the oppressed tended to be: that the regular "release" of tension and rage by drawing one's knife against another colonized person at the slightest vexation was ultimately "collective self-destruction [...] a death wish in the face of danger, a suicidal conduct that enforces the colonist's existence and domination, and reassures him that such men are not rational"[96]. Perhaps Russian journalists were right to see melancholy, hopelessness, and the "loss of taste for life."

If we look ahead to 1917, we see an explicit translation of everyday social violence into directed political violence. But the affinity between what Fanon called self-destructive atmospheric violence and transgressive "violence in motion" means that the boundaries between them are porous and unstable. Perhaps because the wounds went so deep, the purposefulness of revolution could not remove the undirected rage that helped fuel this upheaval. "Excess," again, was a telling sign. Witnesses to the February Revolution (which was relatively

---

92 Cf. FANON, 1961 (2004), e.g. p. 51.
93 Cf. SOREL, 1908 (1950).
94 BENJAMIN, 1921, p. 248-250.
95 SARTRE, JEAN-PAUL, preface to FANON, 1961 (2004), p. lxii.
96 FANON, 1961 (2004), p. 17f.

bloodless compared to the October Revolution and the Civil War that followed) described with dismay the epidemic of street violence that continually crossed the boundaries of reason: people in the streets shooting obsessively into the air or into the windows of apartment buildings, smashing store windows, looting (especially wine stores – a crime not without some instrumental purpose), and, at the extreme, stomping on the lifeless bodies of murdered policemen and officers. The Petrograd Soviet characteristically condemned all this as "hooliganism." Echoing the same older tradition of interpretation, Maxim Gorky (then editor and columnist of a new independent left-wing newspaper in the capital) insisted that this was not revolutionary violence at all, but "Asiatic savagery"[97]. In the months following, organized revolutionaries would repeatedly say the same about the epidemic of crowd violence against perceived enemies of the revolution: as one soldier-socialist declared after witnessing the brutal murder in the street of a dozen officers who had been arrested after the Kornilov mutiny, "this is a disgrace and a shame" and "no one will achieve anything doing it this way"[98]. In other words, violence "under the skin" did not always change its nature when put in political motion. This was a "wound" that "would not heal" (borrowing the classic metaphor of decadence), a violence that could not bring change or redemption, or even consolation, a violence that was no more than a symbolic reminder of injury and rage.

Still, there was politics in this, though an "ugly" politics of ugly feelings and ugly actions. The same may be said of the "traumatic epidemic" of everyday "blood and violence" that the Petersburg press so fulsomely documented in the prerevolutionary years – a politics, yes, but ugly, unable to console, bringing no redemption. At best, this was a politics of disruption and interruption, of being a problem, of presence, of speaking out with physical signs. From a perspective of explicit and conventional politics, this was all terribly inadequate – inadequate for resisting injury and harm, inadequate for producing change. In a way, this violence was too symbolic. Nor did it help that it was shaped by a distorting culture of violent masculinity. Perhaps tragically, these emotions, vocabularies, and actions introduced an ugly politics into the revolution, a time when political and social change actually did become possible. One could argue, and contemporaries certainly did, that this was proof of the trauma and sickness of prerevolutionary society. But one could also argue that even the ugliest popular violence during and especially after 1917 was still political: a dark agency for the unorganized people of Russia's "lower depths," a way of being present in the

---

97 Cited in STEINBERG, 2001, p. 63f.
98 DELO NARODA, No. 147, 06.09.1917, p. 2.

face new postrevolutionary obstructions to plebeian agency, a way of baring and witnessing wounds being inflicted this time by "Soviet" and "socialist" forms of political domination and modernizing "progress."

Acknowledgements: For helping me to clarify my arguments, I am especially grateful to Hans-Christian Petersen, Ilya Gerasimov, Jane Hedges, Rebecca Mitchell, faculty and students at the Havighurst Center at Miami University in Ohio, the workshop on intellectual history at the University of California at Berkeley, and participants in the panel on interpreting and theorizing violence at the 2012 meeting of the Association for Slavic, East European, and Eurasian Studies.

Literature

ABORIGEN [ZARIN, ANDREI EFIMOVICH], Krovavye letopisi Peterburga, St. Petersburg 1914.
ABRAMOVICH, N. IA., Samoubiistvo, in: Samoubiistvo. Sbornik obshchestvennykh, filosofskikh i kriticheskikh statei, Moscow 1911, p. 107-113.
AHMED, SARAH, Cultural Politics of Emotion, New York 2004.
ARENDT, HANNAH, On Violence, New York 1969.
ARNOVA, S., Samoubiistvo v proshlom i nastoiashchem, in: Zhizn' dlia vsekh 3-4 (1911), p. 476-487.
AZ., Deti-nozhevshchiki, in: Gazeta-kopeika, 09.12.1908, p. 4.
BENJAMIN, WALTER, Critique of Violence (1921), in: Benjamin, Selected Writings, ed. by MICHAEL JENNINGS et. al., 4 volumes. Cambridge, Mass. 1996-2003, here vol. 1, p. 236-252.
BENJAMIN, WALTER, Paris, Capital of the Nineteenth Century: Exposé (1939), in: The Arcades Project, transl. by Howard Eiland and Kevin McLaughlin, Cambridge, Mass. 1999, p. 14-27.
BENJAMIN, WALTER, One-Way Street. Berlin 1928.
BERNSTEIN, LAURIE, Sonia's Daughters. Prostitutes and their regulation in imperial Russia. Berkeley 1995.
BEST, STEPHEN/SHARON, MARCUS, Surface Reading. An introduction, in: Representations 108 (2009), p. 1-21.
BLANK, R. , 1909-yi g., in: Zaprosy zhizni, 29.12.1909, p. 1f.
BOURDIEU, PIERRE, Outline of Theory of Practice. Transl. by Richard Nice. Cambridge 1977.

BRONZOV, PROFESSOR A., Progress-li?, in: Tserkovnyi vestnik 1 (1912), 05.01.1909, p. 4-9.
MASSOVYE BUIISTVA KHULIGANOV, in: Peterburgskii listok, 24.11.1905, p. 4.
ÇELIK, ZEYNEP et al., Streets: Critical perspectives on public space, Berkeley 1994.
D., Polovaia vakkhanaliia, in: Gazeta-kopeika, 27.07.1909, p. 3.
Delo naroda, 1917
DUKH BANKO [The Ghost of Banquo], Prodaetsia Bezsmertie, in: Svobodnye mysli 14 (1907), p. 1.
ENGEL'GARDT, MIKH. AL., Bez vykhoda, in: Svobodnye mysli 35 (1908), p. 1.
ENGEL'GARDT, NIKOLAI, Mysli i kartinki, in: Novoe vremia, 20.07.1910, p. 3.
FANON, FRANTZ, Les Damnés de la Terre (1961), transl. by Richard Philcox as "The Wretched of the Earth", New York 2004.
FELSKI, RITA, Context Stinks!, in: New Literary History, 42, 4 (2011), p. 573-591.
FILENKIN, STEPAN, Deshevaia zhizn', in: Gazeta-kopeika, 23.08.1911, p. 3.
FROMMET, BORIS, Deti ulitsy, in: Zhizn' dlia vsekh 6 (1914), p. 696-700.
GAZETA-KOPEIKA, St. Petersburg, 1908-1914.
IZ-ZA GOLODA, in: Peterburgskii listok, 04.03.1909, p. 4.
GORDON, DR. G., Prostitutki i samoubiistvo, in: Rech', 23.04.1910, p. 1f.
GRIDINA, OL'GA, Smert' otvetila!, in: Gazeta-kopeika, 05.03.1910(1), p. 3.
ID., Prostoi vykhod, in: Gazeta-kopeika, 08.05.1910(2), p. 3.
ID., Prevrashchenie, grifelia, in: Gazeta-kopeika, 07.10.1911, p. 3.
ID., Gorod-obmanshchik, in: Gazeta-kopeika, 24.12.1913, p. 3.
HEGEL, GEORG WILHELM FRIEDRICH, The Philosophy of Spirit (Jena Lectures, 1805-1806), Digitized text at http://www.marxists.org/reference/archive/hegel/works/jl/, 07.05.2013.
HOLQUIST, PETER, Violent Russia, Deadly Marxism? Russia in the epoch of violence, 1905–21, in: Kritika. Explorations in Russian and Eurasian History 4 (2003), p. 627–52.
IVANOV, V., Chto takoe khuliganstvo?, in: Novyi zhurnal dlia vsekh 1 (1914), p. 48.
JAY, MARTIN, Songs of Experience. Modern American and European variations on a universal theme, Berkeley 2005.
ZHESTOKOE ISTIAZANIE REBENKA, in: Peterburgskii listok, 11.03.1910, p. 6.
KHOLMSKII, N., Voina i detskaia prestupnost', in: Malen'kaia gazeta, 06./10.10.1914, p. 4.
LIUBOSH, S., Peterburgskie zametki. O detovodstve, in: Sovremennoe slovo 841 (1910), 09.05.1910, p. 2

LIUDI-ZVERY, in: Peterburgskii listok, 02.05.1909, p. 3.
LOVE, HEATHER, Close but not Deep. Literary ethics and the descriptive turn, in: New Literary History, 41, 2 (2010), p. 371-391.
MCREYNOLDS, LOUISE, Murder Most Russian. True crime and punishment in late imperial Russia, Ithaca 2012.
ID., The News under Russia's Old Regime. The development of a mass circulation press, Princeton 1991.
MORRISSEY, SUSAN, Suicide and Civilization in Late Imperial Russia, in: Jahrbücher für Geschichte Osteuropas 43, 2 (1995), p. 201-217.
ID., Suicide and the Body Politic in Imperial Russia, Cambridge, Eng. 2006.
N. V., Itogi minuvshago goda, in: Vesna, 06.01.1908, p. 1.
N., Kak khvoraet i umiraet stolitsa, in: Gorodskoe delo 11 (1909), p. 544-547.
NEMIROVICH-DANCHENKO, VAS., Zhizn' deshevo! (Ocherki epedimii otchaianiia), in: Zaprosy zhizni 10 (1910), p. 581-590
NEUBERGER, JOAN, Hooliganism. Crime, culture, and power in St. Petersburg, 1900-1914, Berkeley 1993.
NGAI, SIANNE, Ugly Feelings, Cambridge, Mass. 2005.
NOVIKOV, M., Bor'ba s vlast'iu ulitsy i pomoshch' besprizornyym detiam, in: Gorodskoe delo 9 (1914), p. 526-532.
NOVITSKII, V., Zver' – v chelovek, in: Peterburgskaia gazeta, 06.04.1909, p. 1.
NOVOE VREMIA, ST. PETERSBURG, 1906-1914.
DIKIE NRAVY, in: Peterburgskii listok, 07.11.1908, p. 3.
OBERLÄNDER, ALEXANDRA, Shame and Modern Subjectivities. The rape of Elizaveta Cheremnova, in: Interpreting Emotions in Russia and Eastern Europe, ed. by MARK D. STEINBERG, MARK D. and VALERIA SOBOL, DeKalb, Ill. 2011, p. 82-102.
GRANDIOZNAIA OBLAVA NA KHULIGANOV I BEZDOMNIKOV, in: Peterburgskii listok, 17.09.1910, p. 2.
OBYVATEL', Samoubiistvo, in: Gazeta-kopeika, 03.01.1909, p. 2.
OMUT ZHIZNI, in: Gazeta-kopeika, 02.07.1908, p. 3.
OMUT ZHIZNI: KHULIGANY, in: Gazeta-kopeika, 21.06.1908, p. 3.
PAPERNO, IRINA, Suicide as a Cultural Institution in Dostoevsky's Russia, Ithaca 1997.
PETERBURGSKII LISTOK, St. Petersburg, 1906-1914.
PINNOW, KENNETH, Lost to the Collective. Suicide and the promise of soviet socialism, 1921-1929, Ithaca, N.Y. 2010.
PODOL'SKII, N., Zhizn'– kopeika, in: Gazeta-kopeika, 17.11.1909, p. 3.
PODPISCHIK ZHURNALA ZHIZN' DLIA VSEKH, Golos iz nedr neveshestva, in: Zhizn' dlia vsekh 9 (1913), p. 1289f.

PODVIGI ULICHNYKH GRABITELEI, in: Peterburgskii listok, 02.08.1910, p. 3.
POSSE, V., Zhestokost', in: Vesna 11.03.1909, p. 83-85.
NE VYNESLI POZORA, in: Peterburgskii listok, 07.05.1909, p. 4.
OKHTENSKIE 'REBIATA', in: Gazeta-kopeika, 19.06.1908, p. 5.
ROZANOV, VASILII, O samoubiistvakh, in: Samoubiistvo. sbornik obshchestvennykh, filosofskikh i kriticheskikh statei, Moscow 1911.
SCOTT, JAMES C., Domination and the Arts of Resistance. Hidden transcripts, New Haven 1992.
SCOTT, JOAN, The Evidence of Experience, in: Critical Inquiry 17 (1991), p. 773-797.
TROINOE UBIISTVO, in: Peterburgskii listok, 14.01.1913, p. 3.
ULICHNAIA SEKTANTSKAIA MISSIIA, in: Peterburgskii listok, 23.09.1908, p. 2.
SHCHIGALEEV, N., Zhizn' ili smert'?, in: Gazeta-kopeika, 03.06.1912, p. 5.
SKITALETS, Prestuplenie i nakazanie, in: Gazeta-kopeika, 09.07.1910, P. 3.
ID., Zimnee pal'to, in: Gazeta-kopeika, 20.10.1911, p. 5.
ID., Ochen' prosto, in: Gazeta-kopeika, 01.04.1913(1), p. 3.
ID., Ozverenie, in: Gazeta-kopeika, 16.04.1913(2), P. 3.
SLEDOPYT, 'Krasnyi fonar' i narodnaia nravstvennost', in: Malen'kaia gazeta, 22.11.1914, p. 4.
SOREL, GEORGES, Réflexions sur la violence (1908), transl. by T. E. Hulme and J. Roth as Reflections on Violence, Glencoe, Ill. 1950.
SPIVAK, GAYATRI CHAKRAVORTY, Can the Subaltern Speak, in: Marxism and the Interpretation of Culture, ed. by CARY NELSON and LAWRENCE GROSSBERG, Urbana 1988, p. 271-313.
STEINBERG, MARK D., Voices of Revolution, 1917, New Haven 2001.
ID., Proletarian Imagination. Self, modernity, and the sacred in Russia, 1910-1925, Ithaca 2002.
ID., Petersburg Fin de Siècle, New Haven 2011.
ID./SOBOL, VALERIA (eds.,), Interpreting Emotions in Russia and Eastern Europe, DeKalb, Ill. 2011.
DETSKII SUD, in: Peterburgskii listok, 11.01.1910, p. 1.
SVIRSKII, A., Peterburgskie khuligany, in: Peterburg i ego zhizni, St. Petersburg 1914.
PREDVARITEL'NYI SVOD STATISTICHESKIKH DANNYKH PO G. S-PETERBURGU ZA 1909 GOD, St. Petersburg 1910.
TAN, Chernye maski, in: Zaprosy zhizni, 05.10.1911, p. 60f.
TROFIMOV, V., 'Zhestoki u nas nravy'…, in: Gazeta-kopeika, 04.04.1909, p. 3.
ZVERSKOE UBIISTVO, in: Gazeta-kopeika, 05.10.1909, p. 3.
V. T., Privykli, in: Gazeta-kopeika, 10.05.1909(1), p. 3.

Id., Na ligovskom bul'vare, in: Gazeta-kopeika, 23.06.1909(2), p. 3.
VADIM, Dukh zla, in: Gazeta-kopeika, 16.02.1913, p. 3.
ZERKALO STOLITSY, in: Malen'kaia gazeta, 27.10.1914, p. 3.
ZHBANKOV, DMITRII, Itogi travmaticheskoi epidemii za noiabr'-dekabr' 1909 g., in: Rech, 14.01.1910(1), p. 2.
ID., Sovremennye samoubiistva, in: Sovremennyi mir 3 (1910)(2), p. 27-55.
ID., Polovaia prestupnost', in: Sovremennyi mir 7 (1910)(3), p. 63-91.
ZHERTVA OBSHCHESTVENNOGO RAVNODUSHIIA, in: Peterburgskii listok, 13.12.1908, p. 4.
ZHIZN' ZA 14 KOPEEK, in: Peterburgskii listok, 05.10.1912, p. 3.
ŽIŽEK, SLAVOJ, Violence, New York 2008.
ZORIN [A. GASTEV], Rabochii mi. Novyi Piter, in: Zhizn' dlia vsekh 10 (1913), p. 1454-1462.

Outcast Vienna 1900

The Politics of Transgression

WOLFGANG MADERTHANER

I

The Vienna of 1900 has been mythologized in recent decades. It has become a historical signet, a highly successful trademark recognized around the world. Its posthumous success has been promoted by masterpieces of historiography such as Carl E. Schorske's *Fin de Siècle Vienna*[1] as well as by a series of spectacular exhibitions at the Vienna Künstlerhaus, the Centre Georges Pompidou in Paris, and the Museum of Modern Art in New York. Nikolaus Sombart, in one example among many, has attributed to the Vienna of 1900 paradigmatic significance for the twentieth century as a whole.[2] According to Sombart, central problems of modernity were articulated here more precisely and radically than elsewhere; they were perceived and conceptualized in a more intelligent and original way as they took on the form and the attitude of cultural innovations such as Arnold Schönberg's anti-music, Karl Kraus's linguistic criticism, Arthur Schnitzler's fictional psychology, Wittgenstein's dismantling of metaphysics, Ernst Mach's empirical criticism, and Sigmund Freud's psychoanalysis.

Vienna 1900 was indeed a peculiar and somehow solitary conglomerate of some of the most divergent yet mutually dependent social, political, and cultural developments of the time. While a liberal bourgeoisie was favoring the monarchy, democratic movements were afflicted with a traditional bureaucracy, populism was associated with Catholicism, and the *Late Enlightenment* was occupied with the conditions of the human soul and the basic psychological conditions of the individual. In the heart of the city, the Hofburg, the aging emperor

---

1 Cf. SCHORSKE, 1981.
2 Cf. SOMBART, 1987, p. 52-54.

Franz Joseph sought desperately to uphold his autocratic regime as well as the myth of the old German *Reich*. On the gorgeous newly constructed Ringstraße Boulevard an economically powerful bourgeoisie showcased the success of a late-coming capitalism in the form of magnificent, historicist architecture. In the lower-middle-class districts, a petite bourgeoisie suspicious of modernity mourned the loss of the "Old Vienna" that had epitomized pre-modern contentment and clarity. In the industrial suburbs which encompassed the inner districts like an iron ring of workers' quarters, serious housing misery, social squalor, mass immigration, and potential political upheavals gathered.

Vienna's symbolic body was distorted in many ways. It was socially segregated and yet contradictorily homogenized by the aesthetic standards and facades of the Ringstraße that dominated the outer appearance of the tenement blocks even in the proletarian outskirts. While the nobility had long passed the zenith of their political power, its cultural heritage dominated the fantasies and longings of a bourgeoisie still striving for social recognition. The liberal and predominantly Jewish bourgeoisie, which only recently had acquired political power, was almost immediately challenged (and finally defeated) by an anti-Semitic, lower-middle-class populism that proved able to combine cultural reaction and municipal modernity. At the same time, an egalitarian utopianism, promoted by progressive Jewish upper-class intellectuals, was unfolding among the masses of suburban proletarians as a reaction to the unfulfilled humanitarian promises of liberalism. In the city's coffeehouses and salons, writers, artists, and scientists searched for a common denominator to all these contradictions and seemed to detect it in psychoanalysis, psychophysics, expressionism, and an aesthetically sophisticated nervousness.[3]

The Vienna of 1900 was at once a laboratory of the Apocalypse and the birthplace of epoch-making modern trends and achievements. It was the place of the last of the Habsburgs as well as that of the young Adolf Hitler, and of Theodor Herzl, the founder of modern Zionism. It was the place of the patriarchal major Karl Lueger, who shaped modern anti-Semitism into a political mass movement, and it was the place of one of the founding fathers of democratic socialism, the Jewish poor man's doctor, psychologist and social reformer Victor Adler. It was the first metropolis in which organized anti-Semitism was able to seize power and it was to become, after the municipal franchise had been democratized, the first city with over one million inhabitants under a social-democratic administration. In Robert Musil's words, Vienna 1900 resembled a boiling blister of

---

3   Cf. MADERTHANER/MUSNER, 1999(2).

initiations and emergences, one gigantic beat and the eternal dissonance and determent of all rhythms against each other:

> "No one knew exactly what was in the making; nobody could have said whether it was to be a new art, a new humanity, a new morality, or perhaps a reshuffling of society. [...] There were those who loved the overman and those who loved the underman; there were health cults and sun cults and the cults of consumptive maidens; there was enthusiasm for the hero worshipers and for the believers in the Common Man; people were devout and skeptical, naturalistic and mannered, robust and morbid; they dreamed of old tree-lined avenues in palace parks, autumnal gardens, glassy ponds, gems, hashish, disease, and demonism, but also of prairies, immense horizons, forges and rolling mills, naked wrestlers, slave uprisings, early man, and the smashing of society. These were certainly opposing and widely varying cries, but uttered in the same breath."[4]

II

Since the 1980s, a specific practice of cultural analysis and discourse on the *Vienna Modern* has been established. This practice was exclusively concerned with the culture of the elites, and was dominated by a discussion of the artistic and intellectual avant-gardes – projecting an embellished image of *Vienna 1900* as an icon of an innovative multiculturalism. The extreme disparities between the social classes and the spatial and cultural segregation that resulted, as well as the nascent anti-Semitism and populist mass politics, are mentioned, if at all, only marginally. This romanticized picture, by focusing on singularities instead of processes, thus obscures an understanding of that long-term logic that led from *fin-de-siècle Vienna* with the posthumously admired creativity of its assimilated Jewish community to the brutal persecution of Jews during the Nazi dictatorship.

Instead of making Carl Schorske's perspective ever more dynamic, *fin de siècle* was ontologically conceptualized as the sum of its intellectual and artistic achievements, and was thus stylized into a kind of precious treasury of high culture. The life-worldly cultures of the suburbs, the worlds of the immigrants, proletarians, and urban pariahs, were persistently ignored in high modern Viennese literature. If the suburbs were mentioned at all they came to be, according

---

4   MUSIL, 1995, p. 53.

to respective ideological dispositions, either places of divergence and disorder, misery, and immorality, or a terrain of utopian prospect, the forthcoming social basis of interwar *Red Vienna*.[5]

On the other hand, the suburbs and outskirts had always been present as a central trope of a popular discourse about the essence of Viennese nature. They had been present in traditional popular songs (*Wienerlied*) and above all in an oral canon of legends and myths. There were rumors about extensive and violent hunger revolts, about a dissipated, lustful *joie de vivre* even under the most miserable living conditions, about frightening and simultaneously idolized juvenile gangs, about grand gangsters or small-time crooks posing as social rebels, supported without reservation by their local neighborhoods. There are numerous reports of the legendary lower class soirees of the washer-girls, the so-called 'freakers' balls' (*Lumpenbälle*), notorious orgiastic feasts at run-down pubs and low dives. And we are told about self-contained territories of insubordination, which were not to be disciplined by any political and social regime whatsoever.

To decipher and decode these popular myths or, to be more precise, to decipher their marginalization by contemporary as well as retrospective elitist cultural discourses, turns out to be an intriguing perspective. This becomes even more fascinating if we take into account one specific feature of Vienna's urban form; poverty and social squalor is, and always has been, hidden behind a facade of impressive beauty that suggests a homogenous urban body inspired by the classical architectural standards of the *Ringstraße*. Judged by their outer appearance, the proletarian tenement blocks of the suburbs were (and are) indeed magnificent buildings, in some cases hardly second to the famous palaces along the *Ringstraße*. Thus they did not constitute an obvious contrast to the center, but rather obscured a characteristic double-folded social and spatial segregation. The Vienna topography unfolded along a concentric pattern by which inner and outer suburbs were clustered around the center according to their respective social status. The actual demarcations were not defined as clearly by architectural or aesthetic differences, but by the social signification of urban territories. Cultural practices, as much as material urban forms, served to locate different social classes and determine the divergent perceptions and appropriations of the urban terrain as well as the extent of communication or separation between these classes.

Against this background it seems promising to focus on the outskirts of Vienna 1900. The 'Other' of suburban culture manifests itself in the popular land-

---

5 Cf. MADERTHANER/MUSNER, 1999(1); HORAK et al., 2000; HORAK et al. 2001; MADERTHANER/MUSNER, 2008.

scapes of pleasure (such as the Prater or the Neulerchenfeld), in beer gardens, saloons, and other sites of indulgence. It becomes manifest in the urban no-man's-land of small crime, gangs, and prostitution – a no-man's-land that does not only signify social and cultural deviance, but is indeed part of a more comprehensive life-worldly spectrum of suburbia. This spectrum combines miserable living conditions with strategies of material and ideal survival, industrial and disciplined work with punctual, short-lived dropouts, and rebelliously veiled criminality with politically articulated insubordination. The tensions inscribed in the town body between high and popular culture, hegemony and social difference, mass identity prescribed, and the disobedience of these very masses, are key for developing an understanding for the modern metropolis. To decipher these concepts means attempting to read the metropolis as a social text.

III

In approaching the literary artifacts of high Viennese modernism as a starting point for such a reading, it soon becomes clear that the misery and scantiness of proletarian, suburban life is neither noticed nor reflected upon, very much in contrast to the literary production in comparable modern metropolises. In this respect Arthur Schnitzler's *Traumnovelle* can be taken as a paradigm. The protagonist undertakes a nightly, mysterious trip to a noble villa situated on the outskirts of the city, where members of the nobility meet in masks for erotic trysts.[6] The track of his coach leads along the Alserstrasse next to the center and heads for an elegant villa at the edge of the forest. Between these lies a terra incognita: the proletarian quarter of Ottakring. Schnitzler comments on Ottakring with only one laconic sentence: "They drove along the Alserstrasse, then underneath a viaduct towards the suburbs and on through badly-lit small side-lanes."[7]

We can detect from Schnitzler's fictions of the urban – and this is the case with an overwhelming majority of his contemporary writers – an urban segregation of *territories intimate* and *territories forbidden*. The mental maps underlying those fictions seem to have constituted an *imaginaire* of the urban that was not only characteristic for the authors but for middle-class patterns of perception as a whole. The other Vienna of the poor and downgraded proletarians, day laborers, servants, and outcasts was obviously beyond that perception and re-

---

6 Stanley Kubrik, by the way, transferred this framework into the New York of the late twentieth century for his last movie *Eyes Wide Shut*.
7 SCHNITZLER, 1992, p. 39.

moved from the world it created. Notions oriented along the standards of courtly and bourgeois culture definitively excluded the suburbs from city life, construing them merely as places best avoided: places of crime, indecency, deviance, and unpredictability. It was left to the new genre of urban reportage by figures such as Emil Kläger[8] or Max Winter[9] to take the minutes of outcast Vienna, thus introducing it to public awareness.

In those records, or in the literary artifacts of writers for whom the outskirts formed the background of a personal experience as a migrant or social outsider, the magnificent Middle-European metropolis is portrayed as a broken and distorted urban space. Ivan Cankar, nowadays generally deemed the founder of modern Slovenian literature, lived in Ottakring during the first decade of the twentieth century. This bohemian and boozer without means found accommodation at the flat of a seamstress, and made his suburban everyday experience the substance of his novels and short stories. We could not conceive of a greater contrast than that of Cankar's world to the splendor and shine of the inner city. Cankar's suburbia is a world of darkness and dirt, a dungeon that cannot be escaped from, as depicted in his 1900 short story *Mimi*:

> "The heavenly sun never shines here. There is smoke from the industrial plants around the roofs and if you stroll along the lanes, soot will fall into your face. The tenement blocks are high and boring; the people you meet are badly dressed, with hollow cheeks, their glances expressing discontent. This dreary suburb is extending over a huge area, no end to the east, no end to the west. I knew a man with a gray beard and a crooked back that had not once in his life reached the end of that seemingly endless street that leads into a world more lucid. The suburbs are a gigantic penitentiary; not one single free man does live there. Every now and then I was reflecting on what crimes these prisoners had committed. One morning I was crossing that street and watched them coming up in long rows, with heavy, tired steps and sleepy eyes; I thought I could hear iron chains jangling under their clothes. They got lost in large, gray buildings without windows, and the doors were heavily closing behind them..."[10]

Cankar's emphatic and personally affected view is paralleled very specifically by the social text inscribed onto suburbia by the medical, distanced, objectified

---

8   Cf. KLÄGER, 1908.
9   Cf. WINTER, 1925; IBID., 1905(1); IBID., 1905(2).
10 CANKAR, 1995, p. 7-8.

diagnosis of the municipal government. Thus given expression, the instrumentality of the Modern takes minutes of a total archeology of desperate housing and living conditions, social deviance, and pathology. Victor Adler first directed, in a very spectacular way, attention to those conditions. In December 1888 Adler published the results of hidden inquiries he had undertaken at the grounds of the Wienerberger brickworks.[11] The series of articles under the title *The Situation of the Brick Layers* in his weekly "Equality" (*Gleichheit*) came as a sensation and a scandal. It disclosed a genuine glance into a hitherto inconceivable social abyss and revealed a counter-world: the hidden, filthy, other side of the fin de siècle coin, the ousted, repressed, forgotten 'Other' of a widely praised metropolis, a world of exploitation, estrangement, and dulling apathy.

Adler reported on the "poorest slaves the sun has ever shed its light upon". Tied to a complex system of hierarchies and dependencies, bricklayers were totally subject to the Company and a carefully conceived truck system. Their salaries, scandalously low to begin with, were not paid in 'normal money' but given out in the form of metal coupons. These coupons were accepted as a means of payment exclusively by the canteen keepers of the Company. The quality of the goods offered was poor, the prices excessively high, and each worker was assigned to one of the canteen keepers as an object of exploitation. "Well aware of his power", Adler wrote, "such a keeper responded to a complaining worker: 'Even if I was going to shit into your dishes you ought to eat it up.' And the guy is right, they would have to."

While the workers were forbidden to purchase anything outside the works premises, they were nonetheless allowed to beg. Adler writes about hordes of people who would set upon the nearby Inzersdorfer cannery every evening, scrounging for waste products. Whoever could arrange it undertook a one-and-a-half hour walk to get hold of one of the eighty portions of vegetable soup the hangman of Vienna distributed daily: "There is more mercy with the hangman than with the Company and its paid slave-drivers."

As if this weren't enough, the bricklayers were forced to live on the premises. Up to ten families lived in every single room of the workers' houses, "men, women, children wildly mixed up". There were so-called sleeping halls for others, where fifty to seventy persons would be herded together on old straw, body next to body. In one of these halls a woman gave birth to her child "in the presence of fifty half-naked, dirty men. We should not talk about modesty, however,

---

11 PARTEIVORSTAND DER SOZIALDEMOKRATISCHEN ARBEITERPARTEI DEUTSCHÖSTERREICHS, vol. 4, 1925, p. 11-35. The citations following are taken from the first article published in *Gleichheit* 49 (1888).

as this is a luxury reserved for property owners only. The life of a mother is actually threatened under those circumstances. But who cares about a poor broad." The main factory grounds at the Laerberg were even more distinguished in that respect. Whole bunches of mainly single workers had to sleep on top of the huge industrial brick ovens, partly exposed to the night freeze, partly almost burnt from below, and covered only meagerly by filthy rags. The prisoners in Siberia, Adler summed up, were better off than these poor sods whose only crime was to work for the profits of the Company.

Adler's sensational revelations led to an epilogue in Parliament without any consequences, while his journal *Gleichheit* was confiscated and Adler himself was fined for non-licensed distribution of a periodical. Yet he was to produce further sensational pieces of investigative journalism. For his most important one, an April 1889 article on the living and working conditions of the tramway drivers, he was sentenced to four months' imprisonment.[12]

IV

In spite of these revealing indicators it would be misleading to regard the urban periphery and the suburbs only as zones of enduring misery or as mere function of the new and rigid industrial paradigm of production. Such a view would ignore essential dimensions of the social and cultural configurations of these areas. The following two scenarios elaborate suburban life-worlds and contexts as emblematic examples of social contradiction and cultural antagonism.

On September 17, 1911 a hunger revolt took place in the proletarian district of Ottakring. Entire quarters and most houses, windows, and streetlamps were damaged. A state of emergency was proclaimed, barricades were erected, streetcars were burned, and street fights with rapidly deployed army units took place. Young men and women, central agents of this revolt, seized and devastated school buildings and set fire to books and papers. For the first time since the revolutionary upheavals of 1848 army units fired on the civilian population, killing four, and the sub-proletariat looted shops and pubs. The young Austro-Marxist librarian of Parliament, to later become chancellor and president of the Austrian Republic, Karl Renner, stated that the most desperate, alienated, and seedy people had left their homes to demonstrate and thereby to protest the conditions held in place by the social order.[13]

---

12   Cf. BRAUNTHAL, 1965, p. 59-64.
13   Cf. RENNER, 1911, p.1-4.

The Vienna Police Department stated in its report that the police units were unable to stop devastation and pillage since the looters and plunderers were anywhere and nowhere and disappeared quickly when confronted by force. According to the department it would have taken all army units stationed in Vienna in order to secure public order and to control the undisciplined crowds in the streets. It took many hours to restore order due to the fact that the revolting crowds were supported and egged on by large segments of the civilian population. From windows and houses stones, glasses, iron pieces and the like were thrown at police and army units.[14] On the side of the young mob, women and mothers, whose objective according to the "Workers' Daily" *(Arbeiterzeitung)* should have been to think clearly and rigorously, took part in street fighting and provided the young mob with stones.[15]

This short day of anarchy stood for more than the harsh political economy of suburban life and more than a battle about power and the hegemony over public space. The "grotesque" character of the hunger revolt, frequently diagnosed by police and media reports, refers to a cultural articulation of difference and antagonism. Those crowds were not only composed of the old urban underclass but also of the many new migrants who brought with them their desire for a better life in the city – something not to be fulfilled in the contemporary urban context of devastating work and poor consumption.

These migrants had left their oral, pre-modern, and rural cultures of origin in order to find a new perspective and better life chances in the metropolis. Still mentally attached to an imaginary village of the past, they searched for a home in a different urban geography that was increasingly linearly and fragmentarily configured by technology, science, and rational conduct. Pushed towards the social margins, they were unable to find a new habitat but ended up in poverty and collective alienation. The seemingly irrational and grotesque character of the hunger revolt and the anarchic strength of its violence, however, reveal an obscure, ambivalent logic and rationality of its own: A largely hopeless venture to call into question the new symbolic order of modernity, modernization, and the metropolis.[16]

One-and-a-half years after the hunger revolt the same crowd showed up in the same Ottakring location but expressed itself in a different way: disciplined and with dignity. But before examining this outstanding event yet to come, a

---

14 Cf. AUSTRIAN STATE ARCHIVES/ÖSTERREICHISCHES STAATSARCHIV, Ministerium des Inneren, Präsidium, 9798, 19.09.1911.
15 Cf. ARBEITER-ZEITUNG, 19.09.1911, p. 2.
16 Cf. MADERTHANER/MUSNER, 1999(1), p. 34-37.

short excursion into the urban development of this proletarian district might be useful. During the so-called *Gründerzeit* in the 1860s and its capitalist restructuring, the preindustrial villages of Ottakring were turned into industrial suburbs, and a 'hard texture' of factories and tenement blocks, of traffic and communication lines was imposed, thereby rationalizing and disciplining everyday life. In parallel, the suburb became a projection screen of power in which economic interests blended with fantasies about the alien 'Other'. The speculative building boom as well as a massive influx of migrants condensed the suburbs into zones of extreme social and spatial density. While the facades of the hastily built tenements imitated the neo-baroque architecture of the center, their interior was characterized by pure capitalist rationality of minimal space sheltering a maximum of tenants. In his 1894 investigation of housing conditions in the Viennese suburbs, the famous Austrian social reformer Eugen von Philippovich concluded that tenants live under spatial circumstances which do not even meet the basic standards of army barracks.[17]

A prototypical example of the capitalist mode of suburban urban development was the so-called *Schmelz*, a former army training ground. In one of the most spectacular undertakings in Vienna's architectural history, the northern part of it was turned into a drawing-board structure of 'Americanized' urban housing characterized by standardized tenement blocks. In spite of the fact that this urban no-man's-land appeared like a final disposal site of the low classes, it became the location of the largest mass demonstration ever held in Vienna. This happened on the occasion of Franz Schuhmeier's funeral on February 16, 1913. Schuhmeier, a popular leader of the workers' movement, had been assassinated shortly before. The social-democratic workers' party had mobilized its already significant organizational apparatus, which covered all the suburbs, but the turnout surpassed all expectations and was to prove almost uncontrollable. Nearly half-a-million people came, literally every fourth inhabitant of Vienna. The funeral service assembled high-ranking representatives of the political, bureaucratic, military, and diplomatic elite. A large choir, composed of court opera and workers' singers, intoned Franz von Suppe's *Ruhe, Müder Wanderer* when the coffin was closed, and the end of the service was marked by Richard Wagner's pilgrim chorus of *Tannhäuser*. A horse-drawn carriage and horsemen in old Spanish costume brought the corpse to its final place of rest, where tens of thousands of mourners covered the grave with a sea of red carnations.

This grandiose funeral was no accident since Franz Schuhmeier was not only the most popular social democrat in Vienna at the turn of the century, but also a

---

17 Cf. FELDBAUER, 1977.

mass politician of the new style, an agitator as talented as he was populist and a stirring speaker; a man of the people who had risen from the poorest background into the highest levels of politics. Unlike any before him, Schuhmeier had managed to lead the politically and socially deprived of the suburbs out of their isolation to form an organized, politically aware, and thus identity-shaping mass movement. With this funeral it was not only a hero of the people who was paid homage according to tradition, the *people* in their new social organization and political expression turned into a public force. The funeral thus became the exposition of a political counterculture, which opposed the dominance of the petty-bourgeois radicalism that the Christian-Social mayor Karl Lueger had two decades before formed into the dominant local political force and brought to municipal power.[18]

Lueger's great political achievement at the time was the creation of an anti-liberal middle-class bloc which reunited the groups that had been split following the Revolution of 1848, the petty bourgeois on one hand and the wealthy middle classes on the other, into a clerical, antisocialist and anti-Semitic citizens' group.[19] Lueger was to prove to be a master of rewriting political history. He created the idea of the *true, authentic Viennese* as a new phenomenon in political life and thus gave the city its own new tradition. He cast the ostensibly true and real Vienna of the lower middle class as opposite to the experience of alienation and the working-world shock of modernity. Lueger created a patriarchal image of Vienna as a *Vaterstadt,* an imagined community of the petite bourgeoisie. Therein he forged an image of the capital city as the paragon of a pre-industrial, middle class, familial, and 'evangelized' city based on authority, paternalism, patrimony, and Christian-Catholic values. Lueger recognized in Schuhmeier a worthy opponent, his congenial popular counterpart. Their clashes in the municipal council were legendary. With both, repartee, wit, sarcasm, and scorn could suddenly turn into profound enmity. But their shouting matches and invectives just as often ended in theatrical gestures of reconciliation, and in such cases Lueger especially would always allude to the *Vienna-ness* so innately a part of the both of them.

Franz Schuhmeier and Karl Lueger, both literally "children of the suburbs", were prototypical exponents, actors and at the same time directors of a period of transition that followed the end of the liberal era in Vienna and of the reformation of political power relations. The period between 1890 and 1910 initiated the politics of the masses, reacting to the unfulfilled social promises of liberalism

---

18 Cf. MADERTHANER/MUSNER, 1999(1), p. 176 - 208.
19 Cf. SCHORSKE, 1981, p. 116.

and at the same time signaling its end. Though social democracy, by creating a modern mass party, successfully managed to take up the unfulfilled political agenda of liberalism, it was largely excluded, on account of a municipal electoral law in force until 1919, from any real political influence in the city. Lueger and his party of Christian Socials, however, destroyed the political power of the liberals, primarily via their "municipalization" (*Verstadtlichung*) projects and by building up a loyal power-base among the municipal civil servants, while leaving the social and political structures intact. Lueger enthroned the lower-middle-class citizen as the new political ruler on a local level; in place of liberal ideology, his own ideas became the basis for a policy agenda.[20]

Social democracy as a mass movement, by contrast, was restricted to proclaiming the city as the site of a different *future* politics, a different society, and a different culture. In this way it developed the idea of a utopia of equality, one that was to take on concrete form after World War I in *Red Vienna*. Lueger, by contrast, relied on a policy of xenophobia and anti-Semitism. Instead of addressing the welfare of the city as a whole, he reinforced social tensions and divisions. His policy was one of 'evangelizing' the poor and excluding those who had recently migrated to the city. If Franz Schuhmeier also played on an anti-Semitic resentment that was already deeply embedded in the attitudes of all the various social groups comprising Viennese society at the turn of the century, this remained fundamentally distinct from Lueger's outright hatred of Jews.[21]

Lueger's marginalization and defamation of Jews as a group was aimed at covering up the problems inherited from liberalism and making the social tensions it had left behind the basis for a xenophobic populism. In this way, his anti-Semitism became not only an instrument of mass mobilization but also an integral component of a new kind of political culture, one that incited the masses against the old elites, and the *integrated* against the *outsiders*. Schuhmeier and the social democrats, by contrast, made the social tensions and contradictions their point of departure; overcoming them became the basis of their political agenda. Lueger used the 'Others', Jews and foreigners as outsiders, to satisfy symbolically the disparate interests of his clientele and thus to remain in power. The social democrats aimed at integration in order to come to power and to create, via an alliance of the working class and the assimilated intellectual Jewish community, a social order in which both would be citizens instead of outsiders, in the center instead of on the periphery. Yet, however different these new forms

---

20 Cf. BOYER, 1995, p. 236, 154.
21 Cf. PULZER, 1988; POLLAK, 1997.

of mass politics were articulated, in their collective dimension they reflected Robert Musil's *common breath*.

Literature

Arbeiter-Zeitung, 19.09.1911.
Boyer, John W., Culture and Political Crisis in Vienna. Christian socialism in power 1897-1918, Chicago 1995.
Braunthal, Julius, Victor und Friedrich Adler. Zwei Generationen Arbeiterbewegung, Vienna 1965.
Canker, Ivan, Pavliceks Krone. Literarische Skizzen aus Wien, Klagenfurt 1995.
Feldbauer, Peter, Stadtwachstum und Wohnungsnot. Determinanten unzureichender Wohnungsversorgung in Wien 1848 bis 1914, Vienna 1977.
Horak, Roman et al. (eds.), Metropole Wien. Texturen der Moderne, 2 vols., Vienna 2000.
Id. et al. (eds.), Stadt. Masse. Raum. Wiener Studien zur Archäologie des Popularen, Vienna 2001.
Kläger, Emil, Durch die Quartiere der Not und des Verbrechens. Wien und die Jahrhundertwende, Vienna 1908.
Maderthaner, Wolfgang/Musner, Lutz, Die Anarchie der Vorstadt. Das andere Wien um 1900, Frankfurt/Main/New York 1999(1);
Id., "Aufstand der Massen", in: Damals. Das aktuelle Magazin für Geschichte und Kultur 3 (1999)(2), p. 12-19.
Id., Unruly Masses. The other side of Fin de Siècle Vienna, New York/Oxford 2008.
Musil, Robert, The Man without Qualities, translated from German by Sophie Wilkins, New York 1995.
Parteivorstand der Sozialdemokratischen Arbeiterpartei Deutschösterreichs (ed.), Victor Adlers Aufsätze, Reden und Briefe. 11 vols., Vienna 1922-1929, here vol. 4, Vienna 1925.
Pulzer, Peter, The Rise of Political Anti-Semitism in Germany and Austria, Cambridge, Mass. 1988.
Pollak, Michael, Wien 1900. Eine verletzte Identität, Konstanz 1997.
Renner, Karl, Soziale Demonstrationen, in: Der Kampf 1 (1911), p. 1-4.
Schnitzler, Arthur, Traumnovelle, Frankfurt am Main 1992.
Schorske, Carl E., Fin-de-Siècle Vienna. Politics and culture, New York 1981.
Sombart, Nikolaus, Nachdenken über Deutschland. Vom Historismus zur Psychoanalyse, München/Zürich 1987.

Winter, Max, Das goldene Wienerherz, Berlin 1905(1).
Id., Im unterirdischen Wien, Leipzig/Berlin 1905(2).
Id., Im dunkelsten Wien. Wiener Schilderungen aus der Luegerzeit, Vienna, 1925.

Austrian State Archives/Österreichisches Staatsarchiv:
- Ministerium des Inneren, Präsidium, 9798, 19.09.1911.

Revisiting Campbell Bunk

JERRY WHITE

Campbell Bunk – more properly Campbell Road in the North London borough of Islington – was an unlikely slum.[1] It was, when laid out from the 1850s, a suburban street of 100-or so quite substantial houses on three floors, designed for respectable clerks and not the poor. Even in the 1920s and 1930s, the interwar years of which I made a detailed study, Campbell Bunk was an atypical slum in spacial terms. The worst run-down housing in London being cleared as slums in those years were mainly two- or even one-storey dwellings built in courts or alleys and tucked behind the main streets of old London, in the ancient districts of Holborn, Finsbury, Stepney and Southwark, all close to the original City of London. They were narrow, congested, largely hidden from view. But Campbell Bunk was a long wide street that opened off one of London's main cross-routes and close to the busy suburban transport interchange of Finsbury Park railway and tube station. On either side and all around were respectable working-class streets which in general were not poor. Yet here it was, the most notorious street in this densely-populated segment of north London and wide open to the public gaze. But slum it was by any definition. It was one of just eighteen or so streets in the whole metropolis coloured entirely black – its population cast as 'semi-criminal and degraded' – in the poverty maps drawn up by the London School of Economics around 1930. It had also been coloured entirely black in Charles Booth's poverty maps of forty years earlier.

It was, then, an unlikely slum. And it had become one by an accident of history, or rather a conjunction of accidents. Its development had been stunted from birth. Not all its building plots were sold in the initial speculation of 1857-8; the

---

1 Cf. WHITE, 2003. This was first published as *The Worst Street in North London: Campbell Bunk, Islington, Between the Wars*, London, 1986. All page references here are to the 2003 edition.

local market for new houses was glutted, so building did not begin until 1865; six years on and the road was still unmade and only half-built on; not all the empty spaces would be filled with houses until the early 1880s, some eighteen years or so after building began. Mud and filth on the ground caused rents to fall and the clerks to leave. Their place was taken by chimney sweeps, general dealers, street sellers, porters and building labourers. The neighbourhood's rough boys and men gambled in the empty spaces. And in 1880 came the fatal tipping point. A large house on the street's middle junction, intended to become a public house, couldn't get a magistrates' licence and was instead converted to a common lodging house for ninety men. The shiftless homeless poor of London had been introduced to Campbell Bunk. Other houses soon followed suit. Within a decade there were more common lodging house beds in Campbell Road than any other street in Islington.

So Campbell Bunk's reputation was established by the 1890s. This is how Charles Booth, who uniquely accorded the street three pages in *Life and Labour of the People in London*, described it at that time:

> "A street fairly broad, with houses of three storeys, not ill-built, many being occupied as common lodging-houses; broken windows, dirty curtains, doors open, a litter of paper, old meat tins, heads of fish and stalks of vegetables. It is a street where thieves and prostitutes congregate. The thieves live in the common lodging-houses, paying fourpence a night, and the prostitutes, generally two together, in a single furnished room, which they rent at four or five shillings a week. They are the lowest class of back-street prostitute, and an hour or two after midnight they may be seen returning home."[2]

A few years later and a local sanitary inspector vented his feelings about the street in a report to Islington Council:

> "This road is the king of all roads. I have been in practically all the slums in London; Notting Hill, Chelsea, Battersea, Fulham, Nine Elms, and also the East End, but there is nothing so lively as this road. Thieves, Prostitutes, cripples, Blind People, Hawkers of all sorts of wares from boot laces to watches and chains are to be found in this road, Pugilists, Card Sharpers, Counter Jumpers, Purse Snatchers, street singers, and Gamblers of all kinds, and things they call men who live on the earnings of women, some of whom I saw outside the Town Hall with the unemployed last week. I could say a lot

---

2   Cited in WHITE, 2003, p. 23f.

more about this road, but I think I have said enough to prove to you the class of people who inhabit it. Of course, there are a few who perhaps get an honest living, but they want a lot of picking-out."[3]

That was written in 1909, and I was myself a sanitary inspector for Islington Council some sixty years after my predecessor wrote these words. My job title had changed by 1970 to public health inspector, but the work was pretty much the same. And although Campbell Bunk had been demolished fifteen years before, its reputation was hardly less vivid than it had been. Indeed, I kept on hearing stories about it and by the end of the 1970s I had determined to investigate its story further by talking to people who had lived there. By this time I had got into the press my first book, an oral history of a Jewish East End tenement block[4] – a different sort of ghetto we might call that – so I was experienced enough with a tape recorder and reasonably adept at finding people to talk to. I wrote an article in "History Workshop Journal" on what I called this 'lumpen community' and thought I'd disposed of the Bunk.[5] In fact I hadn't. The place continued to haunt me. And despite not wanting to write another book about another tiny sliver of London, I spent in all some eight years trying to tease out the many contradictions of this extraordinary place. Central among them, to my mind, was this: Campbell Bunk was a close community where people would steal from one another, and was in numerous other ways at war with itself, as well as at war with the world beyond it.

The book was published twenty-six years ago, and was finished a year or more before that. Since then, of course, our terminology and explanatory frameworks have shifted. I don't recall that 'social exclusion' was much used, if at all, at the time. Had it been, then I believe "Campbell Bunk" would have provided insights into the contradictory mechanisms involved in the social exclusion process, and I'll come back to this point in a moment. The 'underclass' *was* written about at the time, but it's an unsatisfactory term, I think, and I didn't use it: it seems to describe a social formation too inert, too removed from possibilities of change, too far isolated from the shifting dynamics of economic opportunity and class relations, to be a useful descriptor of social reality. Marxism was a far more popular theoretical tool for social historians then than now, and I myself began from a 'base and superstructure' model of change in Campbell Bunk. In the event I found it incomplete and unsatisfying when trying to comprehend a

---

3   Cited in IBID., p. 25.
4   IBID., 1980.
5   IBID., 1979.

'whole society' or 'total way of life', and I needed the introduction of gender fully to explain the street's history. The cultural or linguistic turn, I confess, passed me by at the time – and so have the re-turns and about-turns since then. I remain an unrepentantly old-fashioned social historian.

So looking back, revisiting Campbell Bunk as it were after twenty-six years away, what do I find?

First, it has to be said that in many ways, of course, this really *was* a socially excluded space and culture. But the picture of social exclusion we find there is complex and contingent, as perhaps all historical reality proves to be.

Certainly, though, Campbell Bunk actively set itself apart from – turned its back on - contemporary London in a number of ways.

It was, for instance, distinctively in-bred, with longterm traditions of settlement that were quite unusual. Many families in the street in the 1930s could trace their residence there back to the 1890s and before. Kinship patterns were frequently extensive – one man I spoke to could count more than forty relatives in a street of a hundred or so houses (about a thousand people). It was more frequent for young men and women to marry fellow-Bunkites than was the case in neighbouring streets. And longterm settlements and kinship were reinforced by the street's traditional connection with gypsies, which seems to have developed by the 1880s. This was an element in Bunk culture that strengthened a tendency to economic independence outside wage labour that I found to be a culturally distinctive, almost a defining, component of the Bunk's separateness. I wrote that

There is no documentary evidence for a gypsy connection with Campbell Road, but the oral tradition is overwhelming (although not shared by the street as a whole). A gypsy – or 'pikie' in cockney slang – pedigree was claimed by Harry James and for a number of other families. There were the Brothertons, who moved into the street some time in the 1920s; Dolly Mills and his family put up in Campbell Road whenever they were in the neighbourhood; Gypsy Jack Hobbs sold manure from a horse and cart and later married a girl from the street; Liza Harmer and Mrs Knowles, the street sellers, both had 'Romaner' or 'pikie' backgrounds.

The James family was headed by George, known as Dido. He was a tinker, repairing cane chairs and mats and sharpening scissors, knives, lawnmowers and so on from a richly-decorated barrow which he pushed over the streets of North London. He once fought Ernie Barnes, another knife grinder with a similar heritage, for the title of Campbell Road's 'King of the Pikies'. He went to Barnet Fair every September, a gathering place for gypsies, and he was said to have some sort of title to land there. He taught his son words which were not even in the varied London underworld cant of the 1930s – words like 'jas' for go, 'yog' for fire, 'chokkors' for boots. And at least two of his boys never took to work, becoming professional thieves until after the Second World War.[6]

If this independent economic element was defining, there were numerous other cultural components that separated Campbell Bunk from its neighbours. Its pleasures, for instance, had a rough component about them that had gone out of fashion in working-class London even before the First World War. It retained a culture of heavy drinking and drunkenness among men and older women, in part no doubt an antidote to the foul, crowded and verminous living conditions there. Its collective male pleasures were dominated by illegal street gambling with dice and coins. There was a passion for fighting. Some men were terrors, to their neighbours and to others, but most men seem to have resorted to fists or worse on the slightest provocation. This rubbed off on many Bunk women and girls, some urged by their parents to settle their differences with violence. Violence, illegal pastimes and the way in which many people from the road made their living in the streets as costermongers, hawkers, scrap-metal dealers and so on, brought many Bunk dwellers into a sharp and brutal collective antagonism with the police. And that again was distinctively different from most working-class streets in Islington.

But apart from setting itself apart, it was also cast out, excluded by contemporary London. Take poverty. Not everyone in Campbell Bunk was poor, for its thieves, prostitutes, dealers and rent collectors could make a good return, if only for short and irregular periods; and there were always wage-earners in the local economy who kept well above the poverty line. But the depth of poverty in Campbell Bunk in the 1920s, at least, was sometimes at pre-war, almost Victorian levels. It became a reservoir, perhaps a sanctuary, for the very poorest in interwar North London. Here are some instances.

John Morley, 11 years old, was arrested for begging in November 1919. He had chronic conjunctivitis, 'fassy' eye or sticky eye, common enough in Campbell Road. "He was in a filthy condition. It was a cold, wet day and he has no shirt. When food was offered to him he ate it ravenously." Daisy Booth, 19 years old in 1925, and prosecuted for theft, had a baby to keep: "They were practically starving and without money […]. 'I had no milk and no fire at home, and not a penny coming in.'" When a Campbell Road painter was convicted of stealing milk from a doorstep in February 1932, the Court Missionary "said there was no doubt [his] child was hungry." A police report in May 1933 on a 31-year-old labourer found he "had no food in the house beyond a little bread." "See, we

---

6   Cf. IBID., 2003, p. 55f.

was like animals, we was like animals at home, all of us hungry [...]. I used to sit eating cabbage stalks cos I was that hungry," recalled Ronnie and Marjie Drover from number 25. And Mavis Knight's mother suffered from psoriasis, rheumatoid arthritis and chronic under-feeding: "She has to wear dark glasses cos her eyes was so affected by the malnutrition."[7]

"I've been to school many times with women's shoes on, and women's stockings tied up in a knot there [for socks]," and so did other boys from Campbell Road. "No kids went to school in long trousers in them days," recalled Walter Spencer. "But they did from the Bunk because they were men's trousers cut down with your arse hanging down."[8] Walter and his two brothers slept on a wooden platform with a flock overlay as a mattress, built into the tiny attic at 86 Campbell Road. The makeshift bed was covered with war-surplus blankets and their Uncle Charlie's army greatcoat. There was a paraffin lamp on the wall, and the room was just big enough for the bed and little else:

> "And I remember up there Christmas time. One particular Christmas [...] we used to hang our stockings over for Christmas [...]. I remember this particular year – my brother remembers it, never forgot it. We woke up – I felt mine. 'Oh', I said, 'we're alright [...] we got some ink 'ere!' Cos it felt [...] hard, like. We used to have orange a penny, and a few nuts and that. I thought 'Oh it's all right, we got something,' cos the old man had had a bad year, that Christmas. Oh, when we got up, you know, it was light in the morning, never looked at it until the morning, never forget: it was cinders out the grate and hard bread. And my brother ate that bloody bread! He really ate it – he was crunching it."[9]

The very reputation of the Bunk conspired to keep its residents poor and conspired to exclude them from contemporary London, to some degree at least. Labelling or stigmatization of the street and its residents in the local press, in the police courts and by word of mouth – the myths and exaggerations that persisted long enough after the street's demise to make me interested in it in the first place – directly affected the life-chances of the people living there. They could, indeed, be excluded from the labour market by employers for whom a Campbell-Road address was sufficient to mark out a boy as a thief and a girl as something worse. Perhaps the fear of discrimination was more pervasive than discrimination itself. For example it was said that the Ever Ready battery factory

---

7   IBID., p. 71.
8   IBID., p. 71f.
9   IBID.

in Fonthill Road would not take girls from Campbell Road, but it sometimes did. Yet there was no doubt that discrimination was *felt* to be real, and that it was experienced as a direct and personal rejection by the labour market. "I have written for hundreds of jobs," complained 'A British Legionite (an ex-serviceman) to the local newspaper in 1922, "and when I mention Campbell Road it is all up, simply because the street has been given a bad name." Another wrote "I lived there five years [and] I could never obtain a berth from there. People said to me, you will never get anything while you live there [...]. It is like dynamite to mention the road. Why don't you alter the name? I wish, from the bottom of my heart, I had never known of its existence."[10]

The street's name was indeed changed from Campbell Road in 1938, to Whadcoat Street. There were, though, ways of avoiding the stigma: one youth from number 52 – on the Paddington Street corner – always gave his address as 52 Paddington Street. And in 1924, a charwoman convicted of theft from an employer was said by the police to have "lived in Campbell Road but gave another address."[11]

These then were the traditional 'ghetto' elements, as we might call them, which distinctively isolated – socially excluded - Campbell Bunk from all around it. Yet, and this cannot be stressed too highly, these ghetto walls were porous. The outside influences on the street were numerous, especially in the lives of its young people – school, of course, but also the various clubs for boys and girls run by the missions and working-men's clubs that had Campbell Bunk as their primary focus. Though the street's housing market attracted only the poor, there were many newcomers to the street, residents who came and went and sometimes settled for lengthy periods; they brought connections with other parts of London and no doubt spoke of different ways of doing things.

Even more important, these connections with London, even with a wider world, were strengthened by the expanding cultural life of the metropolis in the 1920s and '30s, and by a growing culture of working-class consumerism. We might mention, for instance, the influence of the cinema. Cinema penetrated everywhere, even to Campbell Bunk. From this new cultural element of talking pictures, with all its baneful influences according to contemporary puritans, and all its richness of new associations and thrills for the young people of Campbell Bunk, some could weave a fantasy world that the old London music-halls had never offered. It was noted in 1934 how, in Islington's 'most notorious café', the conversation was mostly in American accents. Nearly every girl there was

---

10 IBID., p. 51.
11 IBID.

acting a "hard-boiled Kate" role. Nearly every youth, with a very long overcoat and a round black hat on the rear of his head, was to himself a "Chicago nut".[12]

The connections with contemporary London, and the road out of a socially excluded Campbell Bunk, was strengthened most of all by changes in the labour market. Despite the Great Depression and the Crash of 1929, and despite the economic distress common to many parts of industrial Britain, demand for consumer durables in London was fuelled by the suburban growth of the 1920s and the building boom of the decade to come. London prospered, and the demand for factory labour seemed inexhaustible. The demand was strongest for girl labour. Even the girls of Campbell Bunk were invited to find work at the factory bench. And never had there been so many things to spend their earnings on.

It was this dynamic world opening up for young women in Campbell Bunk that sowed the seeds of the street's dissolution during the interwar period, a generation before the bulldozers moved in. It was not an easy process. For the new world opening up for young women in Campbell Bunk was frequently viewed with anger and jealousy by their mothers. Something like an inter-generational struggle took place between mothers left behind in the slum and their daughters trying to make their way out. In true Campbell Bunk fashion it could be accompanied by threats, bullying, theft and violence. We have room for only a couple of instances to stand in for many.

The twenty-year old May Purslowe worked at a North London sweet factory in the early 1920s. Her mother was a hard-drinking charwoman or casual domestic servant, and the family lived in two rooms in Campbell Road, where three girls shared one bed and May's mother and young brother shared another. Rows soon began over how much May should pay her mother for her 'keep'. May and her mother had always been at loggerheads. May, accoding to Mrs Purslowe, "had got too much of what the cat licked its arse with."[13] May became particularly vocal over how she should be clothed. Mrs Purslowe had taken it on herself to clothe May out of the money the girl handed over. But her mother's choice of courier was restricted to totters' barrows in Campbell Road and the Fonthill Road rag shop. Clothes became, for mother and daughter, a fiercely contested symbol of independence:

> "And this one particular day I said to her, 'I'm not giving you all my money, I'm gonna buy my own clothes.' And I went to Chapel Street, Islington market, and I bought a velvet skirt and a blouse. And when I came home, washed

---

12 Cited in IBID., p. 166.
13 IBID., p. 202.

meself, dressed to go out, she says to me, 'And where do you think *you're* going?' I said, 'Well, I'm going out.' So she says, 'Oh are you?' And she did no more, she tore all these clothes off me. And of course I cried and went into me aunt's which was next door but one, number 31 [...] and I said to her, 'Mum's tore all my clothes.' So she said, 'Oh, you'd better stay in here then.' And I had to go indoors back again to get me old clothes to put on."[14]

May chose a route out of Campbell Road that many other girls took – they found a husband as quickly as they could: the mean age of marriage of girls in England and Wales in the 1930s was 25 years; in Campbell Road it was 21.2; in the street next door, fewer than one in eleven girls (under 9 %) were twenty years old or younger when they married; in Campbell Road it was nearly one in three. But May found that her mother did not react well to the prospect:

"First night he took me home I said to him, 'You don't want to come down to my door,' I said, 'because if me mother comes home drunk you'll be sorry.' So he said, 'Well, that's all right,' he said. So of course, home they come from the Duke public house all merry and bright and singing. And when she went to come indoors, there was my boyfriend, Bob, standing there with me and she says to him, 'What the effin' hell are you doing here?' So he said, 'Well, I've brought your daughter home.' So she said, 'Well you can effin' well sling yer 'ook again.' So that was that. So I said to him, 'Come on, stand up on the corner.' She said, 'And you don't want to stop up there all night else I'll have a bucket of piss poured over yer!' So that was the wonderful reception he got."[15]

May had to creep indoors after she had been out with Bob once in case her mother caught her staying out late. And one, when dressed in her finest clothes to go with him to the Wood Green Empire, her mother threw a bucket of slops over her because May hadn't done the washing up. But eventually all ended happily. In 1922, May and Bob were married at Tottenham, and chose a house in respectable Wood Green.

Nancy Tiverton, my second example, had similar experiences a few years later, working at a local brush factory. The job itself she found because of her dissatisfactions with her appearance, especially how she was clothed. She sensibly decided to keep any new paid job secret from her mother and keep paying her the same amount from her previous worse-paid employment:

14 IBID.
15 IBID., p. 203.

> "I thought to meself, I don't know what to do, you know, as I am now I'll never get a rag on me back. I was a disgrace, I was, honest. And it wasn't my fault. So I thought to myself, I know what I'll do. I won't tell mum. I'll go after the Christmas holiday, go down the Star Brush, see if I can get on [...]. So I didn't say a word to her. I come out as though I was coming to work, and down the Star Brush [factory] I went, and got on."[16]

Every penny she had went on clothes. Her mother kept a watchful eye on her purchases:

> "'How much you pay for that costume?' So I said, 'Four guineas.' So she said, 'Oh. How much them boots?' 'Twelve and six.' So she said, 'Oh.' They was down the pawn shop Monday. She asked that so she knew what to ask for, see? Down there Monday."[17]

This was not the only one of Mrs Tiverton's tricks. Nancy's sister Marjie, four years her elder, was courting a print worker from Walthamstow, well-off indeed in Campbell Road's terms. Each time he visited Marjie he'd give young Nancy half a crown. But Mrs Tiverton spotted this the first time it happened and claimed the money as her own thereafter. She cadged, too, from a Campbell Road boy who asked her permission to take Nancy to Finsbury Park Empire:

> "So you know what? Before he could take me out my mum say, 'Lend us half a crown, Freddie?' Nancy had to hide her money in a makeshift money belt tied with string round her waist under her clothes; 'I kept that secret. If I'd told her she would have had it she would.'"[18]

Marjie left home over her mother's depredations. Mrs Tiverton had pawned one of the rings given her by the Walthamstow fiancé. And Nancy, too, fell unwittingly into a similar trap. Mrs Tiverton provoked a row and told Nancy to go. She gave Nancy a parcel of her clothes – "'Take that with you, you haven't got to come back no more here for that.'"[19] But the treasured costume and boots were not in the parcel, and Nancy had to go back to her mother for the pawn ticket. It cost her some 15s to redeem her own clothes from the pawnbroker.

16   IBID., p. 205.
17   IBID., p. 206.
18   IBID.
19   IBID.

Both these young women turned their backs on Campbell Bunk, and so did their sisters, by the end of the 1920s.

If we sum up the picture of social exclusion we find in Campbell Bunk in the two decades after the First World War we might characterise it thus. Social exclusion was a traditional element in the street's make-up and had been for forty or fifty years before. It worked both ways, the street's culture *rejecting* the local economy and the local economy rejecting the people of Campbell Bunk. But this was never watertight, and there have been many economic and cultural connections with a wider London that got stronger from the 1920s. The key element in weakening social exclusion in Campbell Bunk was, I think, first and foremost a combination of economic opportunity and expanding desires affecting young girls and drawing them bodily into a more inclusive working-class and metropolitan world. This helped undermine slum culture from the inside, dissolving as it were the cement that held the street together; traditional life two decades and more before the bulldozers eventually moved in. Finally, if I may, a word on the book's reception. I wrote it very much for myself, to try to understand this most extraordinary place as best I could. For a wider audience I had in mind the intelligent general reader, even though I'd included a lot of what we might call academic baggage. But although I gave a copy to each of the main people I'd interviewed I didn't really think they'd like what I'd done. So I was surprised and delighted when old Bunkites told me they'd read it from cover to cover. One told me that it had helped him come to terms with his parents' behaviour that had troubled him all his life. And I know that some others treasured the book and felt proud that they'd had a hand in it. Even the man – not from the Bunk but well known in it and a famous local bookmaker – who told me on publication that he would sue me for every penny I had if his reputation were tarnished in any way did not need to trouble his solicitors.

There were other surprises. A reunion of Bunkites was arranged at a working men's club in Finsbury Park, and some who hadn't seen each other for years were brought together again. Two plays were made out of material in the book and staged in Finsbury Park and Nottingham. And, astonishingly, another book with the Bunk as a major theme appeared in 1986. Tom McCarthy, who had been born in Campbell Road in 1925 and left in 1986, wrote an autobiography called *Boysie*, brought out by a small publishing firm in Devon.[20] Mr McCarthy had lived in Newcastle and he and I knew nothing of each other. Our approach was very different and it was fascinating to see how this microscope part of

---

20   MCCARTHY, 1986.

London could sustain two entirely contrasted narratives. If I remember right, episodes from Mr McCarthy's life found their way into the plays, too.

Nearly thirty years on, it would not be possible any longer to recover through oral history this sort of dense study of neighbourhood life in the 1920s and 1930s. Memories die out so quickly. It is one of the enduring satisfactions of a book like this that it creates its own archive of tapes and transcripts, for others to listen to and use. And that these recollections were captured *before* memories of life in Campbell Bunk, a representative rough London slum of the first half of the twentieth century, had died out forever.

Literature

MCCARTHY, TOM, Boysie, Braunton (Devon) 1986.

WHITE, JERRY, Campbell Bunk, a Lumpen Community in London between the Wars, in: History Workshop Journal 8 (1979), p. 1-49.

ID., Rothschild Buildings. Life in an East End tenement block, 1887-1920, London, Boston 1980.

ID., Campbell Bunk. The worst street in North London between the wars, London 2003.

Creating the City of Delhi
Stories of Strong Women and Weak Walls

SONJA WENGOBORSKI/JASPAL NAVEEL SINGH

1. Introduction

Situated in the Gangetic plain of northern India, Delhi has been of major economic, military and cultural importance since at least three millennia. In popular portrayal Delhi's history is conceived of as a successive layering of seven, or more, cities. In India's great epic, the Mahābhārata, we find reference to the possible first city, Indraprastha, the mythical capital of the Pāṇḍhavaḥ kingdom, popularly believed to be situated between India Gate and New Delhi Zoo. Painted Grey Ware pottery was excavated between 1954 and 1971 at this site, suggesting the existence of human settlements at around 1000 BCE; yet the factual existence of Indraprastha remains debatable.[1] It becomes apparent from the Mahābhārata description that the city was imagined to have witnessed in-migration from different social milieus – this is not rendered as being necessarily a problematic or chaotic thing:

> "When the city was built, there came, O king, numerous Brahmanas well-acquainted with all the *Vedas* and conversant with every language, wishing to dwell there. And there came also unto that town numerous merchants from every direction, in the hope of earning wealth. There also came numerous persons well-skilled in all the arts, wishing to take up their abode there."[2]

Although this passage suggests a clearly defined social hierarchy or classification, the diversity of social milieus is presented as a vital, or at least a normal,

---

1 Cf. SINGH, 2009, p. 19.
2 GANGULI, 1970, Mahābhārata Book I, Section CCIX, ital. i.o.

feature of a functional city. Similarly, Danu Roy, in his stimulating essay *City makers and city breakers*, makes the somewhat obvious, but oft-forgotten, observation that cities and built environments are always the collective oeuvre of diverse social groups:

> "The visible structure of the city is always imposed upon its social foundations. For instance, when even a casual visitor looks up at the imposing walls of the forts built by the Tughlaqs and the Mughals, it could occur to him that these walls could not have been 'built' by the kings. There must have been masons and stonecutters, water carriers and sand loaders, mixers and helpers, woodcutters and carpenters, ironsmithsand potters, labouring men and women and donkeys by the thousands who did the actual work. So where, in the pages of history, did they all disappear?"[3]

Roy's observation surely alleviates a one-dimensional perception of Delhi's history as a subsequent accomplishment of great kings, emperors, city planners and politicians and calls to put the actual workers, the city makers, into the focus.

However, the near absence of these city makers in historical sources and the overrepresentation of the 'grand' figures like rulers and famous architects leaves us with the difficult task to reconstruct from available sources the astonishing life-stories of the more 'mundane' individuals of history. The status of sources has surely improved in modern times, but still the overwhelming majority of scholarly work (except for perhaps literary studies and ethnographies) makes use of official documents, colonial sources and documented historical caesuras (like wars, or political decisions) and other accounts of those who are and have been powerful. In the first part of this article, exactly such an approach will be presented: we are drawing on official documents of city planning and academic/journalistic writings about the city's management of urban poverty. In the second part, this viewpoint will then be contrasted with insights of modern Hindi literature, which will foreground the lived experiences of the individual social actors in the financially poorer milieus of Delhi.

2. Pre-independence Delhi and the creation of 'slums'

Over the three millennia after Indraprastha, several cities were constructed in the area of contemporary Delhi, first several bastions of indigenous kings, later

---

3   ROY, 2010, p. 144.

fortified cities of Muslim rulers, who were invading the region from central Asia. The most recent of those fortified Muslim cities is Shāhjahānābād, which was founded by the Moghul emperor Shāh Jahān in 1648. After Moghul power began to wane in the late 18th century, the British took possession of the walled city of Shāhjahānābād in 1803, and the control of the Moghul emperors was confined to the palace, the so-called Red Fort.

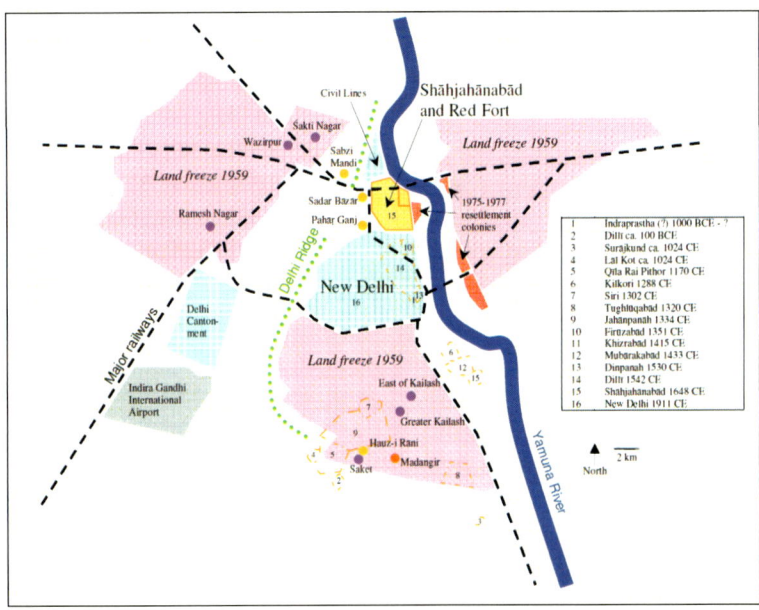

Figure 1: Schematic map of Delhi (adapted from descriptions/map in KACKER, *2005, p. 70, and map in* CHADHA, *2005, p. 94).*

The Indian Mutiny of 1857, an unsuccessful but yet traumatic military upheaval against British rule (the Raj), was a consequential event for Shāhjahānābād. Batra and Mehra regard the Mutiny as something like the founding myth of slums in Delhi. During the skirmishes, the British increasingly regarded the city's small lanes and narrow back alleys, the *mohullas*, as dangerous, unruly and potentially threatening. After the Mutiny, these experienced anxieties were ideologically linked to notions of dirt:[4]

---

4   HOSAGRAHAR, 2005, p. 87, notes: "The events of 1857 had seriously influenced colonial perceptions of disease, dirt, and disloyalty. During the period immediately

"'Native' culture was now admonished for its inferiority, its propensity for dirt, filth, dampness and congestion, and an effort was made to introduce contemporary European ideas of city order and planning to ameliorate the poor condition of the city and its inhabitants."[5]

The British began to demolish almost one third[6] of the seemingly impenetrable housing structures to ensure better surveillance and control (see also Ghalib's accounts in section 4.1). Attempts were even made to raze the entire city of Shāhjahānābād to the ground, but luckily not enough explosive was accessible at the time.[7] Instead, the British removed themselves from the native population and created their own quarter, Civil Lines, north of the walled city of Shāhjahānābād. After the massive clearances following the Mutiny, the area outside the western city walls became increasingly urbanized (Sabzī Mandī, Sadār Bāzār and Pahāṛ Ganj). This created a major concern for colonial city planners in the second half of the 19th century, who endeavoured to plan the western extension in an orderly way.[8]

In 1911, at the height of their imperial power in India, the British decided to transfer the capital of their Indian Empire from Kolkata (spelled 'Calcutta' at the time) to Delhi. A vast area south of Shāhjahānābād was selected to build the imperial city New Delhi, which was completed in 1931. The imperial vision of the British architects Sir Edward Lutyens and Sir Herbert Baker created an imposing assemblage of octagonal axes and broad avenues, inspired by Versailles and Washington, D.C., and monumental buildings in the architectural traditions of classicism and historicism, while maintaining an 'oriental' flavour by incorporating decorative ornaments of Mughal and Hindu architecture; this stylistic pluralism was meant to symbolize British superiority and rationality, and staged New Delhi as the apex of Indian civilization, and perhaps of civilization in general.

New Delhi starkly differs in appearance from Shāhjahānābād, or Old Delhi, as it is now often called. What is more, in spite of its allusions to rationality and orderliness, the creation of New Delhi was itself a cause for further congestion and 'slummifying' of other – now neglected and further enclosed – parts of the

---

following the rebellion, the inhabitants' houses, streets, and ways of living appeared to be even more unclean and diseased than before it."

5   BATRA/MEHRA, 2008, p. 393.
6   Cf. HOSAGRAHAR, 2005, p. 85.
7   Cf. ROY, 2010, p. 145.
8   Cf. HOSAGRAHAR, 2005, p. 115-142.

city. Hosagrahar comments: "In less than a century after they had taken over, colonial officials declared Delhi, the home of Emperors and princes, the mystical and exotic city of the Orient, an uncivilized 'slum.'"[9] In 1936, the entire walled city of Old Delhi was catalogued as 'slum' in the city's planning codes[10] and in more recent documents of city planning, Old Delhi and its adjoining neighbourhoods to the west were dubbed 'Special Area'.[11]

3. A historical outline of city planning of post-independence Delhi

The colonial dichotomies of order – disorder, (western) rationality – (oriental) irregularity and slum – non-slum were taken up in the independent Indian Republic. Chandigarh, the newly created joint capital of the Indian states of Panjāb and Haryāṇa, is one drastic example: a hyper-order of square blocks and straight axes, create functionally separated sectors (e.g. a sector for shopping, a sector for restaurants, residence sectors etc.). However, the architectural mastermind behind Chandigarh was not an Indian, but the Swiss-French modernist Le Corbusier. Likewise, the heads behind Delhi's first master plan (MPD-62) were the American architect and city planner Albert Mayer and a committee of members of the Ford Foundation. These international inputs helped India to overcome colonial associations of a nostalgic 'Orient', while simultaneously maintaining the colonial legacy of rationality.

The post-independence strategies of city planning in Delhi can be roughly structured into three phases: the 1950s and 1960s saw modernist and socialist attempts of centralized city planning and expansion. In the 1970s and 1980s, more pragmatic and rigorous endeavours of coping with the challenges of informal settlements and urban poverty came to the fore. From the 1990s onwards, a globalized alignment of India integrated the corporate and capitalist world-system into city planning. Thus we observe a paradigm shift from what could be described as 'rationalist' to 'cleaning-up' to 'neo-liberalist'. The three phases/mindsets are not necessarily in harmony with each other, and we can actually observe how the 'rationalist' phase of the 1950/60s was in effect overturned by the 'cleaning-up' phase of the 1970/80s, which in turn was rearranged to a degree by the more recent 'neo-liberalist' phase. This development parallels

---

9   IBID., p. 149.
10 Cf. BATRA/MEHRA, 2008, p. 393.
11 Cf. DMP-2001, p. 4; DMP-2021, p. 45.

India's political, economic and societal transition from a socialist to a capitalist system, epitomized in the liberalization of the markets in the early 1990s. It becomes apparent, however, that processes of Delhi's city planning of the pre-1990 era foreshadowed India's capitalist alignment. It is exactly this overlapping and intertwining of the three phases/mindsets that carries a potential for ideological justifications, for example by drawing on historical traditions of city planning on the one hand and by projecting futuristic visions of a 'world-class city' on the other.

3.1 A city for everybody:
The rationalist mindset of the Nehruvian era

When New Delhi became the national capital of the Republic of India in 1947, the city witnessed an unprecedented rate of in-migration. With a decennial population growth rate of 90 percent, Delhi's urban population mushroomed from under 700,000 in 1941 to 1.4 million in 1951,[12] almost doubling the density of persons per square kilometre from 613 to 1174 persons.[13] It can be assumed that most migrants were refugees from north-west India, escaping the civil wars during the India-Pakistan Partition in 1947/48.[14] In addition, the bureaucratic and administrative apparatus, foreign missions and other institutions attracted many civil servants, administrators, functionaries and other professionals. Finally, after Lahore had been included into Pakistan, the trade and wholesale business of northern India concentrated on Delhi, and specifically on the already congested Shāhjahānābād/Old Delhi.

In the 1950s two governmental agencies, the Ministry of Rehabilitation and the Delhi Improvement Trust, were created to restore order and provide adequate housing for the emergent metropolis. Together with numerous private land colonizing companies, the government acquired vast areas in the west, the east and in the south of the city and created housing colonies and, moreover, transformed areas inhabited by 'tribal communities' into middle-class neighbourhoods. Despite these efforts, housing for all Delhiites remained unattainable. Large portions of the city's population lived in unserviced illegal squatter settlements with no prospect of betterment. What is more, in 1955, an outbreak of jaundice, due

---

12 Cf. GAZETTEER, 1976, p. 120. These figures represent the urban population of the Delhi territory. The rural population of the time was ca. 220,000 in 1941 and ca. 306,000 in 1951. Cf. Figure 2 for an overview.
13 Cf. IBID., p. 125. Again, these figures represent Delhi's urban population.
14 Cf. also in the following KACKER, 2005, p. 69.

to inadequate sanitation measures in some of the new colonies, killed approximately 700 people, mainly in the affluent areas of New Delhi and Civil Lines.[15] The government was forced to react, and in 1957 the newly created Delhi Development Authority (DDA) set out to device a Master Plan for Delhi which came to be known as the MPD-62.

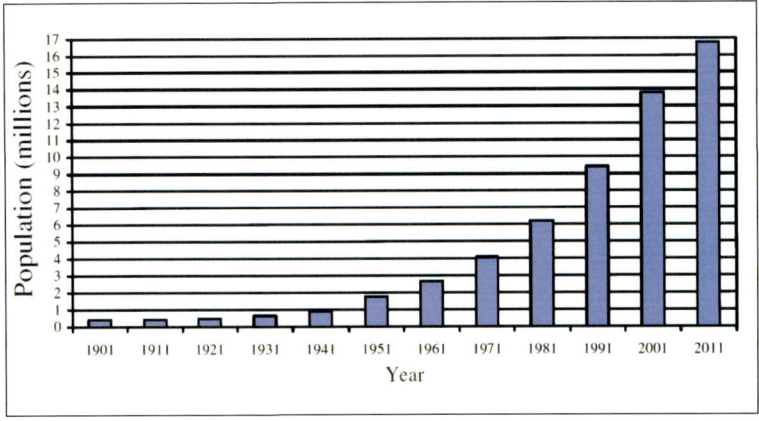

Figure 2: Population of Delhi from 1901 to 2011. Figures are for total population of the National Capital Territory, i.e. Delhi's rural and urban population (adapted from GOVERNMENT OF INDIA, Census of India 2011).

The MPD-62 predicted that the city's population would increase to over five million by 1981.[16] The plan estimated approximately 50,000 "dwelling units in bustis[17] scattered all over the city"[18] and suggested to relocate these squatters to "various parts of the urban area so that they are integrated into the neighborhood community"[19] which, however, should not be "too far away from major work centres".[20] These plans seemed to acknowledge the vital function of squatters

---

15 Cf. ROY, 2010, p. 149
16 Cf. MASTER PLANS FOR DELHI. MPD-62, p. i.
17 A *bustī* or *bastī* is a north Indian term for 'informal settlement.' Other words that are used in the MASTER PLANS FOR DELHI. MPD-62, are *'jugghie jhonpari'* or *'JJ Cluster'* and 'slum.'
18 MASTER PLANS FOR DELHI. MPD-62, p. 5.
19 IBID., p. ii.
20 IBID., p. 27.

and low-income groups, who constitute the majority of workforce in small-scale industries, domestic labour and other low-wage duties.

Such plans were nurtured – on a more ideational level – by the newly established government under Jawaharlal Nehru, which envisaged a 'city for everybody' and announced to subsidise housing for low-income groups.[21] The idea seemed persuasive: to eliminate private speculation and rising land prices, in 1959 the government froze on all vacant or undeveloped land around the city limits, making the land available on reasonable prices at any given time; the DDA would then develop this land and sell or rent 50 percent of the housing plots on the free market, acquiring revenue, which would then be used both to purchase new land and to subsidise the remaining 50 percent of plots for low-income groups.[22]

3.2 Time for some action: The politics of eviction

After Nehru's death in 1964, however, it became apparent that his vision was unattainable: only eleven percent of the plots had reached lower-income groups, while most plots were openly auctioned with the aim to maximize profits: "Land was released in a staggered manner, and plots in developed areas were deliberately withheld, to push prices up."[23] By the 1970s it became clear that the size of the city's population would significantly surpass the DDA's predictions and that attempts to provide housing for low-income groups and labouring squatters had drastically failed. In a "frenetic burst of activity, the administrative machinery swung into action"[24] and between 1975 and 1977 around one million squatters were forcibly relocated from the city centres to the low-lying flood plains on the eastern bank of the Yamuna River. Each family was entitled to a 25-square-yard plot with common water, electricity and sanitation services. The vacated spaces in the city were used for building an infrastructure required for the Asian Games, which Delhi was to host in 1982.

Paradoxically, to construct all the necessary roads, flyovers, hotels, offices, apartments and stadiums, around one million migrant workers immigrated to the city during 1979 and 1982, squatting on the construction sites or nearby,[25] and making up, as it were, for the one million squatters who had been relocated

---

21 Cf. KACKER, 2005, p. 73.
22 Cf. IBID., p. 74.
23 IBID.
24 Also in the following ROY, 2010, p. 151.
25 Cf. BATRA/MEHRA, 2008, p. 398.

a few years earlier. Moreover, most of these workers stayed in the city after the games, inflating the population of Delhi to over six million in 1981.

The radical resettlement politics of the 1970s were in fact rather attempts to demolish informal settlements than to relocate them in an ordered or rational manner as the MPD-62 proposed. Batra and Mehra (2008) call this the 'Emergency Period'[26] and the authors provide some insights of how the processes of slum demolitions work in practice:[27] first, a notice is given to the local *pradhāns*, the spokespersons or 'strong men' of an informal settlement. These then might or might not pass on this information to the local residents. Several practices are employed that divide the residents along various lines. For instance, a certain cut-off date is usually announced, which is perhaps set 15 or 20 years prior to the eviction. The residents who stayed in the settlement before this cut-off date are either exempt from demolition or can claim for reparation or a plot in the resettlement area. Such residents are sometimes in support of demolition, either covertly or overtly, in hope of acquiring more plots or gaining financial benefits. Others, often under assistance of non-governmental organizations, launch legal cases and instigate public protests in order to prevent or delay the arrival of the demolition squads. This short glimpse into the potential communal conflicts resulting from the politics of eviction shows that we cannot conceive of dwellers of informal settlements as monolithic groups, but rather we deal with actors who have different beliefs about and interests in the settlement which are created *inter alia* by individual biographies and differing socio-economic statuses. In Section 4 of this chapter we will provide a discussion of some accounts of such local and personal life-stories of residents in informal settlements in modern Indian literature. First, however, we would like to outline the more recent developments of the politics of city planning in Delhi.

3.3 Visions of a world-class city: The neo-liberalist strategy of city planning

A second Master Plan was drafted in 1985, and notified in 1990, this plan came to be known as the DMP-2001. In 1988, a cholera outbreak, again due to inadequate sanitation measures contaminating the groundwater, killed ca. 1500 people, but unlike in the jaundice epidemic of 1955, the 1988 victims were all from the 1975-77 resettlement areas across the Yamuna River and from other

---

26 IBID., p. 397.
27 Cf. IBID. p. 407, also in the following.

illegal squatter settlements.[28] And unlike 1955, the cholera disaster of 1988 did not prompt the DDA to react. Instead the DDA concentrated on constructing spaces that were to become visible emblems of India's modernity and that catered predominantly for the emerging middle classes.[29]

Sunil Kumar provides us with an example. His ethnography in the South Delhi medieval village Hauz-i Rāni describes how the village was suddenly surrounded by the middle-class housing colonies Saket and Puṣp Vihār. The village, which was first mentioned in Persian documents in 1246, is inhabited predominantly by a traditional Muslim population, who used the *hauz* (a large water reservoir), after it has been silted in the 19th century, as a graveyard for their community.[30] When the Delhi authorities acquired the land surrounding Hauz-i Rāni and the DDA started constructing the housing colony Saket in the mid-1970s, half of the area of the *hauz* was turned into a sports complex. At first, this sports complex was nothing more than three large fields without any barriers, thus the area was accessible for both Hauz-i Rāni villagers and Saket residents. Kumar observed how children from Saket played football against their Hauz-i Rāni peers and he notes that the "very absence of a structured sports regime allowed for an unregulated fraternising between the residents of the two neighbourhoods."[31] In 1990, however, the DDA constructed the 'Saket Sports Complex', with facilities for more up-scale sports like badminton, squash, tennis and aerobics, and upon Kumar's inquiry the DDA engineers were forthright in saying that the facilities were oriented towards the middle-class neighbourhood of Saket. Furthermore, the Muslim graveyard was seen as a disturbing, unclean 'problem' which the Hindu engineers of the DDA found repulsive. The Hauz-i Rāni villagers perceived this exclusion and denial of access as accentuating the distance and mistrust between the communities. In turn they began to build buffalo and goat pens on their half of the *hauz*, to emphasize their stake and they barricaded all paths to their area with thorn and bistle bushes; they also put up placards that underlined the historicity of the village and the graveyard and constructed the inhabitants as *Sayyads* (descendents of the Prophet Mohammed), again emphasizing their right to occupy the space.

This example shows how city development can produce communal conflict and alienation. In the post-1990 era, India's rural and poorer population has been drastically othered and made redundant in the country's scramble for mo-

---

28 Cf. ROY, 2010, p. 153.
29 Cf. KACKER, 2005, p. 76f.
30 Cf. also in the following KUMAR, 1999, p. 160-169.
31 IBID., p. 168.

dernity. A globalized and capitalist vision has created – and still creates – spaces for consumption, business, service, 'high'-culture and recreation, which can be showcased to national and international visitors and construct the nation's capital as an epitome of the new India. In 2004, for instance, the Yamuna resettlement area mentioned above has been 'cleared' in order to 'develop' the area.[32] Some of the large-scale restructurings completed until now are: the Delhi Metro Rail Corporation headquarters, the colossal Akṣardhām Temple, the Yamuna bio-diversity park and the games village for athletes and officials who were participating in the 2010 Commonwealth Games, for which the city, mirroring the developments before the 1982 Asian Games, delved into a massive urban renewal programme.[33]

Although the liberalization of the Indian markets in the early 1990s has allowed for wide-ranging investments of the (multinational) private sector, the vision of a world-class city is not only a market-driven process, it is also pressed forward by both grassroots organizations and state institutions. Under the banner of democratic rights, environmentalism, urban development and beautification, middle-class lobbying associations increasingly petition for urban renewal, all too often with drastic consequences for inhabitants of informal settlements. These petitioners take advantage of new procedures introduced to legal redressal in India. In the so-called 'Public Interest Litigations' basically anyone, from powerful trade or industrial interest groups to residents' associations to 'concerned' individual citizens, can use the legal apparatus to put forward claims about urban 'problems'. The Public Interest Litigation is not a regular legal case, in which two parties have equal voice; rather it is a proactive investigation, in which courts constitute committees of specialists to present evidence which, however, is never assessed in cross-examination.[34] This process "brings together city officials, court commissions and amicus curiae on a democratically non-accountable platform to administratively and logistically work out solutions to the urban 'problems'".[35] The voices of the affected parties, those who will lose their dwellings, their belongings and their right to centrality, are lost in the legal apparatus.

Although the Public Interest Litigations clearly mark a paradigm shift in the practices of Indian state institutions, the courts surprisingly use the MPD-62 as

---

32 Cf. MASTER PLANS FOR DELHI. MPD-2021, p. 118.
33 Cf. BATRA/MEHRA, 2008, p. 404f.
34 Cf. IBID., p. 403, refer to Vandenhole, 2000.
35 IBID., also in the following.

an "imaginary reference"[36] and ordered to demolish all 'illegal' housing structures and 'polluting' small industries. Sundaram comments:

> "Egged on by sympathetic media and advocacy groups, courts appointed special committees spread over every aspect of civic life, causing terror and fear in the neighborhoods they visited. A phantom civic subject emerged in this very public legal discourse, identifiable middle-class, post-political, and projected as the injured legatee of the urban body."[37]

The latest of the Master Plans (DMP-2021) accentuates this post-political, and consumption-oriented activism of the model middle-class citizens. To upgrade the physical structure of Delhi, the plan proposes 'user pays' facilities and public-private partnership models for managing investments and calls for more community participation and decentralization.[38] The effects of the latest Master Plan are still unclear. With the globalized, post-political ideologies that are emerging currently, any centralized master planning appears superfluous. The state can do hardly more than provide the best possible legal and economic options for citizens and organizations to plan and construct 'their own' cities, according to their aspirations and needs. As it appears until now, the emphasis has been put on middle-class life modes and the multinational cooperate world; the general model, in theory, would however allow for *any* group to participate in the processes of city planning. It is possibly the cultural differences between the underprivileged and the powerful that are incommensurable and that have excluded the underprivileged from participation. In the next part, we will illustrate some aspects of these cultures of urban poverty as they are represented in modern Hindi literature, and we thereby provide one avenue for understanding and perhaps overcoming the discrepancies of participation in the planning and construction of Indian cities like Delhi.

4. The capital in Hindi-literature

In this part of the chapter we shall first pay a visit to the observations of the destruction of parts of Delhi in the time after the Mutiny as communicated in some letters of an Urdu und Persian writing poet. The section to follow is devoted

---

36 SUNDARAM, 2010, p. 247.
37 IBID., p. 248.
38 Cf. DMP-2021, p. 181.

to novels and short stories dealing with the life of the inhabitants of informal settlements.

4.1 Delhi after the Mutiny

The famous poet Ghalib (1797-1869) who spent many years of his life in Delhi, comments in his letters on the proceeding destruction of Shāhjahānābād after the Mutiny:

> "Agha Baqir's Imambara [...] is an ancient foundation of exalted fame. Who would not grieve at its destruction? [...] More than that, barracks for the British soldiers are to be built in the city, and in front of the Fort, where Lal Diggi is, there is to be a great area of open ground. It will take in the whole area right up to the Khas Bazaar [...]. Put it this way: from Ammu Jan's Gate to the moat of the Fort, except for Lal Diggi and one or two wells, no trace of any building will remain. Today they have begun demolishing the houses of Jan Nisar Khan Chatta."[39]

Six months later he notes:

> "All the buildings in Fil-Khana, and Falak Paira and around Lal Diggi have been pulled down. The fate of Bulaqi Begam's Lane is still undecided. The military is for pulling it down, but the civil authorities want to preserve it."[40]

One year later he draws a picture of utter desolateness:

> "[...] in all the wells in Lal Diggi the water has suddenly turned brackish. [...] I tell you without exaggeration that from the Jama Masjid to the Rajghat Gate is a barren wilderness, and if the bricks piled here and there were taken away it would be absolutely bare. [...] Now they have cleared a path for the railway from the Calcutta Gate to the Kabuli Gate. Panjabi Katra, Dhobi Wara, Ramji Ganj, Saadat Khan's Katra, Jarnail ki Bibi ki Haveli... [and other localities] – you won't find a trace of them. In short the city has become a desert, and now that the wells are gone and water is something rare and precious, it will

---

39 GHALIB, 1969, p. 213 (dated July 26, 1859). We want to thank Arnd Bruns M.A., Institute for Indology, Johannes Gutenberg University Mainz, for drawing our attention to this publication.
40 IBID. p. 225 (dated December 16, 1859).

be a desert like that of Karbala.[41] [...] Delhi is no more a city, but a camp, a cantonment. No Fort, no city, no bazaars, no watercourses [...]."[42]

4.2 Post-independence Hindi-literature and urbanization

In her study on three novels of Bhisham Sahni, Ines Fornell outlines the development of the progressive literary movement in India which is held in high esteem. It was in the 1930s that the term '*pragativād*,' lit. 'progressivism,' was coined in the context of Hindi literature. Fornell emphasizes the fact that literates such as Premcand had taken up social issues of the poor already before the emergence of this movement. The first All India Progressive Writer's Conference took place in April 1936 in Lucknow. One of its prominent participants, though never member, was Premcand. In his keynote address which was published as an essay titled *Sāhitya kā uddeśya* (The objective of literature), he explained his ideas on matters of style, theme, such as ordinary worker's and peasant's lives, and his conception of literature as criticism of life, '*jīvan kī ālocanā*.'

Mishra, in his study on modern Hindi fiction, acknowledges the influence of the prerevolutionary Russian author Anton Chekhov on the development of the Hindi short story and its authors,[43] while Knirsch observes the relevance of social and humanitarian issues in the development of the Hindi short stories after 1960 up to the end of the second millennium.[44] However, one should not forget that the majority of India's population is until today rural rather than urban,[45] a fact which is reflected in the phenomenon of regionalism in Indian literature.

The capital of Bhārat, India, happens to be situated in a Hindi-speaking region. Thus Delhi is the location of many novels and short stories written in this language. Following the phases of city planning in post-independence Delhi as outlined in the previous sections (3), the following part deals with literary works reflecting everyday lives of the city's less well-off inhabitants.

---

41 [Fn. 1]: "The place where Husain and his companions were martyred, after their access to water had been cut off."
42 IBID. p. 252 (dated January 11, 1861).
43 Cf. MISHRA, 1983, p. 2-3 and 26.
44 Cf. KNIRSCH, 2012, p. 58-99.
45 Cf. THE WORLD FACT BOOK. SOUTH ASIA. INDIA: https://www.cia.gov/library/publications/the-world-factbook/geos/in.html, 07.05.2013.

4.2.1 Heading towards the capital

Young Yashpal became a revolutionary.[46] Born in 1903 in Firozpur, Panjāb, he graduated at Lahore. After trying to assassinate a leading British official in 1929 he was arrested in 1932. It was then that he devoted himself to writing. In 1938 he was released. During his life he published more than 50 books, mainly collections of short stories, novels, and essays. Yashpal died in 1976, as the recipient of that year's Sahitya Academy Award conferred to him for his Hindi-novel *Merī Terī Uskī Bāt*.

In the short story *Devī kī līlā*, *The game of the goddess*, Yashpal introduces his readers to the life of Devīlāl, a man originating from Jālandhar (Panjāb), the region the clerks working in the Accounting Department of New Delhi's Central Secretariat usually come from. Housing prices are exorbitantly high in Delhi. Thus he gave up the idea to find a room in Pahāṛ Ganj and took a room for his wife and himself in a compound inhabited by people from his native region, situated in Śakti Nagar about six miles away from his place of employment. Having to spend 40 Rupees on monthly rent, he regrets paying another 19 Rupees on bus fares in order to get to work. Though he never envied the great *Sāhibs* driving along in their own cars, he dreams of joining the *Bābūs* (clerks) who ride home on their pushbikes. Selling her golden bangles, his wife makes her husband's dream of an own bicycle come true.

It could be interpreted as a clash of village life with city life that Devīlāl leaves his new bicycle standing at a bus stop, when unaware for a moment, chatting with a colleague and entering the bus that he used to catch until this day. After realizing a few moments later, he immediately gets down from the bus and heads back to the bus stop. Luckily he finds the cycle still there, takes it and goes to worship in the Devī's temple in order to thank the great Goddess for having spared him the loss of the valuable means of transportation, but ironically his new unlocked cycle gets stolen from the entrance.

---

46   Cf. also in the following, MEISIG, 2001, p.120-127; SAHITYA ACADEMY AWARDS. YASHPAL: http://indiapicks.com/Literature/Sahitya_Academy/Hindi/Hindi-1976.htm, 07.05.2013; THE HINDU. 07.05.2006: http://www.hindu.com/lr/2006/05/07/stories/2006050700010200.htm, 07.05.2013.

4.2.2 Accepting one's fate in silent rebellion: Basanti and Anaro

Basanti
Bhisham Sahni was born in 1915. In the times of disturbance that woke after gaining independence from the Raj, the famous Hindi author, originating from Rawalpindi (what was to become part of Pakistan in 1947), shifted with his family to India. He published his novel *Basanti* in 1980.

The story is set out between two instances of slum eviction. The protagonist is the young woman Basanti living in a *bastī*, in Delhi. Her father, the barber Chaudhri, belongs to a caste, onto which the leading Rājput members of the community look down as inferior. However, this time the imminent danger of eviction cannot be averted by a delegation of theirs. Clad into their traditional Rājasthānī clothes the men return empty handed from meeting an influential *Sāhib* who turns the group over to his deputy rather than listening to its cause himself.

In the introduction to his translation of Bhisham Sahni's *Basanti*, Jaidev elaborates:

> "[...] even their modest basti in Delhi is never secure. Any day, it can be busted by a callous state apparatus which holds out to them nothing more than bogus promises. There is no going back home (the novelist doesn't waste even a line on spurious nostalgia of the countryside), but even in Delhi displacement returns inevitably, like seasons. A basti is built, only to be pulled down by the administration, another is built, that too is going to be demolished one day [...]."[47]

Jaidev elucidates the capital's attitude towards its recently immigrated inhabitants:[48] "In its relentless urge for expansion, the city of Delhi sucks in the labour and lives of people whom it soon discards as dirt." In this case the huts of the bastī, "near Ramesh Nagar remained intact even after that colony was ready. This happened because they did not touch it but were built upon an uninhabited mound in between two forking roads."[49] Since its male inhabitants are masons and artisans, the place evolves to resemble a Rājasthānī town. The women have taken up relations with the neighbouring middle-class settlements doing house-

---

47 JAIDEV, 1997, p. xi.
48 Cf. IBID., p. x.
49 SAHNI, 1997, p. 6.

hold-scores in a communal framework which the translator refers to in a preceding note: "Hindi and Urdu words for which there are no equivalents in English have been retained as such. For example, chauka-bartan is not simply washing dishes or performing household scores, let alone handling the kitchen work."[50] Though the settlement is "far from being a slum",[51] its lack regarding legality keeps up a state of uncertainty and insecurity that rests on its inhabitants.

Again Jaidev explains that things are not as plain as one might expect them to be:

> "Within this overall frame where survival is posited as the lone virtue for the victims of an inequitable class system, the novelist introduces a variety of complex threads. For the basti is not a simple, homogenized class space. It is split from inside along caste and gender lines. What the administration and its Sahibs, with the help of law and police, do to the basti, the basti Rajputs do to those below them in the caste hierarchy, and in turn the latter do the same to their daughters and wives."[52]

Thus her father treats Basanti as a kind of commodity, marrying her off for an attractive sum to an old tailor – a marriage Basanti refuses not in open rebellion but rather she runs away from what was supposed to be her home.

Chance has it, that Basanti is saved from this marriage. Her father and the tailor had the date fixed spontaneously, yet at this very morning police and trucks arrive at the site in order to clear the basti that is meant to be torn down. Everybody grabs whatever household-goods the families are able to take along with them. Basanti's father treats his wife as if she was a pack mule and he just bothers not waking up his young son whom he carries protectively in his own arms. Meanwhile some of the unemployed inhabitants of the bastī are paid to lay hand on what used to be their own homes.

Regarding Basanti Jaidev remarks:

> "Even before she is sixteen, she has seen enough of men, families, classes. [...] It is a homage to her resilience and natural vivacity that she can take in all these blasts of wisdom without shedding her spontaneous laughter, her delicate dreams, or her zest for living."[53]

---

50   JAIDEV, 1997, p. xvii.
51   SAHNI, 1997, p. 5.
52   JAIDEV, 1997, p. xi.
53   IBID.

Anaro
Mañjul Bhāgat (Manjul Bhagat) was born in 1936 in Meerut, but brought up in Delhi where she devoted herself to writing. She died in 1998. *Anaro* is a short Hindi novel that was published in 1977 and laid the foundation for Bhagat's fame as an awarded writer. It was translated into several languages; the author herself translated it into English.

Anaro is the tough mother of a girl and a boy. Her husband, Nandlal, a mechanic, had brought her from Bareilly, Uttar Pradesh, to Delhi at the age of 14. During his wife's first pregnancy, he had started a relationship with a mistress. He either lives on Anaro's costs or runs off and vanishes for months. Anaro scratches a living out of doing household scores at several middle-class homes situated at Greater Kailash and East of Kailash.

> "Anaro was still ignorant of the mysteries of married life, when she conceived Ganji. That winter, all of them had to shift to Madangir. The Golden Bridge slum settlement was being demolished. Each hut was in shambles. They were all bundled on to a waiting truck and left standing on the bare grounds of Madangir. Nandlal was on one of his sprees. He had vanished days earlier. For a couple of days she had a covered cot, standing close to her head to shield her from the icy winds. Then she could bear it now longer. She collected torn bits of tarpaulin, straw, tin, wood and jute rags, and proceeded to build a hut. The neighbours lent a hand. Thereafter, she built and rebuilt her little hut into a stronger home, never asking her husband for help."[54]

Living in Madangir, she brings up her children alone. She managed to fix a concrete roof on her hut that does not ever leak even during the monsoon. Though illiterate, she holds a saving account. She yet ends up with almost unlimited obligations to all those households from which she borrowed money in order to meet her sense of duty of what is traditionally supposed to be taken care of by the bride's parents. Her life's aim is to see her daughter married decently and she readily even ruins her health to achieve this goal. She fulfils what should be a father's duty, making her husband return from Mumbai only for the sake of formality. She devotes herself to this task, striving to fulfil what she considers to be done to keep up pride and honour, ever willing to stick to caste rules. In doing so she transcends the framework of the role model of a traditional wife without ever reflecting on this point. At the end of the novel Nandlal acknowledges his

---

54 BHAGAT, 2001, p. 55.

wife's capabilities by assigning her an imaginary place of honour traditionally reserved to males:

> "Listen! Listen to me, all of you gathered here. This day, I honour my wife, declaring my deep-felt admiration for her. She is indeed not my wife... but my elder brother. I am proud that she has so enhanced my prestige in the community."[55]

4.2.3 In times of disillusionment: Pollution

The author Gaurinath was born in 1972, holds an M.A. degree in Hindi and worked for several years as an Assistant Editor for the monthly magazine Haṁs in which the short story *Pradūṣaṇ* was published in 1998.[56] Its protagonist is Manoramā, a young woman born in a village and brought to Delhi by her husband Vinay.

The story begins with memories of her first encounter with Delhi. For a start the young couple lived in a small room in Wazirpur. Reaching there the place gave her an impression as if entering a mound of dirt and garbage, the acidic air had caused her cuffing. As for that first home Manoramā remembers a horrible mixture of dust, dirt, saliva and slime with acid as soon as she set her foot in front of the door of their room, the stinking drainage and the factory noise added to the nuisance caused by a complete lack of facilities such like a toilet, a decent space for having a bath or washing clothes. Feeling ashamed to defecate openly in public, her husband had to accompany her in the darkness of early mornings or after the setting of the sun, to do so at the faeces besmeared banks of a nearby drain ditch. Adding to these difficulties Vinay worked far away from Wazirpur at a shop behind Old Delhi Railway Station near Chandni Chowk. In the following month they had shifted to Sīlampur where living conditions were perceptibly better and both of them could make use of the nearby public toilets. But in spite of the improvement of the outward living conditions, the mother of a now four-year-old daughter experiences another kind of pollution: Santosh, a far off relative of her husband's, tries to court her during the head of the household's absence. The main part of the short story deals with these temptations that Manoramā somehow manages to resist. Thereby she also resists the social

---

55 IBID., p. 62.
56 GAURĪNĀTH (GAURI NATH), p. 42: http://in.linkedin.com/pub/gouri-nath/33/a82/72b, 07.05.2013.

'pollution' of urban poverty. The social organization of the urban settlement is far removed from what the inhabitants were used to from their villages.

5. Conclusion

In this contribution we have first outlined a post-colonial history of Delhi's official management of urban poverty. We have identified three major trends in this management: an idealistic approach of the 1950s and 1960s, a hasty interventional phase of the 1970s and 1980s, and finally the contemporary neo-liberalist strategy. These phases represent India's grapple with coming to terms with both its colonial past and its place in a globalized modernity, in which Delhi certainly takes a principal position. Urban poverty is somewhat orthogonal to these developments and the double standards that emerge from dealing with it are manifestations of Delhi's paradoxical disposition. The literary accounts that we have presented show how individuals themselves deal with this situation; for instance when Anaro tries to reconcile her sense of duty with her disintegrating family structures, or when Manoramā for time being effectively resists Santosh's courtship and thereby saves her family from splitting up. The role of strong women in these literary accounts is perhaps no coincidence. It appears as such Anaros, Basantis and Manoramās, are an integral element in keeping families and communities functioning; although their incredible efforts and their careful manoeuvres remain largely veiled behind the grand designs of official city planners, politicians and other 'strong men.' We hope our contribution alleviates such misrepresentations to a degree.

Acknowledgements: We would like to thank Professor Dr. Konrad Meisig, Dr. Hans-Christian Petersen, Arnd Bruns M.A. and Mustafa Hameed M.A. for valuable comments on earlier drafts of this article. All remaining shortcomings are of course our own.

Literature

BHAGAT, MAÑJUL (MANJUL BHAGAT), Anāro. 2nd ed. Dillī 1978.
ID., Anaro and Other Stories. Transl. from the Hindi by MANJUL BHAGAT, New Delhi 2001.
BATRA, LALIT/MEHRA, DIYA, Slum Demolition and Production of Neo-liberal Space. Delhi, in: Inside the Transforming Urban Asia. Processes, policies

and public actions, ed. by DARSHINI MAHADEVIA, New Delhi 2008, p. 391-414.

CHADHA, S. M., Mapping Delhi, in: The idea of Delhi, ed. by ROMI KHOSLA, Mumbai 2005, p. 94-108.

FORNELL, INES, Der Hindi-Romançier Bhīṣm Sāhnī. Eine Analyse seiner realistischen Methode am Beispiel der Werke Kaṛiyā˜, Tamas und Basantī, Marburg 1997.

GAURĪNĀTH (GAURI NATH), Pradūṣaṇ [Pollution], in: Haṁs, September (1998), p. 41-46: http://in.linkedin.com/pub/gouri-nath/33/a82/72b, 07.05.2013.

[GHALIB, MIRZA ASADULLAH KHAN], GHALIB, 1797-1869; transl. [from the Urdu and Persian] and ed. by RALPH RUSSELL/KHURSHIDUL ISLAM, vol. 1: Life and letters (UNESCO collection of representative works: Indian series), London 1969.

GANGULI, KISARI MOHAN, The Mahabharata of Krishna-Dwaipayana Vyasa, vol. I Adi Parva, New Delhi 1970.

GAZETTEER UNIT, Delhi Administration, Gazetteer of India: Delhi, ed. by PRABA CHOPRA, New Delhi 1976.

HOSAGRAHAR, JYOTI, Indigenous Modernities. Negotiating architecture and urbanism, London 2005.

JAIDEV, Introduction, in: SĀHNĪ, BHĪṢMA (BHISHAM SAHNI), Basanti, transl. by JAIDEV, Shimla 1997, p. ix-xvi.

ID., Tranlator's Note, in: SĀHNĪ, BHĪṢMA (BHISHAM SAHNI), Basanti, transl. by JAIDEV, Shimla 1997, p. xvii-xix.

KACKER, SUNEETHA DASAPPA, The DDA and the Idea of Delhi, in: The Idea of Delhi, ed. by ROMI KHOSLA, Mumbai 2005, p. 68-77.

KNIRSCH, VOLKER, Trends und Tendenzen in der Hindi-Kurzgeschichte am Beispiel der Literaturzeitschrift Hams, Wiesbaden 2012.

KUMAR, SUNIL, Perceiving 'your' land. Neighbourhood settlements and the Hauz-i Rani, in: The Archaeology and Anthropology of Landscape. Shaping your landscape, ed. by PETER J. UCKO/ROBERT LAYTON, London 1999, p. 159-174.

MISRA, RĀMA DARASA, Modern Hindi Fiction, Delhi 1983.

MEISIG, KONRAD, Nachwort, in: YAŚPĀL (YASHPAL): Phūlos Hemdchen: Erzählungen von Yashpal, ed. by KONRAD MEISIG, transl. from the Hindi by HANNELORE BAUHAUS-LÖTZKE et al., Wiesbaden 2001, p.120-127.

ROY, DANU, City Breakers and City Makers, in: Celebrating Delhi, ed. by MALA DAYAL, New Delhi 2010, p. 143-161.

SĀHNĪ, BHĪṢMA (BHISHAM SAHNI), Basantī, Nayī Dillī 1982[1980].

ID., Basanti, transl. by JAIDEV, Shimla 1997.

SINGH, UPINDER, A History of Ancient and Medieval India. From the stone Age to the 12th century, Delhi 2009.

SUNDARAM, RAVI, Imagining Urban Breakdown. Delhi in the 1990s, in: Noir Urbanism. Dystopic images of the modern city, ed. by GYAN PRAKASH, Princeton 2010, p. 241-260.

YAŚPĀL (YASHPAL), Devī kī līlā, in: O Bhairavī (kahānī saṃgrah [collection of short stories]), ed. by YAŚPĀL (YASHPAL) (Viplav pustakmālā 34), Lakhnaū (Lucknow) 1958, p. 48-55.

GOVERNMENT OF INDIA, Census of India 2011, Provisional Population Totals: NCT of Delhi, Series 8, Delhi 2008: http://www.censusindia.gov.in/2011-prov-results/prov_data_products_delhi.html, 07.05.2013

THE HINDU. 07.05.2006: http://www.hindu.com/lr/2006/05/07/stories/2006050700010200.htm, 07.05.2013.

MASTER PLANS FOR DELHI:

MPD-62 (1957):
http://rgplan.org/delhi/MASTER-PLAN-FOR-DELHI_1962.pdf, 07.05.2013.

DMP-2001 (1990):
http://www.rgplan.org/delhi/MASTER-PLAN-FOR-DELHI_2.pdf, 07.05.2013.

DMP-2021 (2007):
http://www.rgplan.org/delhi/MASTER%20PLAN%20FOR%20DELHI%202021.pdf, 07.05.2013.

SAHITYA ACADEMY AWARDS. YASHPAL: http://indiapicks.com/Literature/Sahitya_Academy/Hindi/Hindi-1976.htm, 07.05.2013.

THE WORLD FACT BOOK. SOUTH ASIA. INDIA: https://www.cia.gov/library/publications/the-world-factbook/geos/in.html, 07.05.2013.

Urban Meeting Locations of Nicaraguan Migrants in Costa Rica's Metropolitan Area and the Spatial Effects on their Social Support Networks

Hauke Jan Rolf

1. Introduction

After a brief review of the theoretical framework, key historical and current migration processes of Nicaraguans to Costa Rica are presented. Furthermore, the general urban development of Latin American cities and more specifically of the metropolitan region of Costa Rica's Central Valley are discussed to respond to the spatial distribution or rather concentration of Nicaraguan migrants within this urban area. Subsequently, three exemplary places of the case study are described and compared to illustrate the specific relationship between locations and the local and transnational support networks of Nicaraguan migrants in the urban area. The article finishes with some conclusions about the presented places and the reciprocal impacts between these locations and the local and transnational support networks.

2. Theoretical framework of the case study

The migration from Nicaragua to Costa Rica has a long historical tradition and has always been transnational even though the term *transnationalism* had not been used in social sciences until the appearance of the so-called globalization, that is the increasing social, political, and above all economic interconnection and interdependence of the world, induced by technological innovations of new transport and communication media.[1] Instead of unidirectional movement of people with a gradual process of an inevitably long-term settlement and socio-cultural assimilation, the Nicaraguan migration to the neighbouring country in the south has always been characterised as durable, circular, pendular or rather multidirectional movements. This resulted in bi-national economic, cultural and familiar interrelations, plural socio-cultural identification and, last but not least, political tensions between the two involved nations and societies.[2] These processes correspond with the features of *transmigration* defined by Linda Basch, Nina Glick Schiller and Cristina Blanc-Szanton:

> "We define 'transnationalism' as the processes by which immigrants forge and sustain multi-stranded social relations that link together their societies of origin and settlement. [...] Immigrants who develop and maintain multiple relationships – familial, economic, social, organizational, religious, and political – that span borders we call 'transmigrants'. [...] Transmigrants take actions, make decisions, and develop subjectivities and identities embedded in networks of relationships that connect them simultaneously to two or more nation-states."[3]

Particularly over the last twenty years, the migration of Nicaraguans to Costa Rica has been highly politicised in Costa Rican immigration policy debates. It is not only due to a rapidly increasing inflow of migrants since the beginning of the 1990s and its transnational character as "[...] the ongoing interconnection or flow of people, ideas, objects, and capital across the borders of nation-states, in contexts in which the state shapes but does not contain such linkages and movements [...]"[4]. But the increase in attention to the Nicaraguan immigration (and related problematisation) is also because of its new directions. While historically the migration from Nicaragua has always been characterised by movements within the frontier region and towards the rural areas, urban immigration dynamics of Nicaraguans to Costa Rica' s metropolitan Central Valley are still a new phenomenon.

---

1   Cf. CASTELLS, 1996; BECK, 1997; URRY, 2001; SASSEN, 2002; DÜRRSCHMIDT, 2002.
2   Cf. MORALES GAMBOA/CASTRO VALVERDE, 2006; SANDÓVAL GARCÍA, 2003; JIMÉNEZ MATARRITA, 2009.
3   BASCH et al., 1994, p. 7-8. Cf. also PRIES, 2010; FAIST, 2000; LEVITT et al., 2003; PORTES et al., 1999.
4   GLICK SCHILLER/LEVITT, 2006, p. 5.

Looking at the urban migration movements of Nicaraguans to Costa Rica, it is fruitful to explore the specific structure and functions of the local and transnational networks that they have created within and beyond the metropolitan area. In this context, a focus on migrant networks is useful to explain not only the dynamics of the so-called *chain migration* (that is the effect of following migration processes as a result of pioneering emigration paths) but also to explore the migrants' social resources. On one hand, due to the precarious living conditions of the majority of Nicaraguans in Costa Rica's urban area, they have established reciprocal social support networks that help them cope with the everyday struggle for socioeconomic and spatial resources on a local level. On the other hand, they stretch their social ties to kin, friends and other affiliated actors in their country of origin on a transnational level. In a multidirectional perspective, these transnational ties serve as much to broaden the potentials of the migrants' social resources as to fulfil social obligations towards their descendants and other relatives, close friends and sometimes informal creditors, who stayed behind in Nicaragua.

The approach of social support, for its part, is an activity-oriented focus on social networks that highlights not only the structural relationships and social positioning of the network's members (for example by focusing on the ability to stabilise horizontal and/or vertical socio-economic linkages of social *bonding* and *bridging*) but also the quality of such relationships and the functional contents of social interactions.[5] According to the activity-focus, social resources of networks are not just understood as potentially available social capital of a somehow solidarity bonded and homophilic structured community but as concrete social interactions that generates collective opportunities and orientations. In consequence, this approach is markedly appropriate to explore the specific character of a social relationship (if it is unidirectional or reciprocal, unidimensional or multiplex et cetera) in correlation to the particular constitution of the social ties (if they are primarily family-, community- and/or work-based). By this means, it is possible to focus not only on structural elements of social networks, predicated for example on their size and relational density,[6] but also to highlight the dynamics of social interactions. This approach offers the opportunity to differentiate between potential and actual support, received and perceived help, autonomy and dependence or positive and negative impacts. In addition, the focus of social support provides the possibility to distinguish

---

5   Cf. PUTNAM, 2000; RYAN et al., 2008.
6   Cf. HOLLSTEIN, 2006; HOLZER, 2006.

between different kinds of support capacities upon which the social networks depend, such as functional, economic, informative or emotional functions.[7]

However, it could be criticised that the spatial dimension of social support networks has been neglected or even rejected within this concept. In consideration of the diverse character of social networks and their different structural and functional interlinkages with regard to distinctive localities of socio-spatial settings such as an urban area, it seems to be extremely important to focus on the spatial effects of social networks.

When analysing the collected data of ethnographic interviews and observations resulting from a fieldwork period in Costa Rica's metropolitan highlands in 2009-10, one of the main questions the researcher had to deal with was how these social networks are organised and reproduced within the urban space and to what extent migrants' meeting locations influence their social support relationships both locally and transnationally.

The ethnographic fieldwork was launched on two assumptions. First, it had been supposed that such concrete meeting places would serve not only as a precondition for social linkages by providing direct face-to-face contacts for the exchange of information, goods and different types of support, but also as localities of socio-cultural representation within the foreign society to highlight the distinctive collective identity as Nicaraguan migrants. In this perspective, the physical space can only be reflected on as socially generated or rather occupied and is therefore always an expression of the social structure and the socio-political struggle of power relationships. As Pierre Bourdieu says,

> "The physical space could only be thought of as an abstraction, [...] as a lived and occupied space that means a social construction and a projection of the social space, a social structure in an objectivated condition [...], the objectivation and naturalisation of past and current social relations."[8]

The conceptualization of the physical space as a reproduction of past and current social power relationships thus demonstrates the importance of focusing not only the contemporary structure of the urban space, but to adopt an entirely historical perspective of the urban and socio-spatial development in all its sedimentary complexity (equivalent to a biographical exploration of the city and its society, its physical materialisation and social milieus).

---

7 Cf. DIEWALD, 1990; NESTMANN, 2001; KEUPP, RÖHRLE, 1987.
8 BOURDIEU, 1991, p. 28 (translation by the author).

The second prior assumption was that these locations cannot be understood as separate places that exist independently from the spatial and social surrounding. Instead of defining these places as internally coherent and static, it is argued that their uniqueness results especially from the dynamic interconnections with other locations and social constellations. Inspired by Doreen Massey, these localities are considered to be interrelated with the socio-spatial environment of the city as a whole. To quote Massey,

> "With such a set of connections, and such a history, it becomes clear that to romanticize places as settled, coherent and unchanging is highly dubious. [...] to see places as bounded can lead to their interconnections being ignored, and thus may result in parochialism. To see them [...] as particular sets of interconnections in a wider field might hold open the possibility of both appreciating their local uniqueness and recognizing their wider interlinkages."[9]

In a relational socio-spatial perspective, as it has been framed by Bourdieu and Massey, such localities can hardly be seen as internally closed. Focusing on the social interactions it is obvious that spatial-related activities are as much directed to local strategies and orientations as to interconnections to the entire urban space and society. According to this theoretical comprehension, the social interrelations are not just contextualised within an intrinsic logic of the very local places themselves. These locations are reciprocally interlinked with the physical and social environment and also with other external socio-spatial constellations on an urban scale, but also on a national and even transnational level. From this perspective, these places not only interrelate to different social networks within an urban setting, in addition they may also function as gateways between local and transnational ties. Moreover, it remains to be seen if these urban places themselves have been transformed on the basis of the diverse interactive processes of local and transnational exchanges into kinds of *transnational localities*.

The illustrated assumptions have led to the comparison of several urban locations where the social interactions of Nicaraguan migrants' networking take place in a different manner. To this end, characteristic localities of activity and settlement of the Nicaraguan migrant population have been investigated, such as two precarious residential districts, diverse inner-city parks, certain restaurants and bars, clubs and dancing halls as well as churches and the offices of migrants' associations and civic organisations. Out of this broad variety of places, three

---

9 MASSEY, 1995, p. 66.

particular locations are discussed in this article to identify the interconnections between specific local and transnational networks of social support and distinctive spatial settings. The exemplarily compared locations are (1) a suburban squat named *La Carpio* with a remarkable proportion of Nicaraguan inhabitants, (2) the main baseball stadium of San José, the capital of Costa Rica, and (3) the inner-city park called *La Merced* that is mostly frequented by Nicaraguan migrants.

3. Historical and current migration processes of Nicaraguans to Costa Rica[10]

Currently, as well as historically, Nicaraguans are and have been the most important migrant group in Costa Rica with more than 50 % of all foreigners living in the country (see the table below). Approximations vary between six and ten percent of the national population without knowing the precise proportion of temporary, seasonal and particularly irregular migrants. Moreover, updated representative statistics are not available since the last national census in the year of 2000. Supposed approximations resulting from selective case studies mostly act on the assumption that more or less 50 % of the Nicaraguan migrants are in the country illegally.

Populace of Costa Rica and the proportion of inhabitants born outside the nation concerning their country of origin between 1950 and 2000					
National Census					
	1950	1963	1973	1984	2000
Populace	800,875	1,336,274	1,871,780	2,416,809	3,810,179
Foreigners	33,251	35,605	22,264	88,954	296,461
Nicaragua	**18,954**	**18,722**	**11,871**	**45,918**	**226,374**
Panama	2064	3255	1598	4794	10,270
USA	956	2001	2151	5369	9511
El Salvador	574	769	766	8748	8714
Columbia	610	676	517	1678	5898
Others	10,143	10,182	5361	22,447	35,694

---

10 The historical review of Nicaraguan migration to Costa Rica is based on the work of: MORALES GAMBOA, CASTRO VALVERDE, 2006; ROSERO-BIXBY, 2004; ALVARENGA VENUTOLO, 1997. Cf. also HUHN, 2005; PÉREZ, 2006; FUNKHOUSER et al., 2002.

Percentage of inhabitants born outside the nation concerning their country of origin relative to the populace of Costa Rica between 1950 and 2000					
	1950	1963	1973	1984	2000
Born outside the country	4,2	2,7	1,2	3,7	7,8
Nicaragua	-	**2,4**	**1,4**	**0,6**	**1,9**
Panama	-	0,3	0,2	0,1	0,2
USA	0,1	0,1	0,1	0,2	0,2
El Salvador	-	0,1	0,1	0,0	0,4
Colombia	-	0,1	0,1	0,0	0,1
Others	-	1,3	0,8	0,3	0,9

Percentage of inhabitants born outside the nation concerning their country of origin and relative to all foreigners in Costa Rica between 1950 and 2000					
	1950	1963	1973	1984	2000
Nicaragua	-	**57,0**	**52,6**	**53,3**	**51,6**
Panama	-	6,2	9,1	7,2	5,4
USA	2,9	5,6	9,7	6,0	3,2
El Salvador	-	1,7	2,2	3,4	9,8
Colombia	-	1,8	1,9	2,3	1,9
Others	-	30,5	28,6	24,1	25,2

Source: INEC (Instituto Nacional de Estadística y Censos de Costa Rica).
From the national census 2000.

There have always been migratory movements from Nicaragua to Costa Rica for economic, cultural and familial reasons. Traditionally, these dynamics occurred in the border region of the two neighbouring countries and could be explained by the narrow historical and socio-cultural interrelationships within this region and by the minor influences of the historically weak central nation states. Moreover, in the 19th century the political boundary had changed in bellicose conflicts when the province Guanacaste became part of the Costa Rican territory after the failure of a Nicaraguan military invasion in 1856. Furthermore, the definite borderline had still not been clearly defined until the beginning of the 20th century – and still is the cause of bilateral tensions. Even after the declaration of a contractually fixed line of demarcation, systematic border control had not been established for decades until the appearance of the first migration movements for political reasons due to the rise of the Somoza dictatorship in Nicaragua. Even today, the frontier is still not controlled like in other immigration countries, but the Costa Rican state spends much more public funds to check the legal entrance to the territory than before.

While traditionally the Nicaraguan immigration to Costa Rica had mainly been directed towards rural areas to work in the seasonal agricultural production of coffee and bananas, the urban migration of Nicaraguans to Costa Rica's metropolitan area is still a quite new phenomenon, appearing only within the last twenty years. The main explanation for historical movements from Nicaragua to Costa Rica is the migration for labour reasons, forced by the distinctive economic development of the two states. While Nicaragua is one of the poorest countries of the whole Latin American hemisphere Costa Rica is one of the wealthiest and is also called *Switzerland of Central America* with regard to the numerous mountains and the relative socio-economic prosperity. In distinction to former movements and migratory intentions of Nicaraguans towards Costa Rica, the first significant wave had resulted from the earthquake of 1972 in the Managua region and the rates accelerated each year to reach a preliminary peak in the 1980th due to the civil war in Nicaragua (at first against the Somoza regime and afterwards against the Sandinista authority). In the time of civil war the former political emigration of a few intellectuals and opposition members became increasingly a mass phenomenon of the Nicaraguan population that originated mostly from the devastated rural regions. In conjunction with the high rates of Nicaraguan immigration, the demand for a stricter regulation of the immigration policy within the Costa Rican society also increased. In spite of a more restrictive legislation in Costa Rica in the 1990s, the Nicaraguan migration did not decline even though the civil war had ended. In contrast, the established social networks between former refugees and latter newcomers had created a constant chain of migration no longer led by seasonal labour intents but rather by the aim for a permanent life in a wealthier country. With regard to the concept of dual labour markets, the predominately young migrants mainly found work in labour segments of lower income, mostly without any access to insurance or a formalised contract.[11] For example, in 2001 64 % of the workers hired in the coffee production were migrants and a remarkable 94 % did not possess all of the necessary documents to work in this sector.

Finally, the new phenomenon of the Nicaraguan migration to the metropolitan Central Valley is also characterised by an economic integration into the lower segments of the urban dual labour market, although the types of activity differ. Accordingly, the male Nicaraguans work predominantly in the sectors of lower services and construction or are hired as informal vendors and security guards. Female migrants mostly work as housemaids, employees in restaurants and other

---

11 Cf. PIORE, 1979.

unqualified services or in the so-called *maquiladora* industry that is mainly characterised by textile processing, and in some cases they work as prostitutes. In distinction to their marginal proportion in the agricultural sector, the female population represents more than 50 % of the urban migrants (see the table below).

Proportional Distribution of Nicaraguan and Costa Rican males and females in selected labour segments in comparison (2000)		
	Nicaraguans	Costa Ricans
Labour segment	Males	
Agricultural unskilled worker	28,8	14,5
Mason/carpenter	8,7	3,7
Unskilled worker in the sector of mining and construction	8,3	2,3
Security guard	5,9	4,6
Formal vendor	3,4	5,6
Agricultural skilled worker	3,2	6,0
Unskilled worker in manufacturing industry	2,7	2,0
Welder/mechanic/metal worker	2,3	1,5
Truck or personal driver	2,0	7,5
House employee/concierge	2,0	1,6
Percentage	67,3	49,3
	Nicaraguans	Costa Ricans
Labour segment	Females	
House maid	48,4	14,9
Service in restaurants	10,3	5,7
Formal vendor	7,1	9,9
Unskilled worker in the textile industry (*maquiliadora*)	4,2	2,6
Agricultural unskilled worker	3,5	1,8
Skilled worker in the textile and leather production	2,9	4,8
Street vendor	2,3	1,7
Nursing service	2,1	1,9
Cashier	2,0	3,1
Other non qualified services	1,9	0,7
Percentage	84,7	47,1

Source: FLACSO *(Facultad Latinoamericana de Ciencias Sociales, Costa Rica), 2005.*

In consideration of the historically restricted migration to the Central Valley – for example, it had been forbidden to the black Caribbean national population to move to the metropolitan area up to the declaration of the Second Republic in 1948 – this new type of urban migration meant a profound change for the Costa Rican society. As the centre of cultural, political and economic activities as well as the core of national self-identification, Costa Rica's urbanised Central Valley has always played a quite important role for the country's development and was treated like an exclusive and precious space of – not only topographically – higher spheres.

4. The urban development of Latin American cities and Costa Rica's metropolitan area

To explain the specific location, spatial distribution and clustering of Nicaraguan migrants within Costa Rica's metropolitan Central Valley relative to their settlement, economic and socio-cultural activities, it seems to be important to explore the genealogical context of the urbanised space. Therefore, it is quite useful to highlight some benchmarks of the general urban development in Latin America and of Costa Rica's metropolitan highlands specifically. These outlines could serve for a better comprehension of the current aspects of socio-spatial fragmentation within the urban space into which the Nicaraguan migrants have settled.

In the era of globalization, significant processes of urbanisation and migration are seen as two closely meshed phenomena of contemporary social transformation.[12] In Latin America, for its part, the process of urbanisation has begun much earlier than in Africa or Asia, and much faster than previously in North America or Europe. In consequence of a policy of the so-called *import substituted industrialisation*, high levels of internal migration and urban birth rates have accelerated the relative percentage of the urban Latin American populace from 17 to 70 percent just between the years of 1965 and 1987. Nowadays, the proportion of the urban populace in Latin America has reached almost 80 percent. While historically the process was mainly characterised by a tendency of *metropolisation,* meaning a high concentration of the populace in the most important urban agglomerations (mostly the capital), by now the process of urbanisation predominately takes place in metropolitan areas of smaller scales.

---

12 Cf. SASSEN, 2002; ROLF, 2006.

The metropolitan area of Costa Rica's central highlands is such a mid-size urban agglomeration that contains the four main cities (San José, Alajuela, Cartago and Heredia) with a populace of almost 3 million inhabitants, corresponding to more or less 50 percent of the national population. Even if the rapid urban growth of the 1960s and 70s has decelerated, the annual growth still represents 2,8 %, representing a duplication within 25 years. (In comparison: in 1990 the annual growth still corresponded to a proportion of 3,7 %)

Referring to the typology developed by Axel Borsdorf, Jürgen Bähr and Michael Janoschka, the urban transformation of Latin American cities is characterised by four steps from the dense colonial city to the fragmented urban agglomeration of current days.[13] The originally Hispanic *colonial city* – in distinction to the Portuguese – was structured in the strict logic of a military camp according to a grid with a central square, the *plaza mayor*, surrounded by the main buildings such as the cathedral, the city hall, other administrative buildings and the residents of the most important families. The farther the inhabitants lived from this central core, the poorer they were.

This centralised structure has been transformed in a second step of urban transformation in the beginning of the 20th century, which the authors call the emergence of the *sectoral city*. This corresponds to a partial and linear suburban development that depended on the infrastructural subdivisions with a strict segmentation between places of economic production and residence as well as between the residential districts of the urban rich and the working class.

In a third step, Borsdorf et al. describe the era of the rapid growth and industrialisation of Latin American agglomerations during the 1960s and 70s as a development which they call the *polarised city*. This era of urban expansion is basically characterised by high rates of rural-urban migration, a significant lack of housing and the appearance of activities such as the taking over of peripheral or rural public land and the construction of huge marginal squats by the urban poor while the centres were still predominantly occupied by the richer ones.

The last and current step represented by the *fragmented city* corresponds to a more diverse and sometimes opposite transformation of a so-called *archipelagoisation* on a micro level with downgraded and abandoned inner-city spaces next to the central business districts, peripheral *gated communities* of the upper and middle class next to consolidated or precarious squats, and residential islands within industrial districts. Last but not least, this transformation process was strengthened by the effects of the IMF and World Bank structural

---

13   Cf. BORSDORF et al., 2002.

adjustment programs of the 1980s which had induced the de-formalization of the urban labour markets on one hand and on the other the informalisation of urban development. The privatisation of urban space and infrastructure was on the one hand accompanied by the appearance of *gated community*-projects of different size and on the other by the emergence of an informal and commercialised housing and rental market within the various squats. At the same time, the establishment of a few countable social housing programs during the 1960s and 70s has mostly ended due to the constraints of reduced public investment budgets.

The described panorama of the *fragmented city* also coincides with the current situation of Costa Rica's urbanised Central Valley. In distinction to some other agglomerations, the uncontrolled spatial expansion in the metropolitan highlands is restricted in size due to the surrounding mountains that delimit the Central Valley. Nevertheless, the urban region is characterised by a mainly horizontal urban sprawl corresponding to aspects such as the high frequency of earthquakes and a traditional culture of estate property.

As in other Latin American cities the climax of land takeover ended in the 1980s and the current process is mainly characterised by a densification of the populace within the existing squats in terms of parcelling out the already occupied space. Even if Costa Rica has not experienced such a process of economic decline and de-industrialisation like other Latin American nations and cities during the so-called *lost decade* of the 1980s – a process which Mike Davis has identified as an urban expansion without economic growth[14] - the metropolitan region of the Central Valley is confronted with a tendency to urbanised pauperisation. And remarkable proportion of these urban poor equates to the segment of Nicaraguan migrants.

In consideration of the socio-spatial fragmentation it is finally quite important to ask how the Nicaraguan migrants are spatially distributed and where they settle, work and live within the metropolitan area. According to Davis' opinion, the spatial locations of social inequality do not necessarily correspond with processes of *ghettoization*. On one hand, the so-called *slumlords*, which are local estate agents, do not necessarily fit in with the characteristics of poverty, on the other, many construction workers live within the building yards where they work and most of the house maids live directly in the houses and *gated communities* of their employers. Nevertheless, a spatial concentration of poverty is verifiable, and these are in consequence also the districts where many of the Nicaraguan migrants are located (that is in the South, the North and the North-West of the metropolitan area). The comparison of the average housing conditions of Nicaraguans and Costa Ricans also shows high rates of Nicaraguans in precarious dwellings (see table below).

14   DAVIS, 2007.

Indicators of the Housing Conditions corresponding to the origin of the head of a household 2000 (in %)		
Characteristics	Costa Rican	Nicaraguan
Type: slum dwelling (*tugurio*)	1,2	7,2
Housing in bad condition	9,6	25,3
Without connection to water	10,1	18,2
Without connection to canalisation	6,8	17,0
Sanitarian equipment but without canalisation or sewage work (*tanque séptico*)	7,1	28,4
High density	9,5	27,3

Source: INEC *(Instituto Nacional de Estadística y Censos de Costa Rica). Data from the national census 2000.*

5. Presentation of three exemplary urban locations

In the following three exemplary urban locations are presented to show that especially in a fragmented metropolitan area such as the San José region the migrants' socio-spatial orientation and operating range is not just exclusively limited to their places of settlement, but also to different meeting places in public and (semi-)private spaces. Referring to some results of the own research project, these places serve to illustrate the specific relationship between the spatial distribution or rather concentration of Nicaraguan migrants in the urban area and the impacts that spatial effects could have on the formation of their social support networks. To this end, the comparative presentation contains: first a suburban squat with a remarkable proportion of Nicaraguan inhabitants; second, the baseball stadium in San José; and third, an inner-city park which is mainly frequented by Nicaraguan migrants. Even if it is not possible to compare these quite distinctive places by their size, structure and social diversity in all their dimensions, it is still fruitful to compare these locations with respect to their functional role for specific types of social networks.

5.1. The suburban squat *La Carpio*

The suburban squat called *La Carpio* with about 20,000 inhabitants is one of the largest in Costa Rica's metropolitan area and has a considerable concentration of the Nicaraguan population with a proportion of almost 50 %. As opposed to other squats, in the case of *La Carpio* the Nicaraguan households did not move into precarious dwellings of an area already occupied by Costa Ricans, but rather were part of the original land takeover in 1993, which was one of the latest.

The social support networks within this area were mainly led by a common strategy of all inhabitants (Nicaraguans as well as Costa Ricans and a few other migrant groups) to pursue local interests such as the regulation of their property rights, access to basic infrastructure (like paved roads, electricity, fresh water and drainage), access to public housing programs, the establishment of educational and health services, playgrounds and so on.

The social networks are predominately structured by local family- and community-based neighbourhood associations and semi-institutionalised organisations centred on very local activities without any transnational ties that exceed personal contacts to visitors or newcomers from the country of origin. While practical and material help is predominantly based on social support networks resulting from the neighbourhood associations and the resident family members, mostly emotional support is contextualised with transnational ties by the interviewees from *La Carpio*. In contrast, transnational exchanges, for their part, are quite a rare phenomenon in the squat. Apart from some political campaigns of Nicaraguan politicians that visited *La Carpio* during their stay in Costa Rica to engage the migrants' sympathy for their candidature in the native country, political activity in *La Carpio* is mainly represented by debates and conflicts with the city council, the public administration and the state. The economic activities are also locally based, even if some of the stores and stalls sell traditional food from Nicaragua that is demanded from Nicaraguans as much as from Costa Ricans.

In a socio-cultural perspective, an interesting fact about *La Carpio* is that the *Purísima*, one of the most important traditional festivities in Nicaragua, is today celebrated in the squat by almost all inhabitants. Instead of representing an exotic and exclusively Nicaraguan festivity, the *Purísima* has become more and more a symbol for the entire district to show their community-based intercultural identity and function in part as a nostalgic retrospective view by the Nicaraguans. As numerous interviewees from *La Carpio* stressed, they do not really distinguish between Costa Rican and Nicaraguan inhabitants in the squat and highlight the political and infrastructural achievements they have fought for collectively. Moreover, after a long period of shame and stigmatisation due to living in this squat, today they feel proud to call themselves *Carpeños*, which has become a more important feature of self-identification for many interviewees than their Nicaraguan origin. As Martha Lidia A., a 24 year old Nicaraguan resident of *La Carpio*, said:

> "Before, hmm (...) before I always felt in a way (...) kind of ashamed to be from La Carpio. And, well (...) additionally to be Nicaraguan, hmm (...) I always told the people that I live in Uruca because (.) because I was afraid of what they might think. (...) If they think that I am a criminal, that I have a bad education, that, hmm (.) that I am not a trustworthy person. (...) But now I feel something like (.) proud in a way, (...) to be *Carpeña*. (...) proud of all

that my parents have achieved, the whole community has reached. [...] We are all proud now, proud to call ourselves *Carpeños*."[15]

5.2. San José's baseball stadium

---

15 Martha Lidia A., 24, resident of *La Carpio*, in Costa Rica since 1998. Interview from 25.11.2009.

Another location that has been studied during the ethnographic fieldwork in Costa Rica is the main baseball stadium of San José. It serves as a meeting place not only for the Nicaraguan population but also to connect them with other groups of migrants from the Caribbean and from Central and South America. While Costa Ricans are mainly interested in soccer, the baseball stadium is frequented mostly by Nicaraguans, but also by Puerto Ricans, Cubans, Columbians and other migrant groups and people (so for example a single retired US-citizen), according to the predominant sport of their home country.

As a somehow protected place that is partly open, partly separated from the outside world, the stadium has a strong family-oriented character, where migrant families can go for a weekend activity without spending much money (for example, in contrast to shopping malls, where they can hardly remain for an entire day-trip without being forced to buy something). Normally they just pay the symbolic entrance fee and bring their own lunch. Due to the shared interest in baseball, the stadium serves as a meeting place not only between migrants and the national population, but also, and predominantly, between different migrant groups that would not interact in such a way in other public areas. Moreover, the visitors come from all parts of the urbanised Central Valley and use the location of the stadium to get in contact with others whom they could not meet elsewhere because of the lack of alternative time and spatial opportunities.

Reactively, the importance of the migrants for the Costa Rican Baseball is not just reflected in the physical and symbolical occupation of the once abandoned and neglected stadium by Costa Ricans, but also in the constellation of the teams. While some teams are composed of players of different nationalities, others signal their predominantly Nicaraguan origins by giving themselves names like the *Tiburones Nicaraguenses*, the Nicaraguan Sharks, or the *Equípo Managua*, the Managua team, to refer to their home country or even city. Moreover, while the baseball stadium is mainly a place that brings together people of different nationalities at the local level, it has also been used (or misused) in a transnational way during the election campaign in Nicaragua when the candidate of a Nicaraguan political party came to Costa Rica and held a speech in the stadium to his ex-compatriots, in full recognition of their importance for their home country as they send remittances, start investments and keep transnational ties alive.

Additionally, Julio César R., the general director of the Costa Rican National Baseball League, a Nicaraguan who moved to Costa Rica more than 20 years ago, also reported about a special event when a famous team from the Nicaraguan capitol Managua has been invited to play against a selection of Nicaraguan migrant players in San José:

"They all (.) all the Nicaraguan migrants have been very thankful that we could have organised this game. (...) Well, our team lost but (.) the stadium was almost overcrowded. (.) And such an ambiance! Almost like in Nicaragua, with all the banners, the equipment, (.) the music. (...) The event has also been noted in the Nicaraguan newspaper."[16]

5.3. The inner-city park *La Merced*

---

16 Julio César R., 37, the general director of the Costa Rican National Baseball League, in Costa Rica since 1991. Interview from 13.11.2009.

The third place being discussed in greater detail here is the inner-city park *La Merced*, also called the *Nica Park* by Costa Ricans as well as by Nicaraguans themselves. For about 15 years now, the once abandoned park has been occupied physically and symbolically by Nicaraguan migrants and serves as a central location with a variety of support functions for the Nicaraguan communities. Surrounded by a church, a hospital and low-rise buildings, the inner-city park has a rural character that might fit with the predominately rural origin of many Nicaraguan migrants. Moreover, next to the park is an important bus station where many buses arrive from the outskirts like *La Carpio* where most of the Nicaraguan migrants live. The park is frequented during the entire week and especially on the weekends – and even during the rainy season it serves as a central meeting location until the afternoon when the thunder storms usually start.

In a way, the park is a place of cultural reproduction where Nicaraguan festivities are celebrated, traditional Nicaraguan food and utensils are sold by informal vendors and where Nicaraguan music is played by traditional musicians. Moreover, it is also a place of collective socialising and emotional support, a first connection for newcomers as well as the last resort for long-time migrants in precarious situations.

The support functions within the park are quite diverse and range from brief informational support about employment, housing or legalising the immigration status to a profound kind of support concerning the reunion of family members and friends and the creation, maintaining and stabilising of a durable social network between compatriots and - more specific - certain occupational groups like the housemaids that only have public spaces such as these to meet and interact.

Apart from these local support functions, the park is embedded in transnational ties in ways that go far beyond the regular queues in front of the public phones to call the family in Nicaragua and to indulge in the reproduction of a socio-cultural nostalgia. It is because the park environment has profoundly changed over the past 15 years. The entire district around the park, once abandoned by the Costa Rican population, has now become an area of so-called *ethnic businesses*, with numerous remittance banks, typical bars and restaurants, lawyer offices and NGO accommodations for legal support, hotels for newcomers and postal, travel and goods transport agencies to Nicaragua.

At the same time, the park itself has witnessed a dramatic social change. Long-term migrants recount in a nostalgic way that the park used to be a place for socialising, familial meetings and even served as a marriage market, and lament the park's socio-spatial decline into a place which is today characterised by criminality, alcoholism and prostitution. Moreover, the informal vendors within the park have a lot of trouble with the municipal police, which was not the case in the past. As Danélia C., a 50 year old political activist for the rights of the Nicaraguan migrants, reported:

> "Always, always. I am going to the park since I have come to San José (...). This is the place where the Nicaraguan community is gathering, where you can meet your folks. The park is the park. The park has always been the park. [...] But the problem is that the park has changed a lot, you see, you've got all this proliferation of, (.) of *prostitution*, of *alcoholism*, of *drugs*, of *criminality* (...). Before, the park has been a much more familial place (.) but (.) with the time it has lost, hmm, (.) a little bit it's spirit."[17]

In contrast, newcomers, the informal vendors or the prostitutes, as some of them ascertained in the interviews, still see the importance of the park to meet and link together with their compatriots, to support each other or just to do their business.

While there has been some kind of institutionalisation of the migrant activities in the entire district around the park which originated from the park itself, the park has changed its symbolic relevance for the heterogeneously structured community of Nicaraguan migrants over time.

In this sense, one's symbolic self-positioning towards the park seems to be not only a possibility of social differentiation towards the Costa Rican society but also among the Nicaraguan migrants themselves to distinguish, for example, between newcomers and long-term migrants, between well established and precarious migrants, and to point out (or conceal) one's social status within the migrant group *and* the Costa Rican society. Accordingly, Javier M., a 34 year old Nicaraguan musician, noted:

> "Yes, there are differences (...) I would say that, hmm, the people who go to the *Parque de la Merced* (...) they, hmm, they are just the men on the street, (.) the people originally from the countryside. [...] I would say that the Nicaraguans who go to the *Plaza de la Cultura* or to the *Parque Central* have a kind of (.) a little bit more like, hmm, (...) they have a higher cultural level. (.) Or they think that they are something better (.) or something like that. They go to Kentucky to eat a chicken and they wouldn't eat the food from the park, I think."[18]

---

17 Danélia C., 50, Nicaraguan political activist, in Costa Rica since 2002. Interview from 18.10.2009.
18 Javier A., 34, Nicaraguan musician, in Costa Rica since 2005. Interview from 10.12.2009.

6. Conclusions

By contrasting and comparing these different locations, the particular connections between different types of social support networks and the specific conditions of concrete meeting places have been identified. In this context, it has been assumed that the collective linkages to a certain place reinforce as much the network's composition as the socialised place is produced and reproduced reactively by the social action and the physical and symbolic occupation of a particular group such as the Nicaraguan migrants.

The previous assumptions and the comparison of the different places in a fragmented urban agglomeration such as Costa Rica's central highlands have led to a differentiation between more locally-oriented places with a high importance for the direct migrant's networking and of more transnationally related locations for the reciprocal exchange between the host and the native country.

While, for example, in the *La Carpio* squat only locally-based entrepreneurial activities could be set up sustainably and other activities, such as the establishment of a remittance bank or a transport agency, have been implemented but have never been successful, the district around the park as a central hub of the socio-spatial activities of locally widespread Nicaraguan migrants has changed into a space of semi-professional transnational activities. Therefore, it is questioned, whether this area is not only a transnational interlinked location with constant and multiple interconnections across national borders that are anchored in the migrant's daily live or if such a park could also be called a significantly *transnationalised place*.

Further investigation could probably focus on the interconnections between specific *transnational localities* on both sides of the border to highlight the interlinkages among different types of networks. Such investigation in the tradition of *multi-sited ethnography*[19] could explore for example the mutual exchange relations of the diverse business persons involved in the fields of remittance banking, transborder travel or goods transportation agencies. The spatial clustering of such activities on both sides of the border could be understood as a geographical mapping of transnational social networks.

---

19   MARCUS, 1995.

Literature

ALVARENGA VENUTOLO, PATRICIA, Conflictiva Convivencia. Los Nicaragüenses en Costa Rica, in: Facultad Latinoamericana de Ciencias Sociales (FLACSO), Cuaderno de Ciencias Sociales, 101 (1997).

BASCH, LINDA et al. (eds.), Nations Unbound. Transnational projects, postcolonial predicaments and territorialized nation-states, New York 1994.

BECK, ULRICH, Was ist Globalisierung? Irrtümer des Globalismus – Antworten auf Globalisierung, Frankfurt a.M. 1997.

BORSDORF, AXEL et al., Die Dynamik stadtstrukturellen Wandels in Lateinamerika im Modell der lateinamerikanischen Stadt, in: Geographica Helvetica, 57, 4 (2002), p. 300-309.

BOURDIEU, PIERRE, Physischer, sozialer und angeeigneter physischer Raum, in: Stadt-Räume ed. by MARTIN WENTZ, Frankfurt a.M./New York 1991, p. 25-34.

CASTELLS, MANUEL, The Rise of the Network Society, Malden 1996.

DAVIS, MIKE, Planet der Slums, Berlin/Hamburg 2007.

DIEWALD, MARTIN, Soziale Beziehungen. Verlust oder Liberalisierung? Soziale Unterstützung in informellen Netzwerken, Berlin 1990.

DÜRRSCHMIDT, JÖRG, Globalisierung, Bielefeld 2002.

FAIST, THOMAS, Transnationalization in international Migration. Implications for the study of citizenship and culture, in: Ethnic and Racial Studies, 23, 2 (2000), p. 189-222.

FLACSO (Facultad Latinoamericana de Ciencias Sociales), Centroamérica en cifras. 1980-2005. San José, CR 2005.

FUNKHOUSER, EDWARD et al., Social Exclusion of Nicaraguans in the Urban Metropolitan Area of San José, Costa Rica, in: Inter-American Development Bank, Latin American Research Network. Working Paper No. R-437 (2002).

GLICK SCHILLER, NINA/LEVITT, PEGGY, Haven't We Heard This Somewhere Before? A substantive view of transnational migration studies by way of a reply to Waldinger and Fitzgerald, in: The Center for Migration and Development, CMD Working Paper 06-01 (2006).

HOLLSTEIN, BETINA/ STRAUS, FLORIAN (eds.), Qualitative Netzwerkanalyse. Konzepte, Methoden, Anwendungen, Wiesbaden 2006.

HOLZER, BORIS, Netzwerke, Bielefeld 2006.

HUHN, SEBASTIAN, Einwanderungsdiskurse und Migrationspolitik in Costa Rica. Wandel und Konstanzen in der gesellschaftlichen Auseinandersetzung mit der nikaraguanischen Migration seit den 1980er Jahren, Hamburg 2005.

INEC (Instituto Nacional de Estadística y Censos de Costa Rica).

JIMÉNEZ MATARRITA, ALEXANDER, La vida en otra parte. Migraciones y cambios culturales en Costa Rica, San José, CR 2009.

KEUPP, HEINER/RÖHRLE, BERND, Soziale Netzwerke, Frankfurt a.M./New York 1987.

LEVITT, PEGGY et al. (eds.), Transnational Migration. International perspectives, in: Special Issue of International Migration Review, 37, 3 (2003), p. 565-575.

MARCUS, GEORGE E., Ethnography in/of the World System. The emergence of multi-sited ethnography, in: Annual Review of Anthropology, 24 (1995), p. 95-117.

MASSEY, DOREEN, The Conceptualization of Place, in: A Place in the World? Places, Cultures and Globalization, ed. by DOREEN MASSEY/PAT JESS, Oxford 1995, p. 45-86.

MOLINA, IVÁN/PALMER, STEVEN, The History of Costa Rica, in: Universidad de Costa Rica (UCR). 3rd ed., San José, CR 2004.

MORALES GAMBOA, ABELARDO/CASTRO VALVERDE, CARLOS, Migración, empleo y pobreza, San José, CR 2006.

NESTMANN, FRANK, Soziale Netzwerke – Soziale Unterstützung, in: Handbuch zur Sozialarbeit und Sozialpädagogik, ed. by HANS-UWE OTTO, 2nd ed., Neuwied 2001, p. 1684-1692.

PÉREZ, MARIAN, Los impactos perversos de la segregación socio-espacial en la ciudad de San José, in: La segregación socio-espacial urbana. Una Mirada sobre Puebla, Puerto España, San José y San Salvador, ed. by ANNE-MARIE SÉGUIN, San José, CR 2006, p. 147-178.

PIORE, MICHAEL J., Birds of Passage. Migrant labor and industrial societies, Cambridge 1979.

PORTES, ALEJANDRO et al. The Study of Transnationalism. Pitfalls and promise of an emergent research field, in: Ethnic and Racial Studies, 22, 2 (1999), p. 21-37.

PRIES, LUDGER, Transnationalisierung. Theorie und Empirie grenzüberschreitender Vergesellschaftung, Wiesbaden 2010.

PUTNAM, ROBERT D., Bowling Alone. The collapse and revival of American community, New York 2000.

ROLF, HAUKE JAN, Urbane Globalisierung. Bedeutung und Wandel der Stadt im Globalisierungsprozess, Wiesbaden 2006.

ROSERO-BIXBY, LUIS (ed.), Costa Rica a la Luz del Censo del 2000, San José, Costa Rica, 2004.

RYAN, LOUISE et al., Social Networks, Social Support and Social Capital. The experiences of recent Polish migrants in London, in: Sociology, 42, 4 (2008), p. 672-690.

SANDÓVAL GARCÍA, CARLOS, Otras Amenazantes. Los Nicaragüenses y la Formación de Identidades Nacionales en Costa Rica, San José, CR 2003.

SASSEN, SASKIA (ed.), Global Networks, Linked Cities, New York 2002.

URRY, JOHN, Sociology beyond Societies. Mobilities for the twenty-first century, London/New York 2001.

Urban Poverty and Gentrification
A Comparative View on Different Areas in Hamburg

INGRID BRECKNER

Since the end of the 20th century, German cities with population growth such as Munich, Berlin, Hamburg or Cologne are facing a strong spatial polarisation due to economic, cultural and political diversities, which more and more influences the access to labor and housing. In this context, gentrification became a keyword for such types of urban changes in media and scientific discussions, although convincing empirical data explaining and generalising such developments are still lacking.[1] According to Tom Slater "[...] a careful analytical indictment of the mainstream research output (typified by scholarship concluding that gentrification is acceptable if it is 'managed' by policy) is necessary but not sufficient. Such an indictment needs to be coupled with further research that seeks to document displacement (in any or all of its forms) 'from below' in the sobering terms of those who experience it. The absence of qualitative accounts of displacement is striking and shocking when juxtaposed with quantitative measures, or with all those accounts of the trials and tribulations of the new middle class."[2]

The critical reflection of literature on gentrification over four decades[3] shows that quite different reasons and procedures of urban transformation are summarised under the term of gentrification, which tends to lose its descriptive and explanatory capacity. In order not to enter into such a precarious discussion, the following arguments shall focus on three differently structured urban spaces in Hamburg: Ottensen, St. Pauli and Wilhelmsburg. Their different stages of urban transformation are related to specific economic, political, social and cul-

---

1   Cf. BRECKNER, 2010.
2   SLATER, 2011, p. 580.
3   Cf. LEE et al., 2008.

tural structures and processes, however, all of them are labeled as more or less gentrified. These examples show different aspects of the relationship between urban poverty, gentrification and urban policies and underline the necessity of scientific analysis with a focus on displacements of poor populations based both on quantitative and qualitative empirical findings.

As the complexity of micro-spaces can never be understood without relating them to their interferences with an always specific meso- and macro-spatial context[4] and the overlapping of different urban functions, I shall start my argumentation with a brief presentation of poverty in Hamburg, followed by a view on structural specificities and developments in the urban spaces under investigation and a final discussion of relations between poverty and gentrification in the development of the selected urban areas and in a general perspective.

Poverty pockets in a wealthy city: The case of Hamburg

Hamburg is the second biggest metropolis in Germany with approximately 1,800,000 inhabitants. Situated on the Northern and Southern shores of the river Elbe, the city had the chance to develop the largest German harbor since medieval times. Nowadays, commercial relations with China are dominating the business on a growing number of container terminals. Therefore, the harbor moved step by step to the West because the new large container ships needed more and more depth and the digging of sand from the river became increasingly difficult due to costs, lacking storage space for contaminated sands and an old tunnel under the river, which cannot be removed. The port is politically still considered as the heart of the urban economy, although the port businesses lost their central importance for the local labor market due to technological innovations. New economic activities in the sectors of aviation, biotechnology, health, media, entertainment, tourism and other services created growing job opportunities mostly for educated people. They attract increasing numbers of students as well as regional, national and international immigrants. At the same time, many low skilled elderly people lost their jobs with few perspectives to access the postindustrial labor market. They represent the group of long-term unemployed labor force more or less hidden by the way of diverse statistical tricks.

The long lasting tradition of international relations related to port activities and those based on service economies lead to a population of more than 100 na-

---

4   Cf. LÄPPLE, 1993.

tionalities speaking more than 300 languages in Hamburg. 2012 nearly 30 % of the population had a migration background, meaning that these persons or their parents were not born in Germany. Because a lot of these inhabitants had the chance or were forced to get a German citizenship, the percentage of foreigners – as people without a German passport – in Hamburg is much lower (14 %). Both figures show huge differences regarding urban spaces: In Hamburg's central district nearly half of the population has a migratory background, while those with the highest percentage cope with up to 70 % of immigrants; low numbers of immigrants are characteristic for semi-central and marginal districts with high percentages of middle and high income residents.

Beside immigration the growing regional, national and international tourism and a high number of commuters to the city from the suburban surrounding (see chart 1) contribute to the cities diverse labor force as well as to its importance as a rich consumer capital in northern Germany.

Chart 1: Commuters to the City (Green Arrows) and from the City (Red Arrows) 2002

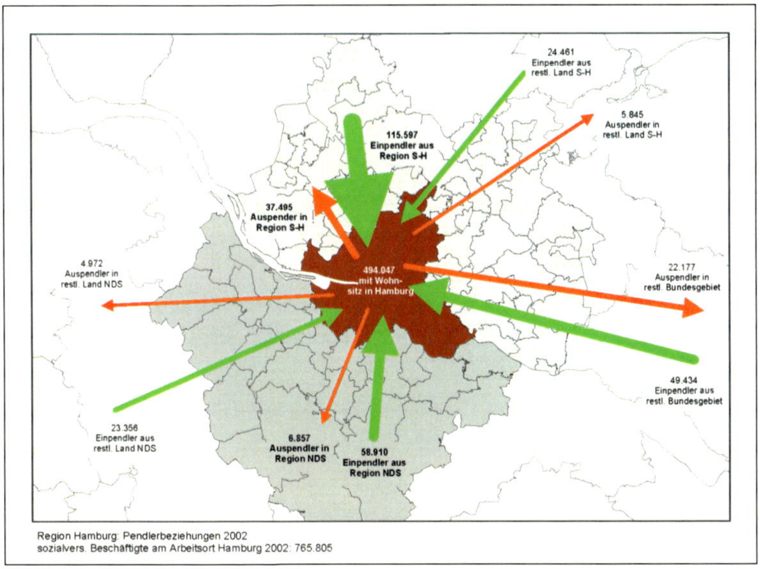

Source: Soyka, 2006, p. 2

This inflow of consumer capital changed the perspective of urban policies: In Hamburg, many administrative, political and economic capacities are invested for the marketing of the city while neglecting the serious effects of social and spatial polarisation on the increasingly difficult living conditions of poor and/ or excluded people.

The City-State of Hamburg[5] is administratively subdivided into seven districts and a huge number of highly diverse neighborhoods.

The map in chart 2 has been updated recently in the context of the regular Social Monitoring, provided by the federal administration with responsibility for urban and environmental development, planning and construction. Green colors in the legend indicate a high socioeconomic status with positive, stabile or negative dynamics in the micro-spatial development of the last year. Blue colors indicate a mid-range status with different dynamic aspects. Low and very low status is indicated by yellow and red colors and shows risky urban developments in Wilhelmsburg as part of the inner city district as well as on the margins of the city center and some peripheries. This picture shows that Hamburg has poverty pockets with specific characteristics referring to their history, their social and economic structure, policy-interventions and activities of the civil society in place.

The selected neighborhoods under investigation in this article are Wilhelmsburg, Ottensen and St. Pauli, all of them situated near the city center with its low density of inhabitants. They are marked dominantly with red and dark yellow colors but in different extensions. The population of Ottensen and St. Pauli were of similar size in 1990 but St. Pauli lost nearly a third of its population in the last 20 years; Wilhelmsburg was always much more populated and had to cope with a growing number of inhabitants in the last 20 years (see table 1).

Spatial mobility patterns for the investigated neighborhoods show decreasing numbers of immigrants but – with the exception of Ottensen in 2010 – a still positive migration balance. The reason for this difference is the fact that urban renewal of residential buildings from the 19th century was completed in Ottensen during the 1990s and there is not very much space for new construction activities. Urban renewal led to bigger flats and a decrease of social density so that there is no more capacity for many interested newcomers. The figures related to foreign immigrants show the highest concentration in Wilhelmsburg and more

---

5   City-states in Germany as Hamburg, Berlin and Bremen have a double political function: They act as federal states with access to respective taxes and delegate communal responsibilities to their districts. In so far they have more money at their disposal and the right to decide about their federal laws.

Chart 2: Social Fragmentation of Neighborhoods in the City-State Hamburg 2011

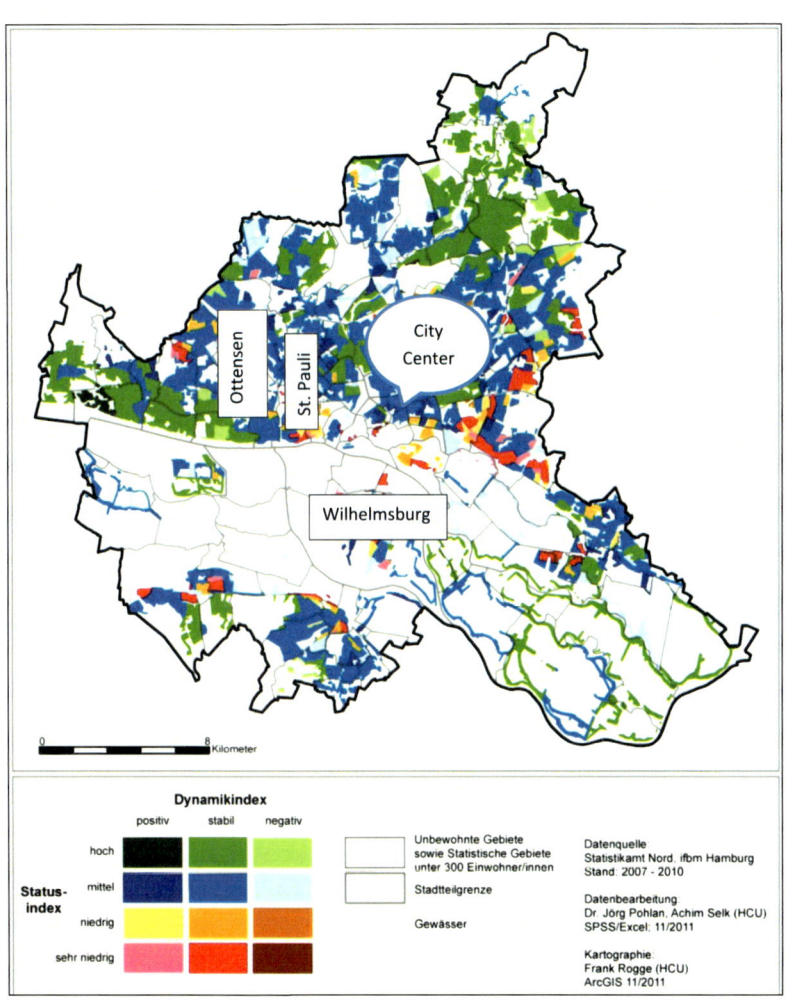

Source: FREIE UND HANSESTADT HAMBURG, 2012, p. 29.

than the cities' average also in St. Pauli. These two areas still offer a higher percentage of social housing and less living space per inhabitant than Ottensen and the average of Hamburg. Ottensen and St. Pauli are dominated by single-households and single-parent families, but access to jobs is much easier in Ottensen than in St. Pauli and Wilhelmsburg and indicates different education levels of the population. Higher education expresses itself also in different income levels, where Ottensen corresponds to the average of Hamburg, while inhabitants of St. Pauli and Wilhelmsburg reach only 2/3 of the average. The dependency on social welfare in Wilhelmsburg ranges between 20 and 26 %, in St. Pauli between 14 and 20 % and in Ottensen between 8 and 14 %.[6]

Table 1: Social Characteristics of Investigated Neighborhoods from 1990 to 2010

	Ottensen		St. Pauli		Wilhelmsburg		Hamburg
	1990	2010	1990	2010	1990	2010	2010
Population	33,161	33,052	31,888	21,469	46,686	50,472	1,7 million
Incomings	8900	3367	9555	2952	6444	4329	0,18 million
Outgoings	7508	3413	8322	2799	5418	4043	0,16 million
migration balance	+1352	-46	+1233	+153	+1,026	+286	+0,02 million
migrant background	-	25,5 %	-	35,8 %	-	56,8 %	29,6 %
social housing	-	7,8 %	-	18,9 %	-	29,4 %	10,7 %
living space p.p.	31,8	37	23,6	31,1	26,9	28	37
Singles	-	60,3 %	-	68,7 %	-	47,9 %	53,1 %
single parents (a)	-	38,8 %	-	41,8 %	-	29,8 %	30,5 %
jobless (15-65)	-	5,7 %	-	9,0 %	-	10,7 %	6,1 %
income 2004	29,270 €		20,509 €		20,354 €		32,505 €

(a) of all households with children

Source: STATISTIKAMT NORD, selected data by Ingrid Breckner

---

6 Cf. KASTENDIECK/BROOCKMANN, 2012, p.6.

Urban transformations in Ottensen, St. Pauli and Wilhelmsburg since the 1980th

Looking back on the long-term history of Ottensen, St. Pauli and Wilhelmsburg we can find some explanations for the diversities in the urban tissue of Hamburg and these areas. An important year for the cities' development is 1937, when Adolf Hitler decided to enlarge the city through the incorporation of huge parts of its surroundings. With his 'Greater Hamburg Law', Altona (including Ottensen) became a district of Hamburg as well as Harburg (including Wilhelmsburg). For a long time, these areas were on the periphery of the traditional Hanseatic City and suffered degradation in the process of industrial decay after 1960.

Ottensen, as a traditional manufacturing area, was first scheduled to be renewed by the way of the demolition of old urban structures. However, the existing plans for physical 'slum clearing' provoked intensive and continuous political protest in the 1970th which succeeded in realizing the first participative 'soft renewal' approach in Hamburg. Physical, social, symbolic and regulative changes of the urban space where negotiated in an integrative perception plot by plot and street by street between inhabitants, advocatory planners and architects, house owners and representatives of the city. This renewal process required more than 30 years and is still ongoing in certain areas; but it achieved highly appreciated results. Today, Ottensen is one of the most sought-after living spaces near to the city center because of its functional and social mix, offering a wide range of life opportunities for different social milieus. It became interesting for so called 'gentrifiers from inside' (e.g. former students engaged in the slow and integrative modernisation and now well paid academics) and people from outside with better salaries, yet still offers public housing for low income people constructed on former industrial plots. The mix of milieus in Ottensen is also evident in the structure of services and commerce in the neighborhood, which allows the residents to satisfy their daily requirements in this multicultural 'urban village'.

Until the beginning of the 21st century *St. Pauli* survived with its image 'poor but sexy'. With its well-known red light district around the Reeperbahn, the area attracted huge numbers of male tourists mostly on weekends and offered living space for different groups of low income people: students, artists, lower working class. The biggest house owner in the area showed a lot of responsibility for the 'left overs' in the postindustrial society: He offered acceptable rents for housing and commercial space, encouraged his tenants to take care of elderly and infirm neighbors and held weekly "open hours" in the lounge of his hotel in order to understand the development process and to find the right moment for necessary interventions. For the last decade the city of Hamburg has been trying to modernize this area full of urban survival spots. An old brewery on the shores of the river Elbe has been replaced by expensive private and rental housing and opened 'the village' for middle class people. Two over-dimensional open air stages became the central place for events. When travelers and homeless people discovered these public places with roofs against rain for sleeping or meeting points, the management of the place installed a water system in the roof of the stages and let it rain at random with the aim to discourage the unexpected und unwanted persons from using this public area. Parts of St. Pauli's low budget milieu started to organise an anti-gentrification protest together with owners of traditional shops and entertainment areas, encouraged by young professionals. However, the pressure of neoliberal renewal continues, forced by local, national and international real estate investors: They buy buildings and plots in advance for hotels, offices and high level housing under minimal formal political control, expecting high revenue in the future. The power of protest from the local and regional civil society is ineffective as long as policies and the cities' middle and upper class mainstream support the modernisation strategy without a solution as to where and how the specific milieu of St. Pauli is to survive under acceptable social, economic and spatial conditions. St. Pauli's traditional social mix faces an extreme risk of erosion and will produce extensive welfare costs together with much individual and collective insecurity.

Since the 1960s, *Wilhelmsburg* suffers from intensive urban decay. The flood in 1962 claimed more than 300 victims because dams in this area where lower than in other parts of the city. After the flood, the whet low standard houses where no longer attractive for those inhabitants who could afford to live in other areas. House owners lost interest in investments and politicians declared that Wilhelmsburg should no longer be treated as a residential, but primarily as an industrial area. Thus, the first "guestworkers" took over the residences considering the low prices and short ways to their jobs in the port or the railway company. In the 1970s, the city changed its policy and decided to build the new public housing quarter Kirchdorf Süd in Wilhelmsburg near the highway, without providing adequate public transport, educational, health and daily life infrastructure. For quite some time the more than 50,000 residents of Wilhelmsburg where forced to organise themselves and to find a way of living in this geographically isolated island in the river Elbe and cosmopolitan 'city in the city'. Until the beginning of the 21st century, Wilhelmsburg was a well-known symbol of marginalisation and exclusion. As housing costs in Hamburg increased, students started to discover this city diaspora in their search of cheap housing. Many of them turned back quickly because they could not find the basic infrastructure for their daily life and felt mostly frightened by the wide range of social and cultural diversities. Better-off immigrants suddenly began to flee their "arrival city"[7] once they could afford it in order to lose the discriminating address. The cities' decision for the "Leap over Elbe" after 2000 was based on the recognition that the city state of Hamburg could not cope with the intended economic growth and rising immigration if everything concentrated on the north side of the river. Under this perspective, Wilhelmsburg and the further south of Hamburg became interesting as economic and social development areas. However, this meant a change of the living conditions in Wilhelmsburg. This difficult task within an urban area neglected for a long time was expected to be solved with the complementary implementation of an International Building Exhibition (IBA) and an International Garden Show (IGS).[8] IBA opened in March 2013 and presents innovative ecological housing concepts, new models of energy supply, renewal of downgraded public housing with immigrant residents under the key themes "Cosmopolis", "Metrozones" and "Cities and Climate Change" until autumn 2013.[9] The opening anniversary was accompanied by anti-gentrification demonstrations of local people and political activists articulating their realistic fear of rising housing costs for low income residents. This risk is structurally given as long as legal rent regulations consider only new rental contracts for the yearly identification of the average rent for different housing stocks which cannot be exceeded by house owners. Thus, if in Wilhelmsburg IBA succeeds in motivating private investments in the housing stock, it will clearly result in rising rents for those residents. Housing security under these conditions is provided only for tenants in the public housing stock as long as their rents are legally limited, which is the case for maximum 15 years. The International Garden Show aims at improving the green spaces and leisure facilities in the area, which again has the effect of increasing property values and attracting well off residents.

The urban transformations in the three areas under investigation can be summarized as follows and will be used as empirical material for the interpretation of relations between poverty and gentrification in these urban spaces.

---

7   Cf. SAUNDERS, 2011.
8   Cf. INTERNATIONALE GARTENSCHAU (IGS) HAMBURG: http://www.igs-hamburg.de, 07.05.2013.
9   INTERNATIONALE BAUAUSSTELLUNG (IBA) HAMBURG: http://www.iba-hamburg.de/en/nc/themes-projects/projekte-a-z.html, 07.05.2013.

Ottensen	District of Altona, since 1937 part of Hamburg suffered degradation and social conflicts until the 1960s. Plans for 'slum clearing' turned to participative urban renewal under professional coordination after huge political protest since the 1970s with effects of stabilisation through gentrification from the in- and outside. This first integrative (physical, social, symbolic and regulative) renewal approach in Hamburg created a mix of spaces for different social and economic milieus coexisting nearly without conflicts. But the loss of poor population and rising living costs are evident.
St. Pauli	This 'poor but sexy district' still hosts a temporary amusement park and touristic spaces with niches for different low budget milieus under pressure of neoliberal renewal since 2000. Local, national and international real estate investors force the modernization of the area with lacking formal political control but accompanied by intensive protest from different groups of Hamburg's civil society.
Wilhelmsburg	Since its integration in the city state of Hamburg in 1937 the Elbe island became the most expensive example of social, economic, political and ecological failures of urban governance. The flood experience in 1962 and disinvestments lead to a neglected infrastructure (schools, public transport, etc.), poor leisure areas and dominating immigrant economies. For a long time, self-regulation of neighborhoods was the only survival strategy and came under pressure of urban renewal strategies with the International Building and Garden Exhibitions (IBA/IGS) opening in 2013 due to local protest and high professional expectations.

Relations between poverty and gentrification in urban developments

The analyzed examples of urban spaces in Hamburg show developments in different stages of post-industrial modernization. The case of Ottensen stands for participative renewal, possibly simultaneously also empowerment and displacement of less educated immigrants with low incomes. Poor young people living independently from their families with high cultural and social capacities are more and more excluded from the housing market in Ottensen because of constantly rising rents. There are no precise data to examine exactly who moved away for what reasons and who arrived in which socioeconomic condition in specific phases of the modernization process. The only fact we know definitely is that immense protest lead to a slow modernization process with the participation of politically oriented residents. Today, there is still a social and functional mixture in the area as long as the existing public housing stock remains under legal rent regulation, thus securing access to people with low income. If this political regulation erodes, the quarter shall become dominated by middle and high income groups and will risk the loss of its urban flair currently consisting of social, cultural and functional diversity and tolerance.

In St.Pauli and Wilhelmsburg the modernisation process initiated much later than in Ottensen under completely different societal conditions. Neoliberal policies had been established for more than a decade and Hamburg, as a tenant metropolis with moderate prices for real estate properties, was discovered by national and international investors seeking good revenues. Since the financial crisis in 2008 there is a huge interest from the in- and outside to use real estate properties as an investment because the trust in banks is decreasing.[10] Under these conditions urban renewal cannot be discussed any more as such: It has to be precisely contextualised with economic, political and social developments on a regional, national and global level. Its immediate or long term micro-spatial effects are much more difficult to relate to their reasons than in the long lasting renewal process in Ottensen since the end of the 1970s. The cases of Wilhelmsburg and St. Pauli show that the post-industrial labor market is less accessible for poor and elderly people without qualifications for rapidly changing and heavily internationalized service jobs. Therefore, overlapping of unemployment or precarious jobs and poor housing or homelessness succeeded to a growing number of the population even being part of the middle class. This explains the wide spectrum of people protesting against urban transformation in general

---

10   Cf. MESTER, 2013, p. 27.

and interventions in the housing market in particular. This is the only reason why the city of Hamburg decided quite quickly to rebuy the inner city area called "Gängeviertel", which was given to an investor from the Netherlands who speculated with the property for more than six years waiting for higher profit. This example shows that members of the local government and the city's public opinion is still traumatised by the 20 years of fights for buildings in Hafenstraße (Harbor Street), which finally resulted in a collective renewal process with the participation of the former squatters and the assistance of advocatory planners.

At the moment it is difficult to foresee how the ongoing protest activities in St. Pauli and Wilhelmsburg will develop in the future. There is some constructive activity from the educated second and third generation of the population with migratory background articulating their identification with the formerly neglected neighborhoods. They protest against possible displacement caused by the political creation of a social mixture, because they do not want to lose their social networks established in the urban diaspora.[11] Those immigrants, who can afford it, buy houses in their well-known quarters by pooling the money of larger families. Even if they earn less than small German households, they become economically successful in concurrence for the same flat or building due to their social capital. This situation often creates jealousy in parts of the German population which does not recognize, that this is the only possible way to keep their living environment in a discriminatory surrounding housing estate.

All over Hamburg the really poor population in central and semi-central districts is increasingly at the risk of displacement to the margins of the city or its suburbs. As chart 3 shows, the city center was highly populated in the 1960th. Until the end of the 20th century the central area of Hamburg lost its residential function because of disinvestment in the old housing stock, lack of green areas and ongoing commercialization of these central spaces. Those who moved to the margins or to the suburbs were the classical middle classes expecting a more homogenous and healthy residential environment. Since the beginning of the 21st century we observe a trend called re-urbanisation (in contradiction to suburbanisation) or 'renaissance of the city' in Hamburg and other German metropolis[12]. New attractive residential opportunities in central areas are highly sought-after by well-off households from the cities' periphery and from outside.[13]

---

11   Cf. BLOKLAND, 2003.
12   Cf. LÄPPLE, 2005; KANAI/LÄPPLE, 2005.
13   Cf. MENZL et al., 2011; BRECKNER/MENZL, 2012.

Chart 3: Distribution of Population in Hamburg in Dependency to the Distance to the City Centre

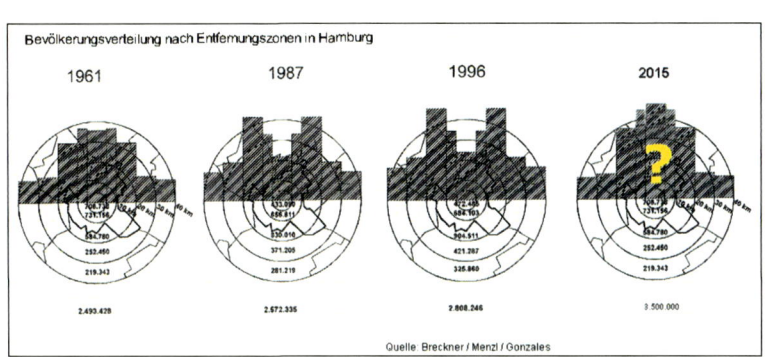

Source: BRECKNER et al., 1998, p. 27

They rent and buy residences while people with lower incomes cannot afford the expensive housing costs in the central areas. Demographic change also creates pressure for the poor population in central city districts because even middle class parents, whose children left home, decide to reduce their living space and prefer to move to central areas.[14] Thus, the attractiveness of central urban living spaces goes hand in hand with risks of displacement for poor elderly and young people, single parent families and new immigrants to closer or further peripheries. These households mostly cannot afford or are not able to drive cars and are in danger to lose their established social contacts and necessary health infrastructure. Therefore, in the future poverty and capacities of self-organisation need to be analyzed in marginal districts of metropolis and in suburbs where we cannot expect yet the same complex competences for the production of space as in megacities of developing countries.[15] The German overregulation of spatial planning and the still existing lack of cooperation between institutions and professions involved in the production of space risk to create new poverty issues outside of the metropolis in cases of low political responsibility and lack of economic resources for societal inclusion.

---

14 Cf. SLAVIK, 2013, p. 25.
15 Cf. DELL, 2009.

Literature

BLOKLAND, TALJA, Urban Bonds: Social relationships in an inner city neighbourhood, Cambridge 2003.

BRECKNER, INGRID/MENZL, MARCUS, Neighbourliness in the City Centre: Reality and potential in the case of the Hamburg HafenCity, in: New Urbanism. Life, Work, and Space in the New Downtown. ed. by ILSE HELBRECHT/PETER DRKSMEIER, Farnham/Burlington 2012, p. 133-148.

BRECKNER, INGRID, Gentrifizierung im 21. Jahrhundert, in: Aus Politik und Zeitgeschichte 17 (2010), p. 27-32.

DELL, CHRISTOPHER, Tacit Urbanism. Hawkers and the production of space in every day Kolkata, Rotterdam 2009.

FREIE UND HANSESTADT HAMBURG/BEHÖRDE FÜR STADTENTWICKLUNG UND UMWELT, Sozialmonitoring Integrierte Stadtteilentwicklung Bericht 2011, Hamburg 2012.

KANAI, MIGUEL/LÄPPLE, DIETER, The Resurgence of Urban Centralities: a look at contemporary New York , ed. by LONDON SCHOOL OF ECONOMICS AND POLITICAL SCIENCE, London 2005.

KASTENDIECK, HANNA/BROOCKMANN, SONJA, Das Hamburg der Gegensätze, in: Hamburger Abendblatt, 22.03.2012, p 6.

LÄPPLE, DIETER, Thesen zu einem Konzept gesellschaftlicher Räume, in: Die aufgeräumte Welt. Raumbilder und Raumkonzepte im Zeitalter globaler Marktwirtschaft, Loccumer Protokolle 74/92, ed. by JÖRG MAYER, Loccum 1993, p. 29-52.

ID., Phoenix aus der Asche : Die Neuerfindung der Stadt, in: Die Wirklichkeit der Städte, ed. by HELMUT BERKING/MARTINA LÖW, Baden-Baden2005, p.397-413.

LEES, LORETTA et al., Gentrification, New York 2008.

MENZL, MARCUS et al., Wohnen in der HafenCity – Zuzugsmotive, Alltagserfahrungen, nachbarschaftliche Aktivitäten. Materialien zur HafenCity Hamburg Nr. 1, ed. by HAFENCITY HAMBURG GmbH, Hamburg 2011.

MESTER, VOLKER, Spekulanten treiben Immobilienpreise hoch, in: Hamburger Abendblatt, 27.03.2013, p. 27.

SAUNDERS, DOUG, Arrival City – The Final Migration and Our Next World, Toronto 2011.

SLATER, TOM, Gentrification oft the City, in: The New Blackwell Companion to the City ed. by GARY BRIDGE/SOPHIE WATSON, Malden (USA)/Oxford (UK), 2011, p. 571-585.

SLAVIK, ANGELIKA, Wer braucht schon ein viertes Zimmer?, in: Süddeutsche Zeitung, 27.03.2013, p. 25.

BRECKNER, INGRID et al, Auswirkungen der Umlandwanderung auf den Hamburger Wohnungsmarkt, ed. by FREIE UND HANSESTADT HAMBURG/BAUBEHÖRDE/AMT FÜR WOHNUNGSWESEN, Hamburg 1998: https://www.hcu-hamburg.de/research/arbeitsgebiete/prof-dr-ingrid-breckner/forschung, 07.05.2013.

INTERNATIONALE BAUAUSSTELLUNG (IBA) HAMBURG: http://www.iba-hamburg.de/en/nc/themes-projects/projekte-a-z.html, 07.05.2013.

INTERNATIONALE GARTENSCHAU (IGS) HAMBURG: http://www.igs-hamburg.de, 07.05.2013.

SOYKA, ANDREA, Arbeit im Kernstadt-Umland-Gefüge, 2006: http://www.suburbanisierung.de/downloads/Verpflechtungsmuster.pdf, 07.05.2013.

Europe's only Megacity

Urban Growth, Migration and Gentrification in 21st Century Moscow

JULIA RÖTTJER/JAN KUSBER

At the beginning of the 21st century, Moscow is the largest city and the only Megacity in the European context.[1] It is therefore a case study to be considered in the frame of this conference volume about perspectives of cultural sciences on urban slum areas and their inhabitants. The capital of the Russian Federation has been growing constantly over the last 20 years and the city itself is currently home to approx. 12,000,000,[2] the Moscow agglomeration to more than 17,000,000 inhabitants, in other words 12 % of the Russian population.[3] Moscow is the true centre of the Russian Federation, not only as the focus of a centralised political system, but also as the hotbed of Russian economy. It has been a widely accepted saying that the Russian capital is "one of the most expensive cities of the world" – it also seems to stand for gated communities, a concentration of powerful oil companies, Soviet city planning heritage, the menacing collapse of traffic and an extremely uneven distribution of wealth. At the same

---

1 One may discuss the case of Istanbul here. Fedor Kudriavcev speaks of European cities in contrast to cities like Istanbul, Cairo and – Moscow. Cf. KUDRIAVCEV, 2012, p. 374. The heritage of the socialist metropolis planning stands against this: LENTZ, 1997, p. 110.

2 Statistical projection on the basis of the last official number in 2010 (11,514,300), the inclusion of new areas into the city, and the development since 2002: VSEROSSIISKAIA PEREPIS' NASELENIIA 2010 GODA: http://www.gks.ru/free_doc/new_site/perepis2010/croc/perepis_itogi1612.htm, 07.05.2013.

3 Cf. MAKHROVA, 2006: http://demoscope.ru/weekly/2006/0247/tema01.php, 07.05.2013.

time, the Moscow of today does not appear to feature the aforementioned "urban slum areas" in a sense that might be associated with other Megacities.[4] Nevertheless, processes of social segregation and gentrification as well as urban migration into and within the city are issues which concern the development of this European Mega-Agglomeration and will be considered in this paper. Its aim is to put Moscow into the debate of this collection, because this Megacity is worth to be researched permanently and interdisciplinary. Within its limited space we shall briefly focus on some points of recent developments in Moscow:

- Urban growth: What are the general stages in Moscow's development until today? What current challenges are there and what is the character of the anticipated future growth?
- Urban migration: Who lives where in this city and what spaces are occupied by different groups of Muscovites? Which groups are migrating into the city? What can be said about the urban poor?
- Gentrification: Who 'owns' the city? What groups are migrating within the city and what are the reasons? How are groups of Muscovites expelled from different areas of the city?

Not all points shall be answered fully, but there always is a historical perspective as a relevant context-setting category. As this article is written by two historians, this may be their appeal for a closer collaboration of historical and social sciences dealing with the phenomena in question.

---

[4] During its history, poverty in Russia has been a topic that was investigated on many levels, and poverty in the city of Moscow has naturally been included in this research. However, at the same time it can be witnessed that St. Petersburg seemed to be more in focus concerning the sketching of urban social issues – cf. for a recent example JAHN, 2010.

Urban growth and development of "The best city in the world"[5]

The city of Moscow gradually grew around the Moscow Kremlin, beginning in the 14th century. It was the capital of the Grand Duchy, after 1547 Tsardom of Muscovy up to 1712, when Peter the Great made the newly founded St. Petersburg his capital. Of course, the loss of the function as the political centre of the state led to a decrease of population of approximately 150,000 down to some 120,000, however, with its location in the Russian heartland and still being centre of commerce the city soon recovered. Moscow once again became capital of the Soviet Union from 1922 to 1991, and of the Russian Federation since 1991.[6]

Situated on either bank of the Moskva River, during the 16th to 17th centuries the city grew up in divisions, formerly separated from one another by walls: the Kremlin, Kitaigorod ("walled town", but interpreted as "Chinatown" by folk etymology), Bielyigorod ("white town"), Zemlianoigorod ("earthworks town"), and Meshchanskiigorod ("bourgeois town") outside the city walls. When Catherine II came to power in 1762, the city's filth and smell of waste and the irregularity of the streets were depicted by observers as a symptom of disorderly lifestyles of lower-class Russians, most of them with a peasant background. Elites called for the improvement of sanitation, which became part of Catherine's plans for increasing control over social life. Although her ambitious General plan for Moscow (1775) as a whole failed, the main achievements were the Mytishchinski water-pipe (built 1784-1804) and the street lightening, which made the centre of the city more secure. After the fire of 1812 as a result of Napoleon's campaign, the city ramparts were replaced with the Boulevard Ring and Garden Ring roads, replacing the walls around Bielyigorod and Zemlianoigorod, respectively.[7] The city's population grew from 250,000 to above 1,000,000 by the end of the 19th century. National political and military successes from 1812 through 1855 calmed the critics and validated efforts to produce a more enlightened and stable society. There was less talk about the smell and the poor hygienic conditions.

---

5 In 2013, Moscow is putting on a festival named "The best city in the world" – see the official Moscow website, presentation for the press March 29th, 2013: PRAVITEL'STVO MOSKVY(1): http://www.mos.ru/press-center/presentations, 07.05.2013.

6 Cf. on the history of the city in general: LUZHKOV, 1997. On the persistence through the political changes of revolution and the breakdown of communism: SCHLÖGEL, 2011.

7 Cf. on the rebuilding of Moscow after 1812: SCHMIDT, 1989, p. 143-202.

However, with Russia's failures in the Crimean War in 1855-56, confidence in the ability of the state to maintain order in the slums eroded and demands for improved public health placed the issue of filth back on the agenda.[8] In the second half of the 19th century, Moscow was connected by railway: The first line was the one to St. Petersburg, opened in 1852. At the end of the 19th century, Moscow had become the centre of the country's railway network and saw an influx of migrating peasants, who were the needed work force for the industrialisation in fin de siècle Moscow. With no general urban planning and no concept for public transport and housing at hand, factories were built at the embankments of the Moskva River, near to Kremlin, for example the chocolate factory "Einem".[9]

After the October Revolution, the Bolsheviks moved the capital from Petrograd to Moscow in order to evade the wakes of the World War and the raging civil war. Whereas the population in Petrograd declined seriously, Moscow became the world capital of socialism with a further increase in population. The first Five-Year-Plan saw Moscow as a centre of light and heavy industry. At the end of the twenties it became a "peasant metropolis"[10]. But the massive influx of peasants was a source of great concern for party officials. In their opinion, peasants, as members of a "petit-bourgeois" class, represented an "uncultured mass" fond of drinking, with no discipline or religious beliefs and a general lack of political consciousness. So, the city with now 2,000,000 inhabitants not only needed outstanding new buildings designed and built by avant-garde architects (Le Corbusier, Mel'nikov, and others) as worker-clubs and houses for leisure entertainment, but a general development plan. This "Master Plan for the Reconstruction of the City of Moscow", devised by a commission under Lazar Kaganovich and co-signed by Stalin and Viacheslav Molotov on July 10th 1935, was intended as an offensive against the old Moscow, which would transform the city as a whole. Four years in the making, the plan called for an expansion of the city's area from 285 to 600 square kilometres that would take in mostly farmland to the south and west beyond the Lenin (nowadays Sparrow) Hills. It involved 16 major highway projects and the construction of sev-

---

8   Cf. MARTIN, 2008, p. 243-274. This subject was important, though a minor one during the revolution of 1905, cf. THURSTON, 1987.

9   Cf. HUBER, 2007, p. 25; DÖNNINGHAUS, 2012. The company became the famous "Red October" in Soviet times. The site was bought by a developer in 2004, the production moved to the rim of Moscow. Since, there have been several fantastical plans for a mix-use project in close proximity to the Kremlin, but nothing could be realised yet. Cf. MAKAROVA, 2010: http://magazines.russ.ru/nz/2010/2/ma25.html, 07.05.2013.

10 So the title of a cultural study by HOFFMANN, 1994.

eral monumental buildings of "state-wide significance", the well-known skyscrapers that were to dominate the boulevards' perspectives.[11] It foresaw 15,000,000 square meters of new housing to accommodate a total population of approximately 5,000,000 within the next decades. Representative streets modelled after Haussmann's boulevards in Paris were built, most prominent the Gorkii street.[12] The city would be surrounded by a green belt up to a width of ten kilometres.

Even while the master plan was being drawn up, old Moscow was giving way to the new. One of the showpieces of the Soviet capital was to be the Moscow Metro, which broke ground in March 1932, went into service in May 1935 and serves, with its successively built lines, especially the ring line, as the backbone of public transportation until today.[13] A second project, begun in the early 1930s, was the Moscow-Volga Canal built by an army of 200,000 forced labourers, which opened in July 1937. The hopes to make the system of rivers and waterways the major route for the transport of goods failed. The railway remained and still is the dominant means of transportation. In the year 1939, the population of Moscow rose to over four million and by 1959, with the banned returning because of the dissolution of the GULAG after Stalin's death in 1953, the number of inhabitants approached the 5,000,000 mark. The General plan of 1935 was superseded ahead of time.

During the Khrushchev-period, entire villages in the Moscow region and farmland that had been cultivated for centuries were ploughed under to make way for new apartment blocks organised in micro-districts.[14] The prototype of such housing developments was Novye Cheremushki, south of the city centre.[15] Later, the neighbourhood of Medvedkovo in the city's south-west and other outlying areas were subjected to the same process. Nevertheless, the new party programme of 1961, which promised that the housing shortage would be eliminated during the first decade of building communism (1961-70), was far from having been realised in the country and in Moscow.

To bring the blue- and especially the white-collar-workers to their working place in the centre of the Soviet Union's capital, the MKAD (Moskovskaia kol'tsevaia avtomobil'naia doroga), a ring road used only for military purposes, was opened to the public in 1962.[16] It had four lanes running 109 kilometres along the city borders.

---

11 Cf. for the Stalinist architecture NOEVER, 1994. The building of the high rises was begun after 1945.
12 Cf. RÜTHERS, 2007, p. 75-152.
13 Cf. NEUTATZ, 2001.
14 Cf. COLTON, 1995, p. 358-381.
15 Cf. RÜTHERS, 2006.
16 Cf. KUDRIAVCEV, 2012, p. 375.

The MKAD marked the administrative boundaries of the city of Moscow until the 1980s, when outlying suburbs beyond the ring road were being incorporated.

Whereas struggling heavily with controlling the migration into Moscow – especially the peasants, who came there just to sell parts of the harvest, melons from Astrakhan and other products to overcome the dysfunctions of planned economy,[17] – the Summer Olympic Games of 1980 presented an unparalleled opportunity to showcase the superiority of Soviet athletes as well as the achievements of Soviet socialism in front of a world-wide audience.[18] Extraordinary measures were taken to prepare for this grand festival. A renaissance of urban planning, typical of host cities, resulted in not only new stadiums, training facilities, and hotels, but also a new airport at Sheremetevo. The city itself was 'polished up': Roads were newly paved, trees were planted – dissidents and the poor were banned or otherwise expelled from the city.[19]

When the USSR was dissolved in 1991, Moscow became the capital of the Russian Federation. Since then, the emergence of market economy in Moscow has produced an explosion of Western-style retailing, services, architecture, and lifestyles. The city has continued to grow during the 1990s to 2000s, its population rising from less than 9,000,000 to more than 11,000,000. Mason and Nigmatullina argue that Soviet-era urban-growth central planning (before 1991) produced controlled and sustainable metropolitan development, typified by the building of the greenbelt in 1935. However, there has been a dramatic growth of low-density suburban sprawl since then, created by a heavy demand for single-family dwellings as opposed to crowded apartments. In 1995-97 the MKAD ring road was widened from the initial four to ten lanes. In December 2002 Bul'var Dmitriia Donskogo became the first Moscow Metro station to open beyond the limits of MKAD. The Third Ring Road, intermediate between the early 19th-century Garden Ring and the Soviet era outer ring road, was completed in 2005.[20] The greenbelt is becoming more and more fragmented and satellite cities are appearing at the fringe. Summer dachas are being converted into year-round residences, and with the proliferation of automobiles there is heavy traffic congestion. These fragmentations of the borders of the megacity and its expansion beyond those rims have to be noted when considering the Moscow agglomeration and its population.[21]

---

17 Cf. on the migration and mixture of population in the 60s and 70s: GAVRILOVA, 2001, p. 130-171.
18 Cf. KUSBER, 2003, p. 108f.
19 Cf. KUPERMANN, 2007.
20 Cf. KUDRIAVCEV, 2012, p. 375.
21 Cf. MASON/NIGMATULLINA, 2011.

A view at the different historical layers of Moscow housing – from the Khrushchevki of the 1950s to later Soviet complexes and postmodern apartment blocks

Urban migration

Moscow is an independent federation subject of the Russian federation. At the same time, the city is the administrative centre of the federation subject it is surrounded by, the "Moscow region" (Moskovskaia *oblast'*). Within the *oblast'*, there are many larger cities and smaller towns located within the direct vicinity of Moscow. More than one million commuters are on their way to Moscow and back every day, while three to four million Muscovites spend the summer on dachas outside the city boundaries. Within this agglomeration there exists not only a close interconnection in terms of traffic, but in the labour and housing markets as well. Tendencies that are true of the housing market of Moscow itself quickly spread into the agglomeration, which has seen an unusually high building activity in the last years; it attracts not only Muscovites but also private housing investors from all over Russia.[22]

---

22 ZUBAREVICH, 2012, p. 265.

Table 1: Population of Moscow, Moscow region and Russia, 1989-2010 (in 000)[23]

	1989	1995	2000	2005	2008	2009	2010	Development		
								1989-2000	2000-2010	1989-2010
Russia	147,400	148,460	146,890	143,474	142,009	141,904	141,914	-0,35 %	-3,39 %	-3,72 %
Moscow City	8,972	9,085	9,933	10,407	10,470	10,509	10,563	10,71 %	6,34 %	17,73 %
Moscow Region	6,689	6,672	6,628	6,630	6,673	6,713	6,753	-0,91 %	1,89 %	0,96 %

---

23 Table is based on numbers from DEMOGRAFICHESKII EZHEGODNIK ROSSII, 2001, p. 22 (1989); DEMOGRAFICHESKII EZHEGODNIK ROSSII, 2010, p. 29 (1995-2009) and from the official site of the 2010 census of the Russian Federation (2010): VSEROSSIISKAIA PEREPIS' NASELENIIA 2010 GODA: http://www.gks.ru/free_doc/new_site/perepis2010/croc/perepis_itogi1612.htm, 07.05.2013.

The table shows the rate of the growth of the Moscow population in comparison to that of the entire country; however, it also demonstrates that the fastest expansion of Moscow population happened between 1995 and 2000 and that it is currently slowing down. While in 1989, the combined population of Moscow city and region made up 10,6 % of the Russian population, in 2010 this rate rose to 12,2 %. According to the census of 2010, Moscow has 11,503,501 inhabitants and the Moscow region 7,095,120, which mostly live in urban-type settlements.[24]

Table 2: Population of Moscow agglomeration in 2002 and 2010; division into Moscow city counties (okrugi) and urban/rural population of Moscow region[25]

	Overall 2002	Overall 2010	Percentage of Population in relation to Moscow city and Region in 2010	Percentage Growth/Decrease in 2010 in relation to 2002
Moscow City and Region	17,001,292	18,598,621	100,0 %	+9,4 %
Moscow City	10,382,754	11,503,501	61,9 %	+10,8 %
Moscow Region	6,618,538	7,095,120	38,1 %	+7,2 %

---

24 Cf. Vserossiiskaia perepis' naseleniia 2010 goda: http://www.gks.ru/free_doc/new_site/perepis2010/croc/perepis_itogi1612.htm, 07.05.2013.

25 The data was taken from the official web sites of the 2002 census: Vserossiiskaia perepis' naseleniia 2002 goda: http://www.perepis2002.ru/index.html?id=42, 07.05.2013, and from Vserossiiskaia perepis' naseleniia 2010 goda: http://www.gks.ru/free_doc/new_site/perepis2010/croc/perepis_itogi1612.htm, 07.05.2013. For the values of 2002, the city of Zelenograd, counted separately in the census, was taken as the city okrug Zelenogradskii. Also, three in 2002 still independent smaller settlements were included in this table in the values of the South-Eastern, Western and Eastern okrugi, of which they became a part later on, in order for comparison with 2010.

	Overall 2002	Overall 2010	Percentage of Population in relation to Moscow city and Region in 2010	Percentage Growth/ Decrease in 2010 in relation to 2002
City okrug Eastern (Vostochnyi)	1,394,497	1,452,759	7,8 %	+4,2 %
City okrug Western (Zapadnyi)	1,049,104	1,285,914	6,9 %	+22,6 %
City okrug Zelenogradskii	215,727	221,712	1,2 %	+2,8 %
City okrug Northern (Severnyi)	1,112,846	1,100,974	5,9 %	-1,1 %
City okrug North-Eastern (Severo-Vostochnyi)	1,240,062	1,359,508	7,3 %	+9,6 %
City okrug North-Western (Severo-Zapadnyi)	779,965	942,223	5,1 %	+20,8 %
City okrug Central (Tsentralnyi)	701,353	741,967	4,0 %	+5,8 %
City okrug South-Eastern (Iugo-Vostochnyi)	1,116,924	1,318,885	7,1 %	+18,1 %
City okrug South-Western (Iugo-Zapadnyi)	1,179,211	1,362,751	7,3 %	+15,6 %
City okrug Southern (Iuzhnyi)	1,593,065	1,716,808	9,2 %	+7,8 %
Moscow Region: urban Population	5,248,534	5,683,710	30,6 %	+8,3 %
Moscow Region: rural Population	1,370,004	1,411,410	7,6 %	+3,0 %

The city itself takes up 2,510 km² and is divided into twelve counties (*okrugi*) which, since the last city extension on July 1st 2012, consist of 146 administrative sub-structures.[26]

In comparison to other big Russian cities, Moscow, as the centre of a centralistic and authoritative state, features many advantages for big companies including the energy sector. Thus, despite the fact that Moscow has a general post-industrial economy with more than 80 % of the gross regional product due to services, it is important that the large producing companies have their headquarters mostly in Moscow. The corporate tax principles in this centralised economic system provided for the payment of taxes at headquarters, at least until the issuing of a new regulation in 2012, which still excludes Gazprom. These taxes, paid to the capital by companies that produce goods elsewhere and offer their services all over the country, make up 43-45 % of the huge Moscow budget which comprised 38 billion Euros in 2011. Not only a high percentage of the Russian population is living in and around Moscow; also, compared to all of Russia, there is an even higher proportional amount of investment, housing construction and retail. The concentration of investment and financial resources is the motor of change to urban society. The share of Muscovites that can be defined as middle class doubles the overall Russian rate – it is about 40 %. The average income in Moscow is comparatively high – in other large Russian cities it is 35-60 % lower than in the capital.[27] In Moscow, the nominal average monthly employment income in 2010 was 908 Euros, and the average pension was 192 Euros, the average living space was 18,7 square metres per person.[28]

Moscow has always featured a low birth rate in comparison to the death rate, not unlike other very large cities. Especially in the 1990s, the birth rate sank to a very low level: While there were 120,000 children born in 1985, the number was only 68,500 in the year 1995. Still, during these years the population of the city

---

26 There were 10 counties (*okrugi*) with 125 districts (*raiony*). In July 2012, with Novomoskovskii and Troitskii two more okrugi were added, consisting of 21 administrative sub-structures, which are called "settlement" (*poselenie*). Cf. the official Moscow city site: PRAVITEL'STVO MOSKVY(2): http://www.mos.ru/authority/structure, 07.05.2013.

27 Cf. ZUBAREVICH, 2012, p. 265-267, based on information by the Moscow Independent Institute for Social Policy. As middle class indicators, Zubarevich uses two out of three of the following: income, education level and self-conception.

28 Cf. Federal agency of state statistics: REGIONY ROSSII. OSNOVNYE SOTSIALNO-ECONOMICHESKIE POKAZATELI GRODOV 2011: http://www.gks.ru/bgd/regl/b11_14t/IssWWW.exe/Stg/centr/moskv-g2011_1.htm, 07.05.2013.

rose. Concerning the average life expectancy, the capital has a lot to offer to its inhabitants and even leaves St. Petersburg far behind: For males the life expectancy is 67 years (for Russia in general: 60), for females it is 77 years (for Russia in general: 73). These facts contribute to the phenomenon that the population of Moscow is increasing while the overall Russian population is declining. But the decisive factor is the migration into the city, which has always been playing an important role in Moscow until today.[29]

Table 3: Migration in Moscow City and Region compared to Russia, in 2009[30]

	Moscow City and Region	Russia	Moscow City and Region	Russia
	Arrivals			
	Total Number of Arrivals		Arrivals, Rate per 1000 Population	
Total Number of Arrivals	191,709	1,987,598	11,1	14,0
Arrivals from Other Regions of Russia	155,805	766,436	9,0	5,4
Arrivals from Foreign Countries	35,904	279,907	2,1	2,0
	Departures			
	Total Number of Departures		Departures, Rate per 1000 Population	
Total Number of Departures	68,156	1,740,149	4,0	12,3
Departures to Other Regions of Russia	64,117	766,436	3,7	5,4
Departures to Foreign Countries	4,039	32,458	0,2	0,2

29 Cf.ZAIONCHKOVSKAYA/MKRTCHYAN,2009:http://www.demoscope.ru/weekly/2009/0389/tema02.php, 07.05.2013.
30 Data was taken from DEMOGRAFICHESKII EZHEGODNIK ROSSII, 2010, p. 29 (table 1.7), p. 408, 411, 414 (table 7.2.).

		Moscow City and Region	Russia	Moscow City and Region	Russia
		Net Migration			
		Total Number of Net Migration		Net Migration, Rate per 1000 Population	
Total Number of Net Migration		123,553	247,449	7,2	1,7
Net Migration from Other Regions of Russia		91,688	0	5,3	0
Net Migration from Foreign Countries		31,865	247,449	1,9	1,7

The aforementioned influx of migrants into the city during the 1920s brought both men and women into the city. They were in search of work, and not intent on founding large families, so a relatively low birth rate and small number of children became a consistent feature of the Moscow population. However, in the 1960s until 1980s the progressing urbanisation in Russia spread this trend and led to an approximation of the overall Russian population age pyramid to that of the capital. Similar features were characteristic of the age pyramid of Moscow in 1989, but at the beginning of the new millennium the migration surge not only balanced the natural decline, it also rejuvenated the city's population.[31] Like in other large cities, the educational level in Moscow is rather high compared to the rest of the country. Being asked about their sources of income in the census of 2010, 57 % of the Muscovites named employment income, including self-employment and family business, as a source, 27 % pensions (including invalidity pensions) and only 3,5 % (other) social benefits or governmental support. One quarter of the respondents stated that their income was dependent on other individuals. Thus, the rate of pensioners, the vast majority of them in the age groups 60 years and older is about the same level in Moscow as it is in all of Russia.[32] It is a phenomenon uncharacteristic for megacities with such high living expenses

---

31 Cf. ZAIONCHKOVSKAYA/MKRTCHYAN, 2009.
32 Respondents were all individuals 15 years or older. Multiple answers were possible, but app. 86 % gave only one and app. 14 % two sources; three answers or more were seldom. Analysed data was taken from 2010 census: VSEROSSIISKAIA PEREPIS' NASELENIIA 2010 GODA: http://www.gks.ru/free_doc/new_site/perepis2010/croc/perepis_itogi1612.htm, 07.05.2013.

that the group of pensioners and the ratio of older population is so strong, fostered by city government, which subsidises the pensions out of its own budget.[33]

The migration history and the present situation which have been forming Moscow's population make it a multi-ethnic and multi-religious city. The strongest groups in the Russian capital who perceive themselves as non-Russian, are inhabitants of former Soviet republics, mainly Ukrainians, Tatars, Armenians, Azerbaijani and Belo-Russians, but there are also other large groups, such as of Mordovians, Jews and Uzbeks:

Table 4: Overall population of Moscow City and Region, according to Nationality[34]

	Population, according to Nationality					
Moscow City and Region	1989	%	2002	%	2010	%
Overall Population			17,001,292	100,0 %	18,598,621	100,0 %
Russians	14,047,917	89,7 %	14,830,772	87,2 %	16,133,082	86,7 %
Ukrainians	438,508	2,8 %	401,452	2,4 %	273,578	1,5 %
Tatars	281,898	1,8 %	218,934	1,3 %	205,245	1,1 %
Armenians	78,305	0,5 %	164,085	1,0 %	169,772	0,9 %
Azerbaijani	31,322	0,2 %	110,214	0,6 %	76,184	0,4 %
Belo-Russians	125,288	0,8 %	101,565	0,6 %	70,890	0,4 %
Jews	313,220	2,0 %	89,258	0,5 %	53,145	0,3 %
Mordovians	46.983	0,3 %	45,243	0,3 %		
Chuvash	31,322	0,2 %	28,541	0,2 %		
Uzbeks	15,661	0,1 %	24,312	0,1 %	61,368	0,3 %
Chechens (city only)			14,465	0,1 %		
Ossetians (city only)			10,561	0,1 %		
Moldavians (region only)			10,418	0,1 %		
Koreans (city only)			8,630	0,1 %		
Kazakhs (city only)			7,997	0,1 %		
Bashkir (city only)			5,941	0,1 %		

---

33 ZUBAREVICH, 2012, p. 268.
34 The data analysed was taken from the census of 2002: VSEROSSIISKAIA PEREPIS' NASELENIIA 2002 GODA: http://www.perepis2002.ru/index.html?id=42, 07.05.2013, and from the census of 2010: VSEROSSIISKAIA PEREPIS' NASELENIIA 2010 GODA: http://www.gks.ru/free_doc/new_site/perepis2010/croc/perepis_itogi1612.htm, 07.05.2013. Cf. for 1989: GAVRILOVA, 2001, p. 420 (table 7).

Official data cannot provide any information about the significant number of nonregistered migrants from Russia and outside Russia living in the capital (table 3 and 4).

Gentrification and segregation in inner Moscow

Prior to 1992, almost all houses in Moscow were state owned, municipal or corporate. There were practically no private houses in Moscow during Soviet times. In the first years following the perestroika period the resources for municipal housing programmes in Moscow were scarce, while new forms of investment and public private partnerships had yet to evolve. The last census of the Soviet Union in 1989 had shown that the housing situation and its problems were an important issue for the Muscovites, but in 1995 there were still about 650,000 households waiting in line for the opportunity to new living quarters and many Muscovites were living in a shared apartment (*kommunalka*).[35] In order to effectively reduce this waiting line, the municipal building company DSK (the former Building Combine No. 1), which had survived the perestroika, continued in the construction of prefabricated housing.[36] But the city was not only short of living quarters, but also of territory. The authorities thus turned to the five-story-buildings with a programme to relocate the dwellers in order to gain area for high rise living quarters. During the first years of the new millennium, the inhabitants in need to be relocated represented competition for those already waiting – so, people from the waiting list who had filed their respective applications in 1987, were able to gain access to new living quarters in 2006.[37]

The capital could not provide nearly enough living quarters to its population and suffered an overall lack of investment into housing and city planning. At the point of dissolution of the Soviet Union, an intense era of construction began

---

35 Cf. KULAKOVA, 2006, p. 238-241. The estimate percentage of kommunalka dwellers reaches from 9 % (KULAKOVA, 2006, p. 238) up to 45 % (BADYINA/GOLUBCHIKOV, 2005, p. 118).

36 The house type P-44/17, first built in 1979, was continued until the year 2000; the 17-story panelled building can boast a total area of 18,814 m² in Moscow. Since 1998, new prefabricated types were introduced, as the P-44T, P44-TM, and the model *Jubilee*, advertised as "the first and only prefabricated house of a new generation with winter gardens (porches) and free layout." Cf. DOMOSTROITEL'NYI KOMBINAT NO. 1: http://www.dsk1.ru/Houses/History, 07.05.2013.

37 Cf. KULAKOVA, 2006, p. 242f.

in Moscow almost immediately. The historic city centre attracted most of the activity, driven by the needs of the emerging market economy with all the new financial and business services and municipal policy alike. The concentration of wealthy companies or financial services and their headquarters in the city centre was followed by a concentration of wealthy inhabitants. So already in the early 1990s, individuals and businesses started to purchase apartments in top quality locations in order to renovate them luxuriously. Badyina and Golubchikov, who analyse these processes, especially in the inner micro-district Ostozhenka, summarise this phenomenon: "However, a central location and an expensive renovation [...] turned out to be not quite enough. [...] The evolution from apartment-by-apartment to house-by-house and then to block-by-block elite housing (re)construction signified the emergence of systematic gentrification in inner Moscow."[38]

The micro-district of Ostozhenka is located south-west to the Kremlin in an area that was used as meadowland until the middle of the 19th century. At the end of the 19th century, the majority of tenants were small-scale retailers, craftsmen, state servants of low ranks, students and impoverished members of the intelligentsia; landlords were mostly merchants. In the case of Ostozhenka, the extreme neglect of building stock in the late Soviet Moscow was even more evident: The general plan of 1935 had designated a site nearby to the megalomaniac – yet never realised – project of the "Palace of Soviets". Thus, there were long existing plans to comprehensively redevelop the entire quarter with the palace, which prevented building or renovation on a smaller scale.[39]

At the beginning of the 1990s, the rate of Ostozhenka inhabitants living in a *kommunalka* was between 60 % and 70 %,[40] and thus significantly higher than the average in central Moscow. With the introduction of housing privatisation in 1991, inhabitants gained the right to privatise their own living quarters free of charge; two years later one third of all flats in Moscow were in private hands. With the developing market economy this served as a basis for the mechanism of well-off private persons and agencies buying the separate *kommunalka* rooms from their inhabitants and combining them into apartments or office floors. The social structure of the micro-district started to change, the overall population declined, and the proportion of wealthier people started to rise, while the for-

---

38 BADYINA/GOLUBCHIKOV, 2005, p. 115.
39 Cf. GDANIEC, 2005, p. 145; BADYINA/GOLUBCHIKOV, 2005, p. 115-117. The 1883 cathedral Christ the Saviour that occupied the lot foreseen for the palace, was demolished in 1931.
40 Cf. GDANIEC, 2005, p. 173 and BADYINA/GOLUBCHIKOV, 2005, p. 118, respectively.

mer *kommunalka* inhabitants left, supported by the city rehousing programmes. After the 1998 Rouble crash and the following economic pause, large development started to invest in the real estate sector. Ostozhenka, where the cathedral "Christ the Saviour" overshadowing the micro-district was being rebuilt on its former site long dedicated to the "Palace of Soviets"-project, was being marketed as an elite location in close proximity to the Kremlin. The new developments did not consist of the mere merging of single rooms into apartments, but of comprehensive building projects and the more there were the more intensive the elite status perception became.[41]

In Moscow, land ownership is separate from building ownership, so the land owner is the municipality, while developers can lease parcels to build on.[42] The city administration took an active part in promoting the physical and social change in areas such as Ostozhenka by resettlement mechanisms that required inhabitants to leave if their building had been marked by the city as in urgent need of repair. The administration had – and still has – to provide the expelled with an alternative housing or, in case of ownership, to compensate them. Often, these terms have been less favourable for the residents than direct negotiations with the investors. The vacated buildings could then be demolished, often ignoring the regulations of the sophisticated Russian monument preservation law, and give way to the new elite projects. Of the 3,725 officially registered tenants in 1992 in Ostozhenka, 1,263 persons were forced to rehouse during this compulsory programme until 2004, while 1,584 persons had been relocated after private negotiations with developers. Additionally, there is a large number of Ostozhenka residents who sold their privatised rooms and flats or rented them

---

41   Cf. BADYINA/GOLUBCHIKOV, 2005, p. 118-120.
42   In 2007 and 2008 Moscow legislation has been altered in order to assimilate it to the federal laws: new possibilities of land ownership or long-term land lease are being introduced. Also, the Moscow mechanism of planning the project in detail beforehand, and only then letting the parcel of land designated to that project, has changed: it is the objective to achieve more competitive and transparent forms of land lease. A row of projects begun in Moscow before the introduction of this legislation which were suspended, have since been revised or cancelled. Supposedly, an emphasis was put on some projects that had been planned in an especially semi-legal or extra-legal relationship between city administration and investor; cf. NOBIS, 2012, p. 130-135. On the network of authorities and developers and its personal, "intimate character" see also BADYINA/GOLUBCHIKOV, 2005, p. 121f.; GDANIEC, 2005, p. 170f.

out and went to live elsewhere. So, the structure of the area's population has undergone a thorough change.[43]

Today, real estate agencies claim that "Ostozhenka Street, 'the Golden Mile', is the most prestigious residential area not only in Moscow, but in entire Russia."[44] According to a ranking by "Financial News", Ostozhenka street made it into the top ten of the "most expensive and desirable streets in the world."[45] In 2010 the average price to buy a flat in one of the developments in Ostozhenka was 19,000 Euros per square metre. In one of the old buildings, depending on the status of renovation, the square metre costs from 5,500 up to 14,000 Euros (the lower end of the range being in proximity to the average price in Moscow city). The "Moscow Times" summarises the new character of this central area:

> "Just next door from the multi-cultural, cross-class and eclectic Arbat, Ostozhenka could be a world away, or anywhere in the world, for that matter. [...] These top-end buildings remain worlds in themselves, with neither obvious links to the city neighbourhood that surrounds them at a distance, nor direct access to immediate infrastructure — although one elite supermarket has finally opened on Korobeinikov lane this year. It has been alleged that most of the apartments here were bought during the gold rush by those who never actually intended to live in them, making the whole place the world's fanciest ghost-town."[46]

This perception of a separate world in itself and the elite concept is fostered by another phenomenon not alien to other Megacities: In order to protect the property of the new owners, concierges and door codes are not enough, but extra security guards and fences have started to arise and produce small islands of gated communities. Up until now, despite discussions about it, not the whole area of Ostozhenka has been fenced off. But elsewhere in and especially around Moscow, larger stretches of settlement have become gated quarters, public space

---

43 Cf. BADYINA/GOLUBCHIKOV, 2005, p. 120-123.
44 AGENCY KNIGHT FRANK; http://www.knightfrank.ru/eng/residential/homes/show/ t6UJ9A0052FN/, 07.05.2013.
45 NEWS AGENCY RIA NOVOSTI, 09.03.2011: http://en.rian.ru/business/20110309/162926700.html, 07.05.2013.
46 Introduction to interview with three real estate agents in THE MOSCOW TIMES, 13.10.2010: http://www.themoscowtimes.com/realestate/residential/analysis/article /ostozhenka-unusual-in-every-way/418724.html#no, 07.05.2013. For average price see also ZUBAREVICH, 2012, p. 265.

has become private in the fenced areas of postmodern cities.[47] The two phases that Badyina and Golubchikov observed in Ostozhenka – "the spontaneous individual-driven process of housing rehabilitation before 1998, and the 'systematic' property-led gentrification thereafter"[48] – can also be paralleled with other global Megacities. However, other phenomena cannot, such as the relatively substantial living space that still remains in Moscow's city centre or the absence of an intermediate phase with artists and creative professionals in the role of "gentrifiers" that later on have to leave themselves after a new wave of reconstruction.[49] Of course, the specific historical circumstances of the Soviet period, such as property legislation, city planning, housing shortage, *kommunalkas* and deteriorated buildings, has had an impact. So had the experience of Soviet society and its collapse, with the subsequent crisis. Some of Moscow's urbanisation features can be compared to other post-socialist capitals such as Budapest, Warsaw or Prague. But the individual historical, cultural and global context points to the unique features of every case study.[50]

As has been shown, the transition from state owned to personal property housing took place especially during the first ten years after the fall of the USSR: two thirds of housing stock became private through privatisation and new construction. The less well-off population generally stayed in state-owned flats they rented or leased. This was the basis for the UN-Habitat-Report human settlements in 2003[51] which aimed at a definition of the term "slum" under such circumstances. It is true that there are no big slum areas in Moscow like the Banlieues in France[52] or the favelas of South-American cities. Slums are intermixed

---

47 Cf. GDANIEC, 2005, p. 182, 193; BADYINA/GOLUBCHIKOV, 2005, p. 120-123; SHEVCHENKO, 2009, p. 167, points out the similarities between erecting fences around luxury buildings and fortifying the doors of quite ordinary apartments with the aim of "warding off outsiders". Her interpretation is that the fencing phenomenon has an identical appearance to that in other globalized cities, but also reacts to a specific post-Soviet utopia aspiration (p. 175).

48 Cf. BADYINA/GOLUBCHIKOV, 2005, p. 127.

49 The latter example refers to the Paris quarter of Roquette. Cf. GDANIEC, 2005, p. 194f. Cf. for the current state of research on gentrification in general LEES, 2010, and for the German debate HOLM, 2010, and TWICKEL, 2010.

50 Cf. BADYINA/GOLUBCHIKOV, 2005, p. 127.

51 Cf. UN-HABITAT, Global Report on Human Settlements 2003, The Challenge of Slums, Earthscan, London; Part IV: 'Summary of City Case Studies', p. 195-228: http://www.unhabitat.org/downloads/docs/GRHS.2003.0.pdf, 07.05.2013.

52 Cf. WEBER et al., 2012, p. 50-56.

into parts of Moscow, as well in Ostozhenka[53], where gentrification has now been underway for almost 20 years, as in other areas. The report's listing for the nuclei of slums names *kommunalkas,* which are used by two or more families who share the kitchen and other facilities (including hostels, dormitories and hotels) and outdated and dilapidated buildings, typically the first generation of mass housing with low quality construction and facilities. They are shabby, consist of so called squatter flats or even look abandoned from the outside. Residents there are entitled to housing improvement or free alternative accommodation, but queues are long and move slowly according to availability of municipal housing stock. The most obvious category in 2003 was deteriorated houses, primarily post-World War II structures that are recognised as damaged or otherwise unsuitable for constant habitation. All these types are sometimes in the periphery but quite often, because of the urban growth, in central areas of the city.[54] The people living there are pensioners, invalids, single parents, student families, refugees, run-away-children, orphans, people of no fixed abode (*"BOMji"*) and other kinds of nonregistered people.

The Putin-government and local administrations tried hard and with some success to alter the situation of the pensioners, who live in Moscow probably better than in many parts of Russia, but the other groups, especially nonregistered migrant workers (from the former USSR) do not find a place in the housing and social policy of state nor city. They are needed for the growing wealth of Moscow, but are the social losers of the situation because of difficult access to adequate housing, medical care and education.[55] The role of supporting NGOs is tolerated in this context, but unsecure under contemporary political contexts in Russia.

Current growth and future development

The Russian capital is growing at breath-taking speed. Traffic jams, noise and smog are just a few of the negative side effects. Neither the city's infrastructure, nor housing and traffic planning, nor parks and recreational areas can currently meet the demands of the inhabitants. The city's General plan up to 2020 has

---

53 In 2004 there were still 77 shared apartments for 440 people (199 families) in Ostozhenka. Cf. BADYINA/GOLUBCHIKOV 2005, p. 123.
54 Cf. KRASHENINNOKOV, 2003: http://www.ucl.ac.uk/dpu-projects/Global_Report/cities/moscow.htm, 07.05.2013.
55 Cf. NAZAROVA, 2007, p. 364.

already been rendered obsolete.[56] Another aspect of the housing problem is the fact that apartments and houses have become objects of speculation, meaning that speculative vacancies exacerbate the housing shortage. It makes sense to buy apartments as investment and it does not matter much whether or not they are occupied. Of course, this is not true of the majority of flats, but there is still no equilibrium between demand for housing and occupation rates of existing housing.

In 2007, 33 million cars were registered in Moscow, but only 1.6 million parking spaces. Every year sees 200,000 additional cars hit Moscow's streets, 800,000 cars are on the street at any one time. Moscow has 1,300 km of streets, 40 % less than the required road network compared to other major European cities. Moscow's spider-web street grid has not been upgraded, purely because the city planners could not anticipate such explosive urban growth.[57] Michael Blinkin on the other hand argues that these are also the results of socialist planning heritage that conceived the net of streets as a fishbone system and not as a system of urban highways on which the individual transport can flow.[58] In April 2012 the new mayor of Moscow, Sergei Sobianin confirmed the ambitious expansion plan for the Moscow Metro: By 2020, a second Circle line shall help to relieve the city's traffic situation. The costs will be enormous:[59] Over the next eight years, the backbone of the public transport system in the Russian capital will be dramatically strengthened. The expansion plans until 2016 see the construction of 75,6 km of new routes and 37 new stations – at a cost of 460 billion Roubles (11,5 billion Euros). The mayor has recently confirmed the next five-year-plan for the development of the metro: from 2016 to 2020 an additional 75 km and 33 new stations are to be added – 100 billion Roubles (2,5 billion Euros) have to be set aside for this each year. This will bring a change in the architecture of the Metro network – the so-called "third interchange": The first is, in metro-language, the group of interchange stations in the city centre, the second is the current circle line. These are to be relieved through a significantly

---

56   Cf. the official plans: INTEGRATED BODY FOR URBAN DESIGN POLICY AND DEVELOPMENT OF MOSCOW; http://stroi.mos.ru/eng/default.aspx?m=31&d=31, 07.05.2013.

57   Cf. RUSSIA-NOW(1): http://www.russia-now.info/russia/moscow/news/moscow_s_growth_is_causing_headaches_for_planners_31.html, 07.05.2013.

58   Cf. BLINKIN, 2012.

59   Cf. INTEGRATED BODY FOR URBAN DESIGN POLICY AND DEVELOPMENT OF MOSCOW; http://stroi.mos.ru/eng/default.aspx?m=31&d=31, 07.05.2013.

further reaching second circle line.⁶⁰ In comparison to other Megacities, the public transport, although very efficient, is at times beyond its capacities and needs to be adapted to the mass of commuters on their way to work and home again.⁶¹

During the last months of Dmitri Medvedev's presidency, a new plan was announced that will eventually strongly influence the further development of Moscow: the incorporation of vast territories (1,480 additional [!] to the existing 1,070 square kilometres in 2012) in the South of the city centre. This announcement, as so often, came first – and only then began serious planning and talks with the mayor of Moscow and the governor of the surrounding Moscow region, Sergei Shoigu. The intention of Medvedev was obviously to create new administrative quarters for the government and thus to alter the traffic from centre to the periphery. But will this work, as Fedor Kudriavcev remarked, with some ten thousand government clerks dispatched from the centre?⁶²

Last but not least: The brief sketch on urban growth always connected with the problems of expansion, transport and housing, needs one last comment on migration within the context of changing political and ideological times. It poses the question, of whose city one wants to talk. It was the city of the Moscow bourgeois in the 19th century⁶³, of the nationalities of the Tsarist Empire and of the peasants and workers of the Soviet Empire who were attracted by a socialist metropolis – which despite all problems of housing and urban development offered them far more opportunities than other socialist cities in most of the Republics of the USSR. This was especially true for migrants from Central Asia and the Caucasus. They were, not only after the dissolution of the Soviet Union, perceived as unloved guests at the very least and necessary work force at the same time and have been and sometimes still are facing open hatred, as a series of incidents shows.⁶⁴

Conclusion

In 2008 Monica Rüthers stated that megalopolis Moscow will stay a fancy and glamorous city where the rich and the middle class try at any cost to stay as near to the city centre as they can. On the other hand, the gap between the rich and

---

60   Cf. RUSSIA-NOW(2): http://www.russia-now.info/russia/russia_news/moscow_to_build_second_metro-circle_line_cost_22_billion_euro_96.html, 07.05.2013.
61   Cf. BLINKIN, 2012, p. 282.
62   Cf. KUDRIAVCEV, 2012, p. 377 f.
63   Cf. RUCKMANN, 1984.
64   Cf. ZUBAREVICH, 2012, p. 268.

the poor widens.⁶⁵ This is also the tenor in blogs on gentrification.⁶⁶ The gentrification processes were already reflected in public art exhibitions: The project Auditorium Moscow, shown in the White palace *(Belaia palata)* in the heart of old Moscow, was for example initiated by the Museum of Modern Art in Warsaw in cooperation with curators Ekaterina Degot and David Riff.⁶⁷ It also reflected on the changes that have been taking place in Ostozhenka. The fact that this criticism takes an artistic form is notable in itself, such as the dislocation of population cannot happen entirely without upheaval. However, while the more resistant tenants sooner or later had to face violent methods used to expel them from their quarters, very little concerted protest on their side has taken place. This perceived absence of public protest, also against the demolition of historic sites, has been assigned to the fact that during the high tide of new development in the inner city, the list of severe and of everyday problems for the population in this time of crisis was extensive: simply too much to deal with them all, the problem of a sound city planning was easily outranked, if one was not the particular person to be expelled from one's neighbourhood in the city centre.⁶⁸

Indeed, the nearer to the centre, the more coveted the living space. The middle class has been and still is looking for property in the micro-districts or lives in a rented apartment and seeks a dacha. Rüthers has described that there was in fact no suburbia outside of Moscow in 2008, just the province. It remains to be seen whether the plans for a new administrative centre in the South of big Moscow alter the situation. There are slight evidences that suburbs and closely connected cities such as Khimki on the way from the airport Sheremetevo downtown, with a shorter way to work, shopping malls and Ikea, will bring some change. Here, the daily migration does not rise. But it is still an example of neoliberal growth and the absence of comprehensive urban planning that sees city, suburbia and region in a context.⁶⁹

---

65 Cf. RÜTHERS, 2008, p. 505.
66 Cf. GENTRIFICATION BLOG: http://gentrificationblog.wordpress.com/2008/09/30/moskau-stadtumbau-fur-neue-reiche/, 07.05.2013; CHTODELAT NEWS: https://chtodelat.wordpress.com/tag/gentrification/, 07.05.2013.
67 Cf. AUDITORIUM MOSCOW: http://auditorium-moscow.org/en/about.html, 07.05. 2013. While some enterprises and the Polish government supported the project, no participation of the Russian government or the city of Moscow was to be seen.
68 Cf. BADYINA/GOLUBCHIKOV, 2005, p. 123-126. For the prolonged, even "total crisis" and its handling by the Muscovites see SHEVCHENKO, 2009.
69 Cf. GOLUBCHIKOV, 2011.

Literature

BADYINA, ANNA/GOLUBCHIKOV, OLEG, Gentrification in Central Moscow – a Market Process or a Deliberate Policy? Money, Power and People in Housing Regeneration in Ostozhenka, in: Geografiska Annaler 87 B, 2 (2005), p. 113-129.

BLINKIN, MICHAEL, Festgefahren. Moskaus Verkehr – ein Spiegelbild der Gesellschaft, in: Osteuropa 62, 6-8 (2012), p. 279-292.

COLTON, TIMOTHY, Moscow. Governing the socialist metropolis, Cambridge 1995.

DÖNNINGHAUS, VICTOR/NUMEROVA, LJUDMILA, Mehr als ein Lebenswerk. Die Moskauer Schokoladen- und Feingebäckfabrik Einem & Co., in: Russen und Deutsche. 1000 Jahre Kunst, Geschichte und Kultur. Essayband zur Ausstellung. Berlin 2012, p. 294-301.

DEMOGRAFICHESKII EZHEGODNIK ROSSII. STATISTICHESKII SBORNIK, 2001.

ID., 2010.

GAVRILOVA, IRINA N., Naselenie Moskvy. Istoricheskii rakurs, Moscow 2001.

GDANIEC, CORDULA, Kommunalka und Penthouse. Stadt und Stadtgesellschaft im postsowjetischen Moskau, Münster 2005.

GOLUBCHIKOV, OLEG/PHELPS, NICHOLAS A., Post-socialist post-suburbia? Growth machine and the emergence of 'edge city' in the metropolitan context of Moscow, in: Transactions of the Institute of British Geographers 36 (2011), p. 425-440.

HOFFMANN, DAVID L., Peasant Metropolis: Social Identities in Moscow, 1929-1941. Ithaca, New York 1994.

HOLM, ANDREJ, Wir bleiben alle! Gentrifizierung – Städtische Konflikte um Aufwertung und Verdrängung, Münster 2010.

HUBER, WERNER, Moskau – Metropole im Wandel. Ein architektonischer Stadtführer, Köln et al. 2007.

JAHN, HUBERTUS F., Armes Russland. Bettler und Notleidende in der russischen Geschichte vom Mittelalter bis in die Gegenwart, Paderborn et al. 2010.

KUDRIAVCEV, FEDOR, Plan ohne Plan. Das Projekt "Groß-Moskau", in: Osteuropa 62, 6-8 (2012), p. 371-382.

KULAKOVA, IRINA, Istoriia moskovskogo zhil'ia, Moscow 2006.

KUPERMANN, ALEXANDER, Die Olympischen Spiele 1980 in Moskau. Unpublished Masterthesis, Mainz 2007.

KUSBER, JAN, "Heiliges Russland" und "Sowjetmacht". Moskau als Ensemble von Gedächtnisorten. In: Gedächtnisorte in Osteuropa. Vergangenheiten auf dem Prüfstand, ed. by RUDOLF JAWORSKI et al., Frankfurt/Main et al. 2003, p. 97-115.

LEES, LORETTA et al. (eds.), The Gentrification Reader, London, New York 2010.

LENTZ, SEBASTIAN, Cityentwicklung in Moskau. Zwischen Transformation und Globalisierung, in: Zeitschrift für Wirtschaftsgeographie 41, 2-3 (1997), p. 110-122.

LUZHKOV, IU. A. (Red.), Istoriia Moskvy s drevneishich vremen do nashikh dnei, 3 volumes, Moscow 1997.

MARTIN, ALEXANDER M., Sewage and the City: Filth, Smell, and Representations of Urban Life in Moscow, 1770–1880, in: Russian Review 67, 2 (2008), p. 243-274.

MASON, ROBERT J./NIGMATULLINA, LILIIA, Suburbanization and Sustainability in Metropolitan Moscow, in: Geographical Review 101, 3 (2011), p. 316-333.

NAZAROVA, E. A., Nachalo XXI veka – novyi etap formirovaniia natsional'nogo sostava Moskvy, in: Moskva mnogonatsional'naia. Istoki, evoliutsiia, problemy, sovremennosti, ed. by A. N. SACHAROV, Moscow 2007, p. 325-367.

NEUTATZ, DIETMAR, Die Moskauer Metro. Von den ersten Plänen bis zur Großbaustelle des Stalinismus (1897-1935), Köln et al. 2001.

NOBIS, VICTORIA, Rechtliche Rahmenbedingungen für die Abwicklung von Bauvorhaben in der Russischen Föderation, Berlin 2012.

NOEVER, PETER, Tyrannei des Schönen. Architektur der Stalin-Zeit. Ausstellungskatalog. München, New York 1994.

RUCKMANN, JO ANN, The Moscow Business Elite: A Social and Cultural Portrait of Two Generations, 1840-1905. Illinois 1984.

RÜTHERS, MONICA, Schneller wohnen in Moskau: Novye Čeremuški Nr. 9, das erste Viertel in industrieller Massenbauweise, 1956-1970. In: Städteplanung – Planungsstädte, ed. by BRUNO FRITZSCHE et al., Zürich 2006, p. 157-180.

ID., Moskau bauen von Lenin bis Chruščev. Öffentliche Räume zwischen Utopie, Terror und Alltag. Köln et al. 2007.

ID., Moskau als imperiale Stadt. Sowjetische Hauptstadtarchitektur als Medium imperialer Selbstbeschreibung in vergleichender Perspektive, in: Jahrbücher für Geschichte Osteuropas N.F. 56 (2008), S. 481-506.

SCHLÖGEL, KARL, Moskau lesen. Verwandlungen einer Metropole, 3rd ed., München 2011.

SCHMIDT, ALBERT J., The Architecture and Planning of Classical Moscow: A Cultural History. Philadelphia 1989.

SHEVCHENKO, OLGA, Crisis and the Everyday in Postsocialist Moscow, Bloomington 2009.

THURSTON, ROBERT W., Liberal City, Conservative State: Moscow and Russia's Urban Crisis, 1906-1914, Oxford 1987.

TWICKEL, CHRISTOPH, Gentrifidingsbums oder Eine Stadt für alle, Hamburg 2010.

WEBER, FLORIAN et al., Krise der Banlieues und die politique de la ville in Frankreich, in: Geographische Rundschau 64, 6 (2012), p. 50-56.

ZUBAREVICH, NATAL'YA, Russlands Parallelwelten. Dynamische Zentren, stagnierende Peripherie, in: Osteuropa 62, 6-8 (2012), p. 263-278.

AGENCY KNIGHT FRANK: http://www.knightfrank.ru/eng/residential/homes/show/t6UJ9A0052FN/, 07.05.2013.

AUDITORIUM MOSCOW: http://auditorium-moscow.org/en/about.html, 07.05.2013.

INTEGRATED BODY FOR URBAN DESIGN POLICY AND DEVELOPMENT OF MOSCOW: http://stroi.mos.ru/eng/default.aspx?m=31&d=31, 07.05.2013.

CHTODELAT NEWS: https://chtodelat.wordpress.com/tag/gentrification/,07.05.2013.

DOMOSTROITEL'NYI KOMBINAT NO. 1: http://www.dsk1.ru/Houses/History, 07.05.2013.

GENTRIFICATION BLOG: http://gentrificationblog.wordpress.com/2008/09/30/moskau-stadtumbau-fur-neue-reiche/, 07.05.2013.

KRASHENINNOKOV, ALEXEY, Moscow, Russia, in: Understanding Slums: Case Studies for the Global report 2003, ed. by UN-Habitat: http://www.ucl.ac.uk/dpu-projects/Global_Report/cities/moscow.htm, 07.05.2013.

MAKAROVA, KATIA, Postindustrializm, dzhentrifikatsiia i transformatsiia gorodskogo prostranstva v sovremennoi Moskve, in: Neprikosnovennyi Zapas: Debaty o Politike i Kul'ture, 70, 2 (2010), p. 35-53: http://magazines.russ.ru/nz/2010/2/ma25.html, 07.05.2013.

MAKHROVA, ALLA, Dorogaia moia Moskva: tsena prestizha, in: Demoskop weekly (electronic version of the bulletin "Naselenie i obshchestvo"), No. 247-248, May/June 2006: http://demoscope.ru/weekly/2006/0247/tema01.php, 07.05.2013.

THE MOSCOW TIMES, 13.10.2010: http://www.themoscowtimes.com/realestate/residential/analysis/article/ostozhenka-unusual-in-every-way/418724.html#no, 07.05.2013.

NEWS AGENCY RIANOVOSTI, 9.03.2011: http://en.rian.ru/business/20110309/162926700.html, 07.05.2013.

VSEROSSIISKAIA PEREPIS' NASELENIIA 2002 GODA: http://www.perepis2002.ru/index.html?id=42, 07.05.2013.

VSEROSSIISKAIA PEREPIS' NASELENIIA 2010 GODA: http://www.gks.ru/free_doc/new_site/perepis2010/croc/perepis_itogi1612.htm, 07.05.2013.

PRAVITEL'STVO MOSKVY(1): http://www.mos.ru/press-center/presentations, 07.05.2013.

ID.(2): http://www.mos.ru/authority/structure, 07.05.2013.

REGIONY ROSSII. OSNOVNYE SOTSIALNO-ECONOMICHESKIE POKAZATELI GORODOV 2011: http://www.gks.ru/bgd/regl/b11_14t/IssWWW.exe/Stg/centr/moskv-g2011_1.htm, 07.05.2013.

RUSSIA-NOW(1): http://www.russia-now.info/russia/moscow/news/moscow_s_growth_is_causing_headaches_for_planners_31.html, 07.05.2013.

ID.(2), http://www.russia-now.info/russia/russia_news/moscow_to_build_second_metro-circle_line_cost_22_billion_euro_96.html, 07.05.2013.

UN-HABITAT, Global Report on Human Settlements 2003, The Challenge of Slums, Earthscan, London; Part IV: "Summary of City Case Studies", London, Sterling 2003: http://www.unhabitat.org/downloads/docs/GRHS.2003.0.pdf, 07.05.2013.

ZAIONCHKOVSKAIA, ZHANNA/MKRTCHIAN, NIKITA, Moskva i migratsiia, in: Demoskop weekly, No. 389-390 (September 2009): http://www.demoscope.ru/weekly/2009/0389/tema02.php, 07.05.2013.

Contributors

Ingrid Breckner holds the chair of Urban and Regional Sociology at the Hafen-City University Hamburg and is head of the universities PhD-Committee. Her research practice is focused on different social aspects of urban and regional development as housing, social effects of ecological regeneration, migration, multilingualism, poverty, social practices in urban districts et cetera.
Contact: ingrid.breckner@hcu-hamburg.de.

Ilya V. Gerasimov, Ph.D. in History (Rutgers University, USA) and Candidate of Sciences in History (Kazan State University, Russia), is Executive Editor of the Quarterly *Ab Imperio* and Director of the Center for the Studies of Nationalism and Empire in Kazan (Russia). His main research interests are the new imperial history of Russia, social history, anthropology of violence and sociology of criminality, history of Russian Progressivism.
Contact: ig@abimperio.net.

Jan Kusber is Professor and Chair for East European History at the Historical Institute of the Johannes Gutenberg University Mainz. He has published widely on the History of the Russian Empire in the 18th and 19th century.
Contact: kusber@uni-mainz.de.

Wolfgang Maderthaner is Director General of the Austrian State Archive. He is an expert in European Labour and Social History and has published widely in the fields of Urban History/Anthropology, Cultural Studies, industrial and post-industrial accumulation/regulation. His most recent publication (co-edited with Helmut Konrad) is a comparative study on the global crisis in the 1930s (2013).
Contact: wolfgang.maderthaner@oesta.gv.at.

Hans-Christian Petersen is Assistant Professor for East European History at the Historical Institute of the Johannes Gutenberg University Mainz. His main research interests are the history of science, especially the history of the German *Ostforschung*, biographical research and the history of urban poverty and social spaces.
Contact: peters@uni-mainz.de.

Hauke Jan Rolf is a member of the Research Training Group "Transnational Social Support" at the Johannes Gutenberg University Mainz. He is an urban sociologist with the specialisation in urban development, migration studies and transnationalism.
Contact: hauke_janr@web.de.

Julia Röttjer is a historian, art historian and political scientist. Her main research interests are cultures of remembrance, memory politics and politics of history as well as architecture, city planning and urbanism. She is a PhD-Candidate at the Leibniz Institute of European History Mainz (IEG) within the research group "Knowledge of the World – Heritage of Mankind: The History of UNESCO World Cultural and Natural Heritage".
Contact: juliaroettjer@gmx.de.

Jaspal Naveel Singh is a PhD candidate at the Centre for Language and Communication Research at Cardiff University in Wales, UK. His current research explores the upcoming hip hop scene in Delhi as a tool for empowering marginalized youths and emancipating parts of India's urban society.
Contact: singhjn@cardiff.ac.uk.

Mark D. Steinberg is Professor of History at the University of Illinois at Urbana-Champaign. His most recent research and publications have focused on the city, modernities, emotions, religion, violence, revolution, and utopia – in late-imperial Russia, especially, but always in comparative perspective.
Contact: steinb@illinois.edu.

Loïc Wacquant is Professor of Sociology at the University of California, Berkeley, and Researcher at the Centre européen de sociologie et de science politique, Paris. A MacArthur Foundation Fellow and recipient of the Lewis Coser Award of the American Sociological Association, his research spans urban relegation, ethnoracial domination, the penal state, incarnation, and social theory and the politics of reason. His books are translated in some twenty languages

and include the trilogy *Urban Outcasts* (2008), *Punishing the Poor* (2009), and *Deadly Symbiosis* (2013), as well as *The Two Faces of the Ghetto* (2013) and *Tracking the Penal State* (2014). For more information, see loicwacquant.net.
Contact: loic@berkeley.edu.

Sonja Wengoborski is Teaching and Research Associate at the Institute of Indology of the Johannes Gutenberg University Mainz. Contemporary South Asian literature and learning in tandem in second language acquisition in the context of South Asian Studies follow upon her Indological specializations in Sinhalese, Hindi, Sanskrit, Tibetan, and the history of South Asian religions.
Contact: wengobor@yahoo.de.

Jerry White teaches modern London history at Birkbeck College, University of London. He is the author of numerous social histories of London life, and is currently writing a book on London in the First World War for publication in 2014.
Contact: jerry.white@bbk.ac.uk.